THE LEWIS AND CLARK TRAIL
YESTERDAY AND TODAY

THE LEWIS AND CLARK TRAIL
YESTERDAY AND TODAY

William E. Hill

CAXTON PRESS
Caldwell, Idaho
2004

Library of Congress Cataloging-in-Publication Data

Hill, William E.
  The Lewis and Clark trail yesterday and today / William Hill.
    p. cm.
  Includes bibliographical references and index.
  ISBN 0-87004-439-7 (alk. paper)
  1. Lewis and Clark National Historic Trail--Guidebooks. 2. West (U.S.)--Guidebooks. 3. Lewis and Clark Expedition (1804-1806) 4. West (U.S.)--Description and travel. I. Title.

  F592.7.H55 2004
  917.804'34--dc22

                                                        2003027665

Lithographed and bound in the United States of America
CAXTON PRESS
Caldwell, Idaho
170589

CONTENTS

Illustrations

ACKNOWLEDGMENTS

This is the fifth book in my *Yesterday and Today* series. It was one that I started in the late 1990s and then put off in order to work on some other similar projects. Like with my other books, writing it has been an enjoyable and exciting experience from start until finish. I had many helpers and encouragers throughout the project.

As with my other projects there were a few really breathtaking events that were similar in nature to those experienced by Lewis or Clark that made their trail more alive than I thought it could be. Some memorable activities were: canoeing 150 miles down the Missouri River from Fort Benton through the White Cliffs to Kipps Landing, seeing the river and landscape with its wildlife almost unchanged; walking up the last hundred yards or more to see the view from Lemhi Pass unfold before my own eyes; hiking on a portion of the Nez Perce or Lolo Trail on the crest of the mountains with only more mountains around me; and coming over a hill in South Dakota and seeing a large herd of buffalo spread out in the valley and coming over the distant hills. These are experiences that most people will never have in their lifetimes. They all excited me, and made the trail more meaningful and unforgettable. But these are not the special incidents that really took my breath away.

There were no incidents with grizzly bears like the life and death situations the Corps had, for there are no grizzlies along the Missouri today. However, at one of our camps on the Missouri, while walking from our canoe to our tent, I was startled by the sound of rattles that were all too close. While not at the same camp, but at one within a few miles, Lewis had been startled by a rattlesnake on May 26, 1805. He wrote, . . . *on my return to camp I trod within five inches of a rattle snake but being in motion I passed before he could probably put himself in a striking attitude and fortunately escaped his bite, I struck about at random (lying) with my espontoon being directed in some measure by his nois until I killed him.* I too, was in motion, and luckily, my snake was farther away—one foot off the path in some grass. He was not very happy with my passing. I got out of the way in a hurry and yelled excitedly for my wife Jan to come quickly with my camera so I could shoot him. Unfortunately, in my haste, the picture was blurred. But, on a different path, in a different place, with a different snake, I got my shot of an "unhappy" snake.

Another incident happened to Lewis when the expedition was just ten days out. He was climbing on a cliff about 200 or 300 feet high. He slid and fell nearly all the way down and could have killed himself. Fortunately, he was able to stop himself with only minor damage done, and the Corps continued on. While in the Great Falls area I had to climb up the cliffside to take a picture. It was quite steep and I knocked out a few small rocks that rolled down the side. After I finished photographing and finally got back down, my wife told me all she could think about was Lewis's experience falling down a cliff and me falling down and then she having to decide whether to try to catch me and break my fall, possibly injuring both of us, or just letting me fall and being hurt or killed and she remaining unscathed. The next time I was climbing on the side of a steep cliff in the Three Forks area she told me she did not watch until she thought I was safely up or back down. Every other time I did any climbing, she was fast to again remind me of her earlier quandary, thereby hoping to persuade me not to climb.

A third incident, and one that involved no danger, occurred when I was walking up the hillside at Blackbird's gravesite. Clark wrote about how he and Lewis along with ten other men climbed the hill. My imaginative mind had Catlin's painting in view, but my practical mind had me thinking that the hill and area would be all overgrown with little resemblance to his painting. The difficult route we had taken to get there seemed to assure me that the site would be obscured. There was a special feeling of being in that sacred place, but the almost over-powering thrill was all there when I could still see the grass area on the crest and the curved cliffside, knowing that this is where both the Indians and Lewis and Clark had walked. I shouted for Jan and then ran to get her so she could also experience the climb to the top. It was these little experiences and other similar ones that really made the trail come alive for me.

Another part of the enjoyment in traveling on the trails has been in meeting people in various parts of the country from all walks of life. Sometimes the stops and visitations were planned, but more often than not they just happened. Almost all threw us off our schedule, loosely planned as it usually was. Most of the stops involved either trying to locate a site where a painting or sketch was made or trying to identify the probable landowner. In almost every situation the people met were genuinely interested in helping and sharing information. Frequently, they wanted me to tell them more about what I knew. Sometimes what we planned on as a stop of perhaps a few minutes or at most an hour grew to be the better part of a day.

There have been many people and companies who provided information, gave directions, or granted permission for us to wander around their property. These are but a few of the many townspeople, farmers, and ranchers. Some were Indian tribal members.

Teressa Sward, at the Western Historic Trails Center in Council Bluffs, was one of the first to inquire about my future projects and encouraged me to write this.

Lila Daniels was a lady met while researching in Rockport, Indiana. I had the painting by Bodmer of the area and was interested in finding out if there were any earlier sketches or representations. I had stopped in at local drugstore and obtained some information and ended up at the town office. There I met Lila. She provided more information and recounted some of the early history of the area and its Lincoln connection. She noticed I was also interested in the Chester Islands and explained where they were. She offered a private tour of the Lincoln Village that we took the following day.

Especially nice were the people at Doe Run, Inc., a lead plant along the Mississippi River. I wanted to photograph an area on the river that appeared to have been painted from the plant's property. I spoke with Donny Poke, the night manager, and explained to him what I was interested in. He explained he could not grant permission. He did, however, provide the names of people to contact and suggested that I return the next day to inquire of them about getting permission. Upon arrival the next morning everything was all ready. Donny had forwarded the request and information about what I was doing and the two people, Rhonda Read and Richard Batts, were there to assist. They talked about the history of the plant and area, and then Rick took me out and opened up areas so I could get my pictures. The company and its employees were some of the nicest met in all my years.

An institution of a different sort was the Kansas Lansing Correctional Facility. I had my doubts about getting permission to go on it, but permission was graciously granted, and Kyle Deere, Executive Officer and Warden's Assistant, acted as guide on the facility's grounds and took me where I needed to go.

While I was out photographing the Grand Tower on the Mississippi, my wife Jan remained in our car. Two local farmers, Edgar Dreyer and Ted Harnagel came up to see if she needed any help. While I got my photos they were telling my wife all about the area and how their families migrated from Germany to the U.S. and then settled in Missouri in the 1840s. Both families had lived in the area and one had farmed the land near the tower since their arrival. When I returned the conversation continued, while not about Lewis and Clark, but about the local history of the area and the changes in the area surrounding the tower.

While on the Fort Peck Reservation three men, Leroy Headress and Philip Johnston, both Assiniboine, and Peter Olson were in the middle of a one-lane dirt road. They were completing a surveying project. What I thought would be a brief conversation about the local roads, conditions, and access to the river turned out to be a long conversation about the local tribes and their histories, and Prince Maximilian's trip and Karl Bodmer's paintings.

While looking for access to the site of another Bodmer painting in South Dakota, Pat Feyereisen provided more than the help requested. He had lived his whole life ranching in the same area and told us about it and what it was like along the river before all the dams. Then we met some of his grown children, his grandchildren, and neighbors who had stopped by and we talked some more. He gave us permission and directions and also some cautions as we probably looked like some city slickers, but we tried to assure him that we were experienced in off trail travel and not to worry. We took off traveling a few miles out into the fields and prairie. Then I hiked a few miles after the "road" ran out in the hills. By the time I took my pictures and started back, the sun was down. Outside standing by the ranch yard light was Pat. He had been watching our lights as we wound and bounced our way back across the prairies. He said he wanted to make sure we made it back safely and was ready to search for us if we didn't. We talked some more, again extended our appreciation and said our good-byes.

Another enjoyable stop was at the ranch of Deanne and Greg Heen. Again after a short greeting and explanation, the interest showed, permission to roam was granted, the conversation expanded, and time began to pass. The light was changing, and I was again off to locate two more sites.

Sometimes I was just lucky. While driving in the area of one of Mathews' sketches we came to what I thought was the probable location. After taking a number of pictures from the area I decided things just weren't quite right. We did a little backtracking and came to what opened up to be what I thought was the right place. I stopped before the entrance to the long driveway and could see there was no activity or cars at the ranch house. Just when we were ready to leave, a car turned in front of us right into the driveway. We decided to follow. There we met Dan Voyich, and his wife, Marie. We explained what we were doing and they invited us in for something to drink—and again seconds became minutes and then longer. They told us about their families' migration to the United States and their settling in Montana. They told us we could drive or walk around in the pastures as needed. I finally took my pictures, closed the fence gate and said good-bye. On our way back home we stopped in again, met one of their sons, a neighbor and took some more pictures.

We had stopped in at one area in Missouri along the river three different times trying to locate the owner or someone who could give us permission to cross the fields. I decided to try one more time and if not successful, I would settle for a photo from a similar area. I saw someone out in the fields harvesting the crops and walked out to met him. Luckily I was informed the owner, Stewart Morris, who lived in another state, was up by the grain bins. After a brief introduction, we visited for a short time. He told me about the changing course of the river in the area, his interest in steamboat traffic on the river and also in the *Yellow Stone* that Prince Maximilian and Bodmer had sailed on. Then he told me to go get the pictures and to return to visit some more as he had things I might be interested in. When we returned he had a notebook full of the history of the area including information about an old inn that had been built in the early 1800s on the riverbank as a major steamboat stop. It was still standing when he acquired the property. Plans were to develop the area and renovate it as a historical site, but unfortunately, it burned and could not be restored.

While on the Omaha Reservation looking for the locations of both a Bodmer and a Catlin painting we stopped in at the reservation's police department. Explaining the project and what I was interested in to the people in the office, the conversation soon expanded to include more topics and others as they came in. Captain Ed Tyndall was one who was called in because it was thought he might have the information. Ed was familiar with what I was seeking to locate and offered to be our guide. We talked about Chief Blackbird, the history of the Omaha Indians, some of its present problems, and he also suggested other places of interest in the area to visit. It was through his kind assistance that I was able to take my needed pictures.

The canoe trip down the Missouri River was a terrific experience. I must give much of the credit to the outfitters, Mike and Meredith Gregston of Adventure Bound. My wife and I had thought about doing it on our own, but then decided to use an outfitter. We brought some of our own equipment, but they really provided most of it and made our trip a terrific experience and also very "easy"—if you don't mind paddling all day. They took care of providing the food, which was excellent and more than we could eat, the canoes, and all the other needed equipment. Thus, I was freer to focus on my pictures and Jan had a "vacation" from housekeeping. Renee MacDonald, an elementary teacher for most of the year, acted as our guide and took care of the camp. Renee's nephew, Eric Neal, who was visiting from Austin, Texas, came along and helped out. As outfitters and guides they were terrific and would make anyone's trip down the Missouri a pleasure. We stopped at Virgelle and met Dan Johanssen. He was the owner and restorer of the old Virgelle Mercantile which served both as a store and a bed and breakfast. He provided us with more history about the area. For those interested in a different type of camp on the Lewis and Clark Trail, his various rustic cabins and fine hotel rooms above the mercantile are the perfect break from a tent and sleeping bag on the ground.

It was people like the ones mentioned that made the trips and project more interesting than just the history of Lewis and Clark. My wife always says we get to meet the "real Americans" whenever and wherever we are when researching.

I want to put in a special "thank you" to the librarians all across the country, including those in my own backyard—the Middle Country Library. You can ask any of them a question or for help in locating a book and they are right there to assist you. They say it is just part of their job—that may be true, but it makes my work so much easier. And another to the University of Nebraska Press who allowed me to extensively quote from Gary Moulton's thirteen-volume *The Journals of the Lewis and Clark Expedition.*

Another person who has participated in this project and has had to put up with my wanderings is my wife, Jan. She was "required" to read my drafts and rewrites and did so willingly. She was the person who was worrying about me when it appeared that I had no "horse sense" at all and would be off wandering someplace in the hot afternoon sun without my hat or enough water, or climbing a steep hill or hiking miles off the road, or swimming across a river, all just so I could get a better picture, while she had to "patiently" wait in the car. The last couple of years it has gotten somewhat easier for her. Our Chevy Suburban has On-Star, so she knows that at least the car could be located, even if I couldn't be. We even purchased some walkie-talkies that helped, but somehow they never seemed to work all the time.

But enough of this, it is time we proceed on!

PREFACE

The Lewis and Clark Expedition was the brainchild of Thomas Jefferson. This book, while providing information about important events and happenings during the expedition, is not meant to be a detailed daily description of the journey on the now famous trail. There are other books available for that. Rather, this book gives the reader basic but important facts about significant events related to the evolution of the expedition and a broader overview of the Louisiana Purchase and other significant events related to the territory during the lifetimes of the three most important people—Thomas Jefferson, Meriwether Lewis, and William Clark. It also attempts to show, as closely as possible, what the territory and route looked like when the Corps of Discovery passed through it, its present state, and how it looks today. It includes relevant old maps, journal entries, and makes extensive use of early paintings, sketches, a few old photos of scenes along the route and corresponding photos from today. It will take readers along a significant portion of the route, allow them to experience the trail and encourage them to visit the trail itself.

The question of exactly what lands were included in the Louisiana Purchase was never really answered at the time of the purchase, nor was there a complete agreement by the time the land was transferred. France did not know exactly what had been transferred from Spain. Spain hadn't specified what it had given to France. France didn't explain what it sold to the United States. Jefferson and the United States assumed that the drainage of the Arkansas and Red River were included and that perhaps that the southwestern border might be as far as the Rio Grande, but Spain never believed that. The Americans thought they had received New Orleans and West Florida in the deal, but the French didn't agree and the Spanish certainly did not. No one knew exactly where the Rocky Mountains were, nor did they know the specific location of the Continental Divide. Even the northern border was in dispute since the watershed of the Missouri had not been determined. And although the eastern boundary was accepted to be the Mississippi River, the northernmost section of it had not been plotted nor had the river's source been discovered. There would be many years of negotiations and treaties and more explorations before these matters were finally settled.

Now, let us proceed on!

[Throughout this book when primary source materials – letters & journal quotations are used, the spelling and punctuation remains unchanged.]

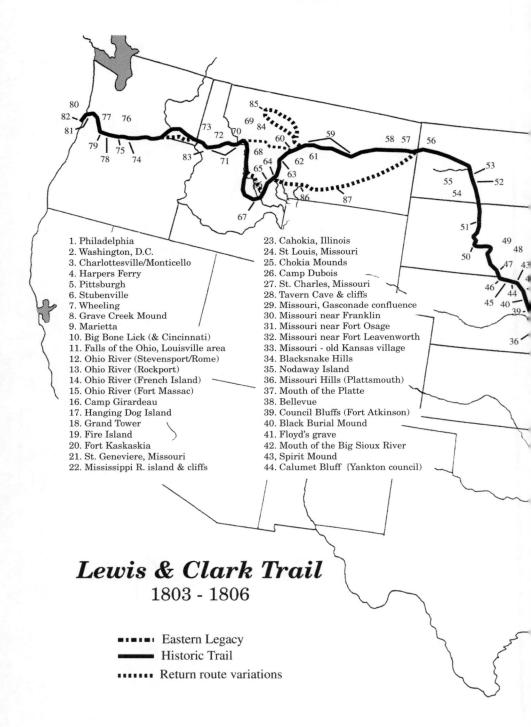

1. Philadelphia
2. Washington, D.C.
3. Charlottesville/Monticello
4. Harpers Ferry
5. Pittsburgh
6. Stubenville
7. Wheeling
8. Grave Creek Mound
9. Marietta
10. Big Bone Lick (& Cincinnati)
11. Falls of the Ohio, Louisville area
12. Ohio River (Stevensport/Rome)
13. Ohio River (Rockport)
14. Ohio River (French Island)
15. Ohio River (Fort Massac)
16. Camp Girardeau
17. Hanging Dog Island
18. Grand Tower
19. Fire Island
20. Fort Kaskaskia
21. St. Geneviere, Missouri
22. Mississippi R. island & cliffs

23. Cahokia, Illinois
24. St Louis, Missouri
25. Chokia Mounds
26. Camp Dubois
27. St. Charles, Missouri
28. Tavern Cave & cliffs
29. Missouri, Gasconade confluence
30. Missouri near Franklin
31. Missouri near Fort Osage
32. Missouri near Fort Leavenworth
33. Missouri - old Kansas village
34. Blacksnake Hills
35. Nodaway Island
36. Missouri Hills (Plattsmouth)
37. Mouth of the Platte
38. Bellevue
39. Council Bluffs (Fort Atkinson)
40. Black Burial Mound
41. Floyd's grave
42. Mouth of the Big Sioux River
43, Spirit Mound
44. Calumet Bluff (Yankton council)

Lewis & Clark Trail
1803 - 1806

■▪■▪■▪ Eastern Legacy
━━━━━ Historic Trail
▪▪▪▪▪▪ Return route variations

45. Ponca Creek & camp
46. Old Baldy/Grand Tower
47. Missouri River banks and hills
48. Bijoux Hills
49. Grand Detour
50. Bad River Teton Sioux camp
51. Arikara Village
52. Village on the Slant
53. Fort Mandan
54. Mandan village/Fort Clark site
55. Knife River Mandan/Hidatsa sites
56. Yellowstone junction (Fort Union)
57. Unusual elevations on the Missouri
58. Bluffs on the Missouri
59. White Cliffs & Badlands area
60. Marias River mouth (Decision Point)
61. Black Bluffs and distant mountains.
62. Great Falls and Giant Springs area
63. Gates of the Rocky Mountains
64. Three Forks of the Missouri
65. Beaverhead Rock
66. Camp Fortunate

67. Lemhi Pass
68. Travelers Rest
69. Lolo Hot Springs
70. Lolo Pass
71. Lolo-Nez Perce Trail
72. Weippe Prairie
73. Canoe Camp
74. Celilo Falls
75. The Dalles
76. Columbia River
77. Beacon Rock
78. Multomah Falls
79. Rooster Rock
80. Cape Disappointment
81. Fort Clatsop
82. Salt Works
83. Long Camp
84. Hellgate
85. Camp Disappointment
86. Yellowstone River Valley
87. Pompey's Pillar

CHAPTER ONE

The Great Trails

T he Lewis and Clark Trail is unlike the other great trails—the Oregon, California, Mormon and Santa Fe trails. The purpose and goals associated with each trail helps to distinguish it from the others. The Lewis and Clark Expedition and its trail were the result of formal government actions, with specific instructions that covered a wide variety of goals and congressional appropriations. It was a military expedition under the command of military officers. The Lewis and Clark Trail was one of exploration and discovery as was made evident by Thomas Jefferson's letter of instruction, June 20, 1803. The other trails were developed mainly as trails of emigration and commerce and were organized primarily by private individuals or commercial groups.

These were Jefferson's instructions to Lewis:

To Meriwether Lewis, esquire, Captain of the 1st regiment of infantry of the United States of America: Your situation as Secretary of the President of the United States has made you acquainted with the objects of my confidential message of January 18, 1803. to the legislature. You have seen the act they passed, which, tho' expressed in general terms, was meant to sanction those objects, and you are appointed to carry them into execution.

Instruments for ascertaining by celestial observations the geography of the country thro' which you will pass, have already been provided. light articles for barter, & presents among the Indians, arms for your attendants, say for from 10 to 12 men, boats, tents, & other travelling apparatus, with ammunition, medicine, surgical instruments & provisions you will have prepared with such aids as the Secretary of

War can yield in his department; & from him also you will receive authority to engage among our troops, by voluntary agreement, the number of attendants above mentioned, over whom you, as their commanding officer are invested with all powers the laws give in such a case.

As your movements while within the limits of the U.S. will be better directed by occasional communications, adapted to circumstances as they arise, they will not be noticed here. what follows will respect your proceedings after you depart from the U.S.

Your Mission has been communicated to the Ministers here from France, Spain & Great Britain, and through them to their respective governments: and such assurances given them as to it's objectives as we trust will satisfy them. the country of Louisiana having been ceded by Spain to France, the passport you have from the Minister of France, the representative of the present sovereign of the country, will be a protection with all it's subjects: And that from the Minister of England will entitle you to the friendly aid of any traders of that allegiance with whom you may happen to meet.

The object of your mission is to explore the Missouri river, & such principal stream of it, as, by it's course & communication with the waters of the Pacific Ocean, may offer the most direct & practicable water communication across this continent, for the purposes of commerce.

Beginning at the mouth of the Missouri, you will take observations of latitude & longitude, at all remarkable points on the river, & especially at the mouths of rivers, at rapids, at island & other places & objects distinguished by such natural marks & characters of a durable kind, as that they may certainly be recognized thereafter. the courses of the river between these points of observation may be supplied by the compass, the log-line & by time, corrected by the observations themselves. the variations of the compass too, in different places, should be noticed.

The interesting points of portage between the heads of the Missouri & the water offering the best communications with the Pacific Ocean should also be fixed by observation, & the course of the water to the ocean, in the same manner as that of the Missouri.

Your observations are to be taken with great pains & accuracy, to be entered distinctly, & intelligibly for others as well as yourself, to comprehend all the elements necessary, with the aid of the usual tables, to fix the latitude and longitude of the places at which they were taken, & are to be rendered to the war office, for the purpose of having the calculations made concurrently by proper persons within the U.S. several copies of these, as well, as your other notes, should be made at leisure times & put into care of the most trustworthy of your attendants, to guard by multiplying them, against the accidental losses to which they will be exposed. a further would be that one of these copies be written on paper of the birch, as less liable to injury from damp than common paper.

The commerce which may be carried on with the people inhabiting the line you pursue, renders a knolege of these people important. you will therefore endeavor to make yourself acquainted, as far as a diligent pursuit of your journey shall admit,

With the names of the nations & their numbers;

the extent & limits of their possessions;

their relations with other tribes or nations;

their ordinary occupations in agriculture, fishing, hunting, war, arts, & the implements for these;

their food, clothing, & domestic accommodations;

the diseases prevalent among them, & the remedies they use;

moral & physical circumstances which distinguish them from the tribes we know;

peculiarities in their laws, customs & dispositions;

and articles of commerce they may need or furnish, & to what extent.

And considering the interest every nation has in extending & strengthening the authority of reason & justice among the people around them, it will be useful to acquire what knolege you can of the state of morality, religion & information among them, as it may better enable those who endeavor to civilize & instruct them, to adapt their measures to the existing notions & practices of those on whom they are top operate.

Other objects worthy of notice will be

the soil & face of the country, it's growth & vegetable productions; especially those not of the U.S.

the animals of the country generally, & especially those not known in the U.S.

the remains and accounts of any which may deemed rare or extinct;

the mineral productions of every kinds; but more particularly metals, limestone, pit coal & salpetre; salins & mineral waters, noting the temperature of the last, & such circumstances as may indicate their character.

Volcanic appearances.

climate as characterized by the thermometer, by the proportion of rainy, cloudy & clear days, by lightening, hail, snow, ice, by the access & recess of frost, by the
winds prevailing at different seasons, the dates at which particular plants put forth or lose their flowers, or leaf, times of appearance of particular birds, reptiles or insects.

Altho' your route will be along the channel of the Missouri, yet you will endeavor to inform yourself, by inquiry, of the character & extent of the country watered by it's branches, & especially on it's southern side. the North river or Rio Bravo which runs into the gulph of Mexico, and the North river, or Rio Colorado, which runs into the gulph of California, are understood to be the principal streams heading opposite to the waters of the Missouri, and running Southwardly. whether the dividing grounds between the Missouri & them are mountains or flatlands, what are their distance from the Missouri, the character of the intermediate country, & the people inhabiting it, are worthy of particular enquiry. The Northern waters of the Missouri are less to be inquired after, because they have been ascertained to a considerable degree, and are still in a course of ascertainment by English traders and travelers. but if you can learn anything certain of the most Northern source of the Missisipi, & of it's position relative to lake of the woods, it will be interesting to us. some account too of the path of the Canadian traders from the Missisipi, at the mouth of the Ouisconsin river, to where it strikes the Missouri and of the soil & rivers in it's course, is desireable.
In all your intercourse with the natives treat them in the most friendly & conciliatory manner which their own conduct will admit; allay all jealousies as to the object of your journey, satisfy them of it's innocence, make them acquainted with the position, extent, character, peaceable & commercial dispositions of the U.S. of our wish to be neighborly, friendly, & useful to them, & of our dispositions to a commercial intercourse with them; confer with them on the points most convenient as mutual emporiums, & the articles of most desireable interchange for them & us. if a few of their influential chiefs, within practicable distance, wish to visit us, arrange such a visit with them, and furnish them with the authority to call on our officers, on their entering the U.S. to have them conveyed to this place at public expence. if any of them should wish to have some of their young people brought up with us, & taught such arts as may be useful to them, we will receive, instruct & take care of them. such a mission, whether of influential chiefs, or of young people, would give some security to your own party. carry with you some matter of the kinepox, inform those of them

with whom you may be of it' efficacy as a preservative from the small-pox; and instruct & incourage them in the use of it. this may be specially done wherever you winter.

As it is impossible for us to forsee in what manner you will be received by those people, whether with hospitality or hostility, so is it impossible to prescribe the exact degree of perseverance with which you are to pursue your journey. we value too much the lives of citizens to offer them to probably destruction. your numbers will be sufficient to secure you against the unauthorised opposition of individuals, or of small parties: but if a superior force, authorised or not authorized, by a nation, should be arrayed against your further passage, & inflexibly determined to arrest it, you must decline it's further pursuit, and return. in the loss of yourselves, we should lose also the information you will have acquired. by returning safely with that, you may enable us to renew the essay with better calculated means. to your own discretion therefore must be left the degree of danger you may risk, & the point at which you should decline, only saying we wish you to err on the side of your safety, & bring back your party safe, even if it be with less information.

As far up the Missouri as the white settlements extend, an intercourse will probably be found to exist between them and the Spanish posts at St. Louis, opposite Cahokia, or Ste. Genevieve opposite Kaskaskia. from still farther up the river, the traders may furnish a conveyance for letters. beyond that you may perhaps be able to engage Indians to bring letters for the government to Cahokia or Kaskaskia, on promising that they shall there receive such special compensation as you shall have stipulate with them. avail yourself of these means to communicate to us, at seasonable intervals, a copy of your journal, notes & observations of every kind, putting into cipher whatever might do injury if betrayed.

Should you reach the Pacific ocean [line illegible-scratched out] inform yourself of the circumstances which may decide whether the furs of those parts may not be collected as advantageously at the head of the Missouri (convenient as is supposed to the waters of the Coroado & Oregon or Columbia) as at Nootka sound or any other point of that coast; & the trade be consequently conducted through the Missouri & U.S. more beneficially than by circumnavigation now practiced.

On your arrival on that coast endeavor to learn if there be any port within your reach frequented by the sea-vessels of any nation, and to send two of your trusted people back by sea, in such way as shall appear practicable, with a copy of your notes. and should you be of the opinion that the return of your party by the way they went will be emi-

nently dangerous, then ship the whole, & return by sea by way of Cape Horn or Cape of Good Hope, as you shall be able. as you will be without money, clothes or provisions, you must endeavor to use the credit of the U.S. to obtain them; for which purpose open letters of credits shall be furnished you authorizing you to draw on the Executive of the U.S. or any of its officers in any part of the world, on which drafts can be disposed of, and to apply with our recommendations to the Consuls, agents, merchants, or citizens of any nation with which we have intercources, assuring them in out name that any aids they may furnish you, shall honorably repaid, and on demand. Our consuls Thomas Howes at Batavia in Java, William Buchanan on the isles of France and Bourbon, & John Elmslie at the Cape of good hope will be able to supply your necessities by draughts on us.

Should you find it safe to return by the way you go, after sending two of your party round by sea, or with the whole party, if no conveyance by sea can be found, do so; making such observations on your return as may serve to supply, correct or confirm those made on your outward journey.

In re-entering the U.S. and reaching s a place of safety, discharge any of your attendants who may desire & deserve it, procuring for them immediate paiment of all arrears of pay & cloathing which may have incurred since their departure; & assure them that they shall be recommended to the liberality of the legislature for the grant of a soldier's portion of land each, as proposed in my message to Congress & repair yourself with your papers to the seat of government.

To provide, on the accident of your death, against anarchy, dispersion & the consequent danger to your party, and total failure of the enterprise, you are hereby authorized, by any instrument signed & written in your hand, to name the person among them who shall succeed to command on your decease, & by like instruments to change the nomination from time to time, as further experience of the characters accompanying you shall points out superior fitness; and all the powers & authorities given to yourself are, in the event of your death, transferred to & vested in the successor so named, with further power to him, & his successors in a like manner to name each successor, who, on the death of his predecessor, shall be invested with all the powers & authorities given to yourself.

Th. Jefferson
Pr. U S. of America

The Lewis and Clark Trail, for the most part was a water route, not a land route. One major goal of the expedition was to find "the most direct and practical water communication across the continent" in other words, a navigable northwest passage. The "communication" would not be a trail for wagons, but hopefully a passage for boats and ships and commerce. Jefferson was hopeful that it would provide an easy way to ship goods across the continent and then on to the Orient. As it turned out, the Lewis and Clark Expedition did not achieve this part of its mission. It wasn't due to lack of effort on the part of the leaders or effort by the Corps of Discovery, but was the result of the geography of the North America itself.

For a long time it was believed that the Missouri River and other major rivers flowed from a high central area where there was a single low chain of mountains. It was thought that there would be a relatively short portage over the mountains, similar to those in the East, bringing one to a major navigable river flowing to the Pacific. Unfortunately, it was not as originally hoped. There was no half-day's journey over a single low mountain range. There was a wide major rugged mountain system with some smaller ones that got in the way. The rivers became too shallow for navigation and rapids and falls became obstacles that at that time could not be overcome except by portage. The land portion of the route over the mountains was also just too long and rugged to haul the large amounts of goods that would have been involved in making the route the major trade route across the continent, as first envisioned by Jefferson. The portion of the trail from where the members of the Corps left their canoes until where they were finally able to build new ones was about 400 miles and took about forty days. It wasn't until the mid-twentieth century that a year-round two-lane highway was developed paralleling the most difficult section of their mountain crossing in the Bitterroot Mountains.

While the Missouri and Columbia rivers later became important routes for riverboats and barges, this was not due to the Lewis and Clark Expedition. Water and river transportation were already a major means of transportation in many places and became so in new areas as people moved in. The rivers were already important to the Indians and early voyageurs and traders who pre-dated Lewis and Clark. The expedition served to increase the pace of development along the rivers as information about the area and the wildlife spread. Steamboats involved in the fur trade were going up the Missouri as far as its junction with the Yellowstone River by the early 1830s. Fort Benton, in western Montana, was founded in 1846, and it soon developed as the head of steamboat traffic on the Missouri River. It was situated about 350 miles farther west. It also became the hub for trails and transportation in the great northern plains until the railroad arrived in 1887. The 1860s Montana gold rush brought even more people and commerce to the area. In one year about 10,000 people and seventy steamboats came to Fort Benton. However, this was regional commerce, not the international commerce to China that Jefferson had originally envisioned for the Missouri.

Fort Benton was still hundreds of miles away from the Columbia River and West Coast. The falls and rapids on the Columbia also made large-scale river traffic on it difficult. It would take more than a century before the Columbia was tamed with its series of dams and locks and large vessels could travel up it to eastern Oregon and Washington. As it turned out, few traders or emigrants ever followed the whole trail west to Oregon and the Pacific. Other trails would be developed to fulfill their needs. The lifetime of the Lewis and Clark Trail in that sense was less than two and a half years. The Corps of Discovery only used the initial route when going to the Pacific. On their return they explored some alternate routes that they had learned about from the Indians.

The other great trails, the Santa Fe, Oregon, California, and Mormon, were almost exclusively land routes. Originally these trails followed old animal, Indian, or trading trails modified as needed for wagon use. It was hoped that they were the safest and shortest. However, cut-offs were constantly searched for in order to speed and ease the trip. While the trails frequently incorporated river valleys into their route, they did not have to follow every meander and bend that the rivers took. The rivers did provide the needed water for the emigrants, traders, and their animals. River crossings were seen as impediments and hazards to be overcome. Often the valleys were flatter and easier on the animals. During the early years, emigrants on the Oregon Trail used rafts built at The Dalles to float down the Columbia to the Fort Vancouver area. However, once the Barlow Road was opened in 1846, it took most of the river traffic. When the trails were in the hilly regions, they tried to follow the crests where it was drier and more level. Instead of winding their way up the hills, when possible, the early trails often went straight up or down.

Hundreds of thousands of pioneers, emigrants, and merchants took these other trails to achieve their goal of establishing new homes in the west hoping to fulfill their dreams of a better life with more freedom—economic, political or religious. These trails were developed as wagon routes. The wagon was the mode of transportation. Thousands of animals followed the trail, and while most of the time the people walked or some rode horses, the route had to accommodate the wagon. The wagon carried the all important supplies and furnishings of the emigrants for their new homes or products to be sold to them. Some of the very first wagons used on portions of these trails were owned by traders who were bringing goods to the fur trading rendezvous in the Rocky Mountains. Later, the traders brought thousands of wagons packed full of goods back and forth across the trails to supply the inhabitants in both the West and the East with the resources and products that enabled the United States to grow and prosper.

When William Becknell opened the Santa Fe Trail he used pack mules for his first trip, but wagons were used the following year. The number of wagons using it continued to grow as the number of traders and merchants increased. Many of the early trading posts and the military forts were established along rivers or near the trails. In later years these wagon trails were followed in part or in whole by the Pony Express, the telegraph, the railroads and more recently by electric power lines, automobile roads, and even gas and oil pipelines.

The government's role in these other great trails was different. It became involved after the routes were established. The government used the trails of commerce and emigration for military purposes. It became involved in identifying the trails and later in setting up military posts near or along them. These trails served as a means of expanding its presence and control over the land and the Indians. The military also used them to move men and supplies. It also helped to provide protection for the emigrants and commerce along the trails.

William Becknell opened the Santa Fe Trail in 1821 and commerce quickly expanded between Mexico and the United States. A few years after the trail opened, the government sponsored a survey and mapping of it. Joseph C. Brown served as the chief surveyor of the 1825 Sibley Commission Survey. In 1829 the first military escort under the command of Major Bennett Riley was sent to protect the traders' caravans. In 1834 the government again provided some escorts. Trade continued to expand almost every year. As a result of the 1846 Mexican War, Santa Fe became part of the United States. In 1846 the U.S. Army sent its invading force over the Santa Fe Trail. Fort Marcy was built in Santa Fe in 1846 and Fort Mann on the Arkansas River in 1847. It was replaced by Fort Atkinson in 1850. Soon other forts were built along the trail—Fort Union in 1851, Fort Larned in 1859 and Fort Lyon in 1860.

The Oregon and California trails developed over time. Parts were first used by fur traders, such as the Astorians in 1812-13. Traders brought the first wagons over part of the route to the 1830 rendezvous in the Rockies. Missionaries started for Oregon in the 1830s. In 1836 Reverend Marcus Whitman and his wife, Narcissa, used the first emigrant wagon on a large segment of the trail. The heyday of these trails lasted almost thirty years, from the 1840s to the development of the railroad by about 1870. The first bona fide emigrant wagon company to Oregon and California headed west in 1841. It was guided by trappers Joseph Meek and Thomas Fitzpatrick and led by John Bidwell and John Bartleson, with both emigrants serving as its captains. Near Soda Springs, Idaho, the company split, some going to Oregon and the others to California. Emigration over the trails increased each year. By 1843 migration to Oregon was nearly 1,000. Hoping to escape religious persecution, in 1847 the Mormons followed the trail west to the Great Salt Lake. In 1846 this same route had been used by some California emigrants. In 1849 about 27,000 emigrants used the trails to Oregon, California, and Utah. A few years later in 1852 over 70,000 emigrants were heading west. Recent estimates place the total trail traffic at nearly a half million people.

The government's role with these other great trails was also developing. By the mid 1840s most of the Oregon Trail had been mapped. Lieutenant John C. Fremont led a number of expeditions west in the 1840s. Mountain man Kit Carson served as his guide. Charles Preuss served as Fremont's cartographer and his map was published in 1846. In 1846 Congress passed legislation that provided for raising a regiment of mounted riflemen, and establishing military forts on the route to Oregon. The Mexican War forced a postponement of the action until 1848-50 when the government established a new Fort Kearny, Fort Laramie, and Fort Dalles along the trail. Sometimes the government became involved in making improvements or developing shortcuts or new routes such as the 1859 Lander Road on the Oregon-California trails from near the South Pass to Fort Hall. This was part of the government's larger program known as the Fort Kearny-South Pass-Honey Lake Wagon Road to California for which Congress granted a $300,000 appropriation in 1857. Sometimes parts of these other great trails incorporated portions of a route that had been used by military expeditions or developed as a military road. This frequently happened when the emigrants spread throughout the lands.

The organization of those associated with the trails differed. The Lewis and Clark expedition was a military operation under the orders of the secretary of the army and guided by the rules of military conduct. With only minor exceptions the permanent members of the Corps were military men. They either volunteered and were accepted by the captains or were recruited or requested by the captains. They had military uniforms and used them until they later wore out or perhaps were traded away. The civilian members that accompanied the Corps were also selected by the captains or came with their consent and were expected to fulfill their obligations.

In the Corps of Discovery there was a chain of command. Orders were to be obeyed. Those who did not obey or do their duty were court martialed and punished military style. The expedition was led by the two "captains." Lewis held the official rank of captain, 1st U.S. Infantry, but through an oversight or perhaps political intrigue, William Clark was only reinstated with a rank of second lieutenant, U.S. Corps of Artillerists. This fact was kept from the men and the public and Clark was always referred to as Captain. Even in the journals of the men they referred to Lewis and Clark with their rank, as either the captains, or as Captain Lewis or Captain Clark.

Lewis and Clark gave the orders, and the Corps was expected to follow. Once the expedition was under way, members could not just leave the company or do as they pleased. While the members were often consulted and allowed to voice their preferences or "vote" as many writers and historians like to point out, such as in the "election" of Patrick Gass to become the Sergeant to fill the position after Charles Floyd died, or when the members "voted" on where to set up winter camp in 1805-6, they were always expected to do as the captains said. This is probably best shown when the Corps faced the problem of determining which river to follow when they came to a river junction in central Montana. After more than a week of exploration up the two rivers all of the members of the Corps felt that the muddy branch, not the clear branch, was the Missouri River. The two captains, however, believed it was the clear river and off they went. The command had been given, and the Corps followed without question. Infractions of the rules or the disobeying of orders could and did result in court martials and appropriate military punishments.

On July 11/12, 1804 Alexander Willard was accused of sleeping while on sentinel duty. The court martial found him guilty, and he received 100 lashes each for four consecutive days. On August 4, Moses Reed deserted. He was apprehended after a few days and brought back. A court-martial was held on August 18, 1804. He was found guilty of desertion, dishonorably discharged, but held until he could be sent back in the spring. Even their daily camp site seem to have been set up according to military regulations regarding the placement of tents, fires, and latrines.

Travel on the other great trails was organized into companies. They were usually formed voluntarily, but they did have leaders and rules. Everyone was expected to follow them, but not everyone did. Members could vote to change their leaders and rules, and sometimes did so. Individuals or families with their wagons could decide to leave a wagon company and join another if they so chose. They could even decide to quit and return back east if the trip became too hard or dangerous. All these things were common occurrences during the westward migration of wagon companies, but they could not be tolerated in the Lewis and Clark Expedition.

The Lewis and Clark Trail was a trail of exploration and discovery, not of emigration and commerce. For the most part, it pre-dates the other great trails mentioned. In one sense it helped to make the others possible. While much information about the Northwest Territories—lands north of the Ohio—was known, knowledge about the lands west of the Mississippi River was only beginning to trickle in. The information that Lewis and Clark brought back about the fertile lands, the great variety of wildlife and plant life, and the inhabitants of the west helped to inspire the dreams of many people.

The expedition did succeed and meet, perhaps even exceeding, its expectations concerning many of its other goals. It did expand the geographical knowledge of the interior of the continent. Clark's map is included later in this book. Samples of the soils, rocks, and minerals were collected. The examination and recording of information about the flora and fauna (plants and animals) of the land occupied much of the time and pages of the captains' reports. The captains made some drawings but most of the time took specimens and used words to describe their items. One hundred seventy-eight species of plants were identified and recorded. Two hundred thirty nine plant specimens were dried and pressed and brought back. Seeds were collected and included. The specimens were given to the American Philosophical Society and most are presently on loan to the Academy of Natural Sciences.

One hundred twenty-two species and subspecies of animals—fish, reptiles and amphibians, birds, and mammals were recorded. Some of those animals were known, while others were new. A few, such as Lewis's Woodpecker and Clark's Nutcracker were named after the captains. Unfortunately, some of the animals mentioned or identified, Audubon's bighorn mountain sheep, the Carolina parakeet, the ivory-billed woodpecker, and the passenger pigeon, have since become extinct. Others, such as the white sturgeon, steelhead trout, black-footed ferret, and California condor, became nearly extinct and were placed on the federal endangered species list. Other animals are on state lists. Lewis and Clark even recorded information about fossils of extinct animals that they uncovered.

Lewis and Clark's ethnological observations about the Indians were detailed and extensive. Doctor Benjamin Rush, whom Lewis studied with at Jefferson's request, also asked Lewis to record information about a variety of areas related to the Indian population. This the captains did as faithfully as they could. Sometimes their cultural biases impacted their behavior and observations. Their observations about the Indians with whom they stayed for an extended time proved to be the most inclusive. Some of the behaviors and information recorded was so culturally different it was hard for people back home to believe. The captains not only recorded information that they observed first-hand, but also information provided by and about other Indians from the Indians and traders with whom they were in contact. It has only been in recent years that this aspect of their expedition has begun to receive the attention it deserves.

CHAPTER TWO

Profiles

The success of any mission is the function of a number of factors, including leadership; composition and skills of the members; outside people who have an impact; planning; and conditions encountered, both those within and outside of the members' control. The focus here will be on the people who became members of the Corps of Volunteers for Northwestern Discovery and some other people the Corps came in contact with who influenced the success of the expedition.

To accomplish the goals given to Lewis by President Jefferson the expedition needed a unique mix of people, commitment and discipline. The expedition was to be lengthy in nature, away from normal contacts and sources of supplies and assistance, with many great unknowns. It required leaders who were respected, trusted, knowledgeable and adaptable. A wide variety of people and skills were needed: soldiers, hunters, cooks, woodsmen, interpreters, blacksmiths, gunsmiths, carpenters, and boatmen. They had to be physically fit, skilled, independent, self-reliant, reliable, yet work well with others and be able to take commands, and be willing to leave their home and family. Originally Jefferson thought of a corps of about twelve people, but that was before the agreement to buy all of Louisiana. Then Jefferson and Lewis expanded the size of the expedition. The Corps of Volunteers for Northwestern Discovery (now referred to as the Corps of Discovery) that started up the Missouri in 1804 was comprised of the two captains, thirty-six selected members, Clark's slave, York, plus about eleven French engagés or boatmen. Writing to Clark on June 19, 1803, Lewis asked him to find "some good hunters, stout, healthy, unmarried men, accustom to the woods, and capable of bearing bodily fatigue in a pretty considerable degree." The selection of the Corps began. Historians often cite a group from the Kentucky area as playing a significant role. They have been called the "nine young men from Kentucky."

During the winter of 1803-04, the captains decided they would divide the Corps into a return party and a permanent party. The individual members of the two parties changed a little over time. That has caused researchers some confusion. A small return party of six, plus the French engagés, and perhaps some Indians were assigned to take the barge or keelboat and return with reports and materials collected, while the rest of the party, designated the permanent party, would continue on west to complete the whole journey. The captains made a final list of those who continued on April 7, 1805, but never comprised one that included all those returning. The permanent party that continued totaled thirty-three—the two captains, three sergeants, twenty-three privates, one civilian hunter/interpreter, one slave, and the three members of the Charbonneau family. In addition, there was one Mandan who hoped to go as far as the Shoshoni village area and return.

Historians have not been able to uncover much information about many members of the Corps, and therefore, one might assume that many were ordinary people who were called to duty, accomplished it, and then were satisfied to return to a normal life. One could surmise that all the men were generally well qualified for their positions and performed their daily duties in an acceptable manner unless otherwise noted. It was a military command, and the captains' journals were for recording information and materials in accordance with their instruction—about their explorations, discoveries, and other noteworthy items. They did not spend time and space describing in detail what each member of the expedition did. It was not necessary to record that the men did their daily duties, but they would probably record information about misconduct and court-martial findings.

Even the men who were given instructions to keep journals were expected to put the significant items in it. Thus, it seems that attention was given to those things that were uncommon occurrences, things that were extraordinary or detrimental. Thus, when an individual messed up or did something above and beyond the call of duty, they were mentioned in a journal. However, if the men fulfilled their many duties and performed up to expectations and completed the difficult daily tasks, the journals could be silent and little would be known about their specifics during the journey. One thing that does seem to be true is that these were relatively young men who faced the unknown. Lewis was twenty-nine, and Clark, thirty-three. The oldest was John Shields, thirty-four, and the youngest, George Shannon, eighteen. The average age for the other men was probably in the mid-twenties.

The military command was comprised of the two commanders, Meriwether Lewis and William Clark who served as co-captains. Lewis still retained his military rank of captain. As noted earlier, Clark was actually a lieutenant with the "captain" title. Three men originally served as sergeants—John Ordway, Nathaniel Pryor, and Charles Floyd. After Floyd died, Patrick Gass, was

Collection of the New York Historical Society #6003
Thomas Jefferson

appointed in his place. There was one corporal, Richard Warfington, and the rest were privates. The "nine young men from Kentucky" are sometimes called the heart of the crew. Two French rivermen: Pierre Cruzatte and Francois Labiche enlisted in St. Charles. Pierre Cruzatte and Private George Gibson brought their fiddles and entertained both the Corps and Indians they met. The civilian members were: George Drouillard, the interpreter/hunter; York, Clark's slave; and Toussaint Charbonneau, his wife Sacagawea and their baby Jean Baptiste Charbonneau, called "Pomp." These last three joined the permanent crew during the winter stay at the Mandan villages.

THOMAS JEFFERSON was one of the founding fathers of the United States, the author of the Declaration of Independence, vice-president under John Adams, and the third president of the United States, serving from 1800-1808. It was during his first term that he doubled the size of the United States with the purchase of the Louisiana Territory.

Jefferson was born on April 13, 1743, at Shadwell, the Jefferson family farm in Albemarle County, Virginia. Jefferson was a true man of the Enlightenment. He had a huge appetite for knowledge. Even before the United States obtained the Louisiana Territory, Jefferson had a vision of a United States that included a nation that stretched across the continent from the Atlantic to the Pacific. It was this vision that culminated in the Lewis and Clark Expedition in 1803.

Jefferson's first attempt to organize an expedition to the West was in 1783. He tried to persuade General George Rogers Clark, older brother of William, to lead the expedition, but nothing materialized. A few years later he encouraged John Ledyard, but the proposal lacked support. In 1793 Jefferson hoped to back a journey by the French botanist André Michaux. A young Lewis asked to accompany Michaux, but again factors arose that halted the venture before it began. Jefferson's election as president gave him the authority and opportunity to make his vision come true.

In 1803, President Jefferson organized the Lewis and Clark Expedition of Northwestern Discovery. While the expedition was going on Jefferson was re-elected president. Other expeditions of exploration and discovery were organized during his presidency. Zebulon Pike was sent north to find the source of the Mississippi River. Next Pike was sent west to explore the Arkansas River and central plains to the Rocky Mountains. The Exploring Expedition of the Red River, also known as the Freeman-Custis Expedition, was sent southwest to explore the Arkansas and Red Rivers. However, none of these were as successful as the Lewis and Clark expedition.

MERIWETHER LEWIS was born August 18, 1774 at Locust Hill in Albemarle County, near Charlottesville, Virginia. He served as a private in the militia in T. Walker's volunteer corps during the Whiskey Rebellion in 1794. In 1795, he was assigned to the army under General Anthony Wayne and then transferred to one of the elite rifle units commanded by William Clark. He continued his military service and was promoted to lieutenant in 1799 and to captain in 1801. Then President Jefferson asked Lewis to come to Washington to work with him. He also retained his military rank at this time.

Lewis was only twenty-nine years old when President Thomas Jefferson selected him to lead of the Corps of Discovery. He was already serving as Jefferson's private secretary and was well respected and trusted. When Lewis was asked to appoint another person to lead the expedition with him, he selected William Clark as co-captain. They had developed a friendship while serving together and knew they could rely on each other.

Lewis was also the scientific leader. Prior to the expedition, Jefferson had Lewis study botany so that he would have a working knowledge about what plants were known and unknown and a

vocabulary for the flora and
fauna. He was taught about
mapmaking, astronomy and
the use of celestial instruments. He studied geology,
zoology and the latest medical
knowledge under Doctor
Benjamin Rush, one of the
most famous physicians of the
day. Lewis served as the doctor
for the Corps and the Indians.
Just prior to the start of the
expedition, he was elected to
the American Philosophical
Society, one of the most presti-
gious scientific organizations
of the day.

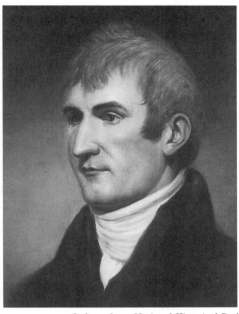

Independence National Historical Park
Meriwether Lewis

After the expedition
returned, Jefferson appointed
Lewis governor of the
Louisiana Territory. He was
supposed to prepare the expe-
dition's journals for publication. Although he started the journal project, his duties associated with his new position and the varied stress-
es he faced never allowed him to finish them. Lewis appears to have
suffered from periods of depression due to a variety of possible medical, psychological and financial issues. He became entwined in a number of disputes. Many involved financial matters related to the expedition or post-expedition matters. In 1809, he decided to return to
Washington to try to straighten out the problems. He never made it.
He died of gunshot wounds while stopped overnight at an inn,
Grinders Stand, on the Natchez Trace. It is thought he committed suicide, but some scholars believe he was murdered. His memorial is
located on the trail at Hohenwald, Tennessee near where he died.

WILLIAM CLARK was only thirty-three years old when he was
selected by Lewis to serve as his co-captain for the Corps of Discovery.
He was born on August 1, 1770 in Caroline County, Virginia. His older
brother, George Rogers Clark, was a famous American Revolutionary
War hero. William Clark joined the militia at nineteen. He fought
against the Cherokee and Creek Indians in 1790. In 1792, he became
a lieutenant in the regular army and served under General Anthony
Wayne. By 1795, Captain Clark became Lewis's commanding officer.

While they did not serve together for very long, they did get to know and trust each other. Clark resigned his commission in 1796 to take care of family matters.

In 1803, Lewis asked him serve as co-commander of the expedition with Jefferson's concurrence. On July 29, 1803, Clark accepted the offer. He was supposed to return to service with the rank of captain, but politics intervened. His official rank was second lieutenant in the Corps of Artillerists. This fact was kept secret from the Corps. He served as co-captain and to all the members of the expedition he had the rank of captain. However, Clark was paid at the rate of a lieutenant, $30.00 a month.

Independence National Historical Park
William Clark

Clark was a skilled cartographer and was responsible for mapping the route they had explored. He also sketched much of the animal life encountered on their voyage of discovery.

Clark developed a friendship with the Indians and had a reputation for honest and fair dealing. He was called the "Red-Headed Chief" by natives. In 1807, he was appointed the Superintendent of Indian Affairs for the Louisiana Territory. He continued to be reappointed by later presidents to similar positions until his death in 1838. In 1808, he constructed Fort (Clark) Osage as part of the American factory system of Indian trade. In 1813, he was appointed governor for the Missouri Territory and held that position until Missouri became a state in 1821. In 1820, he ran for governor for the state of Missouri but was defeated. After assisting Nicholas Biddle, the journals of the expedition were finally published in 1814. In January 1808, Clark married sixteen-year-old Julia Hancock for whom he had named the Judith River in Montana. Together they had five children. After Julia's death in 1821, he married Harriet Radford Kennerly, Julia's cousin. They had two children. Clark died in St. Louis in 1838. In 1850, his body was moved from its original resting place to the Bellefontaine Cemetery outside St. Louis, Missouri.

YORK. As with many of the other members of the expedition there are some disagreements and gaps in the knowledge about York's life. York was probably born in the early 1770s, to Old York and Rose, slaves of John Clark, William's father. After John died in 1799, William inherited York and became his legal owner. It is believed that York may have been raised to serve as William's body servant and companion. Therefore, he was probably a few years younger than William. When William was selected to serve as co-captain of the expedition it was natural for his slave/body servant to go with him.

York was black, big, agile, strong, with "short curling hair" and was thought to have a good sense of humor. Once in the journey Clark described him as fat, but with all the physical work that characteristic, if accurate, probably changed. As the first black man seen by many of the Indians, York was considered to be both a curiosity and "big medicine" by them. That certainly helped the Corps when meeting the Arikaras and Mandans, and later, the Shoshonis and Nez Perce.

In most respects York served as an equal member of the Corps of Discovery. He was allowed to carry a rifle, to participate in discussions, and at times, even in the decision making process. He was sent hunting like other members, participated freely in trading with the Indians for needed food, and was also allowed to send a buffalo robe back to his wife with the return party in 1805. The fact that he was part of the reconnaissance party at Marias River shows the confidence the captains had in him. He even voted as an equal after the Corps arrived at the Pacific when they decided where to spend the winter. Just as other members had places named after them and recorded on the maps, York's name was given to two sites: islands on the Missouri and a small tributary of the Yellowstone River, which is now called Custer Creek.

After the expedition returned, York continued to serve as Clark's slave. However, relations between Clark and York became strained when Clark moved to St. Louis. York's wife belonged to a family near Louisville, Kentucky. Clark finally allowed him to be hired out near there so he could be close to her. By 1811, Clark gave him his freedom and helped to set him up. York operated a freighting business in Kentucky and Tennessee until about 1832 when it failed. While on his way to visit or return to Clark in St. Louis, he died of cholera. Another story holds that he went back west to live with the Crow Indians in the 1830s, but this story is dismissed by most historians.

SACAGAWEA (Bird Woman) was born a member of the Lemhi Shoshoni tribe in about 1788. They lived along the modern day Idaho-Montana border. While the tribe was on a buffalo hunt at Three Forks in 1800, she was captured by the Hidatsa and brought back east to the Knife River area in present-day South Dakota. She became one of two wives of Toussaint Charbonneau. She was about sixteen years old and pregnant when her husband signed on with Lewis and Clark as an interpreter. At times she also helped as an interpreter. She could speak both Hidatsa and Shoshoni. On February 11, 1805, Sacagawea, nicknamed "Janey" by Clark, gave birth to a boy, Jean Baptiste, at Fort Mandan, nicknamed "Pomp" by Clark.

Sacagawea played a significant role in the success of the Corps of Discovery, but her role as a guide was minimal. Her level headedness during crises, her food gathering abilities, her knowledge of the Three Forks area, and her function as an ambassador all helped the expedition to succeed. Clark noted that her presence . . .*confirmed (to) those people of our friendly intentions, as no woman ever accompanies a war party. . .* The captains recorded her gathering a variety of roots and plant foods all along the track.

On May 16, 1805, a powerful wind almost rolled the white pirogue over. Water was coming in and supplies and equipment would have been lost except for the quick thinking and actions of Sacagawea. Lewis recorded, *The Indian woman to whom I ascribe equal fortitude and resolution, with any person on board at the time of the accedent, caught and preserved most of the light articles which were washed overboard.* However, it was her ability to speak Shoshoni that would prove invaluable to the Corps. The Corps needed horses to cross the mountains once they left the Missouri, and she helped with needed translation. When they finally arrived at the Pacific she even had a vote in deciding where to build their winter camp.

When the Corps returned in 1806 to the Mandan Village, Sacagawea remained there with her family. In late 1809, she and Charbonneau visited Clark in St. Louis. They brought Pomp to be educated by Clark as they had agreed to when they parted the Corps at the Mandan Village in 1806. She and Charbonneau returned to the Knife River in 1811. In August 1812 they went to Fort Manuel with their new baby, a girl named Lizette Charbonneau. On December 20, 1812, while at Fort Manuel, Sacagawea was reported to have died of "putrid fever." Lizette was later sent to Clark in St. Louis. Some scholars have questioned this account and claimed Sacagawea lived in western Wyoming where she died in 1884, but most historians today do not accept this story. Other tribes in the West also have traditions related to Sacagawea.

The spelling of her name has been a topic of discussion from since Lewis and Clark met her and tried to write her name in their journals. More recently, it has been spelled with: a 'j,' "Sacajawea; a 'k,' Sakakawea; and a 'g', Sacagawea." It seems editor Biddle decided to first use the 'j,' in the official publication, but the more recent examinations of the original documents tends to support the 'g,' Sacagawea. However, her name and its spelling now have a history of their own, and that is hard to change. The Lemhi Shoshoni recognize only the Sacajawea spelling.

TOUSSAINT CHARBONNEAU was born in Canada of French and Indian descent around 1758. He became a trapper for the North West Company in Canada. He moved to the Knife River area in the late 1790s and acquired two Shoshoni captives as wives. Sacagawea was one of them. Charbonneau was hired as an interpreter in 1804 shortly after Lewis and Clark arrived in the Mandan/Hidatsa area. He was about forty-seven when he signed on and was then the oldest member in the Corps. Charbonneau could speak both French and Hidatsa. References to him were both laudatory and critical. As a cook he made the best "white pudding", but he was the "most timed (timid) waterman in the world." The fact that he could not swim, however, could explain that. When the Corps returned to the Mandan villages, he and his family chose to remain there.

For several years after the expedition he was associated with Manuel Lisa's Missouri Fur Company, often serving as interpreter. In late 1809, Charbonneau and Sacagawea went to visit Clark in St. Louis. It seems that they tried farming for a short time, but were not successful. Leaving Pomp with Clark to be educated, they returned to the Dakotas in April 1811 with Manuel Lisa. In the late summer of 1812, they were at Fort Manuel, near the present North/South Dakota border. Charbonneau was away when Sacagawea died that December. He was often employed as an interpreter for the government when Clark served as the Superintendent of Indian Affairs. During the War of 1812 he ran diplomatic errands for the United States government and the Missouri River tribes. In 1814, he may have returned to the Shoshoni Indians in the Wyoming and western Montana area. Then, in 1815, he joined an expedition to Santa Fe and was briefly imprisoned by the Spanish. By 1819, he was again serving as an interpreter for the Indian Bureau at the Upper Missouri Agency near the Mandan villages. In 1823, he briefly served as an interpreter for Prince Paul Wilhelm, Duke of Wurtemburg. Then, in 1833, when Prince

Maximilian, another German nobleman, visited the West, he served as his interpreter at Fort Clark and appeared in one of Karl Bodmer's paintings. Charbonneau remained on the government payroll as interpreter until 1838. He married again in 1838/39 after his other wife died in 1837. By the early 1840s he was thought to have died. It should be noted that just as there is a dispute over Sacagawea's death and burial, the same is true of his. There are a few who believe that he lived from 1781-1866 and is buried in Richwoods, Missouri.

JEAN BAPTISTE "POMP" CHARBONNEAU was son of Sacagawea and Toussaint Charbonneau. He was born February 11, 1805, at Fort Mandan. It was his presence, as a baby, along with his mother, which provided the Corps' physical evidence of the peaceful nature of the expedition when they met various Indian tribes. Clark became very fond of him and called him "Pomp."

On the return journey Lewis and Clark split up at the camp at Travelers Rest. Lewis headed up to explore the Marias River, and Clark cut over to the Yellowstone River. Janey and Pomp came with Clark. Along the river the party came to a large sandstone rock formation on the south side of the river. Clark named this "Pompys Tower", known today as Pompey's Pillar. When the Corps returned to the Mandan and Hidatsa villages Clark offered to take Pomp back to civilization and have him educated. However, Sacagawea felt that he was too young to be taken from his family, but accepted the idea that at the age of four it would be permissible.

In 1809, Sacagawea and Charbonneau brought Pomp, then almost five years old, to St. Louis and Clark for him to be schooled. Pomp was educated by the Jesuits. He already spoke Hidatsa, Shoshoni, French, and English. The Jesuits taught him Greek and Latin. After he completed his education he returned to the Hidatsa. In 1823, Pomp met Prince Paul Wilhelm, Duke of Wurtemburg for whom his father also served for a time as a guide and interpreter. In 1824, Pomp returned to "Germany" with the Duke to study and travel. There he learned German and Italian. He also learned to play the violin and was reported to have played with Beethoven. In 1829 he returned home to the Hidatsa after stopping to visit with Clark. He then became a mountain man, scout, and guide. He traveled with Jim Bridger, Jim Beckwourth, and Joe Meek. By 1844, he was a hunter for Bent's Fort. In 1846, he served as guide for Philip St. George Cooke and the Mormon Battalion going from Santa Fe to San Diego, California. At other times he acted as a guide for John C. Fremont, W. H. Emory and James Abert. It seems he caught the "gold fever," and eventually he settled in California. He served as the acalde, or mayor, of Mission San

Luis Rey for a short time. It seems that he did not have much success in finding gold in California. He died of pneumonia on May 16, 1866, in Inskip Station, Oregon. He was on his way from California to the goldfields in Montana. Only Patrick Gass lived longer. Pomp is buried at Danner, Oregon.

GEORGE DROUILLARD (Drewyer) was born in Canada in the late 1770s. His father, Pierre, a friend of George Rogers Clark, was French, and his mother was Shawnee. Historians consider him to have been one of the most important members on the expedition. In the late 1790s, he served in the U.S. Army along the Ohio River at Fort Massac enforcing the Pinckney Treaty. He was reported to have known seven of the local Indian languages in the area.

He joined the Lewis and Clark Expedition as a civilian in 1803. He served as an interpreter with his knowledge of French, Shawnee, and Plains Indian sign language. He was considered to be the expedition's best shot, hunter and scout. He was also a good boatman with some knowledge of the Missouri River. These skills were crucial for the success of the expedition. Lewis referred to him as *A man of much merit; he has been peculiarly useful from his knowledge of the common language of gesticulation, and his uncommon skill as a hunter and woodsman; those several duties he performed in good faith, and with an ardor which deserves the highest commendation. It was his fate also to have encountered. . .all the most dangerous and trying scenes of the voyage, in which he uniformly acquitted himself with honor.*

During the winter at Fort Clatsop, Lewis wrote on January 12, 1806, . . .*Dreweyer having killed seven Elk; I scarcely know how we should subsist were it not for the exertion of the excillet hunter.* On the return trip Drouillard was with Lewis's party after the Corps divided at Travelers Rest. In July of 1806, a conflict arose with the Indians on the Two Medicine River. In the ensuing fight two of the Indians were killed. Most historians note the Indians as Blackfeet, but others note them as Gross Ventres.

After the expedition, Drouillard returned to the West to explore and trap. In March 1807, he was employed by Manuel Lisa, a St. Louis entrepeneur, to build a trading post at the confluence of the Bighorn and Yellowstone rivers. John Potts, Peter Weiser and John Colter, all former members of the Corps of Discovery were part of the party that built Fort Lisa. By 1809 Drouillard was one of the minor partners with Lisa. In 1810, he, along with John Colter, was part of the party led by Pierre Menard that went up the Yellowstone, over the Bozeman Pass to the Three Forks to establish Fort Piegan. This was supposed to be a permanent trading post. Relations with the Blackfeet Indians were going from bad to worse. In April, the Blackfeet killed five trappers. Colter and other trappers left, but Drouillard remained. Then, in May, while trapping for beaver on the Jefferson, Drouillard, and two other Indian trappers, were killed by the Blackfeet.

Who were the nine young men from Kentucky often referred to as the heart of the Corps? They were the men that were recruited from the area around the Falls of the Ohio. They came from both sides of the Ohio River, but have been referred to as from Kentucky. Two of them were selected by Lewis, and the other seven selected by Clark.

WILLIAM BRATTON was born on July 27, 1778 in Virginia. It is believed that his parents moved to Kentucky about 1790. By the time he joined the Corps on October 20, 1803, he had developed into a tall and muscular young man. Bratton served as one of two blacksmiths for the expedition, and also as a gunsmith and hunter. He was also one of the salt makers during the stay at Fort Clatsop at the Pacific. He suffered from a back injury that greatly restricted his usefulness for a number of weeks. Finally, John Shields treated him by using a sweathouse and herbs. After his discharge in 1806 Bratton returned to Kentucky but moved to Missouri within a few years. He served in the War of 1812. He married Mary Maxwell on November 25, 1819, lived in Ohio, and moved to Waynetown, Indiana in 1822. They had ten children. He died there on November 11, 1841 at age sixty-one.

JOHN COLTER was born in Staunton, Virginia, in 1775. Little is known about him until October 15, 1803 when Lewis signed him on in what is now Maysville, Kentucky. Colter became one of the expedition's main hunters. This was a very important function since the total rations brought along were estimated to be enough for only forty to forty-five days. Hunting, along with trading, was expected to be the primary method of obtaining food. Colter was the only member allowed to leave the expedition before it returned to St. Louis. While at the Mandan villages he requested permission to join two trappers who were on their way up the Missouri to trade and trap for furs. The captains and Corps voted to allow it. Colter is also well known for his discovery of "Colter's Hell," a land of thermal hot springs and steaming holes. This area is known today as Yellowstone National Park.

While returning from trapping out west in 1807, Colter joined the party led by Manuel Lisa to establish a trading post on the Bighorn River in present-day Montana. There they built Fort Raymond, commonly called Fort Lisa or Fort Manuel. During that winter, alone, he traversed the Yellowstone area. In spring of 1808, he was wounded in the leg during a fight with the Blackfeet. Later that year, he and John

Potts, another former member of the Corps of Discovery, were involved in another fight with the Blackfeet near Three Forks. Potts was killed and Colter captured. He was stripped and allowed to "run for his life." He killed one of the pursuers and escaped by jumping into the Jefferson River and hiding under some logs until the Blackfeet left.

Colter returned to the Mandan villages in the fall of 1809 where he was engaged to serve as a guide by the Missouri Fur Company. In the spring of 1810, he guided the party under Pierre Menard that went up the Yellowstone River, over the Bozeman Pass and out to Three Forks to build Fort Piegan. There hostilities with the Blackfeet resumed. In April, after more trappers were killed, Colter decided he had had enough and decided to leave the area forever. He returned east, married a woman named Sally, and settled on a farm near La Charette, Missouri. Daniel Boone was one of his neighbors. It is said that he served with Nathan Boone's Rangers in the War of 1812. One account holds that he died of jaundice in 1813 and was buried near Dundee, Missouri. The other account indicates that he died on May 7, 1812, and that his grave is near New Haven, Missouri.

CHARLES FLOYD is remembered as the only person who died on the expedition. He was recruited by Clark on August 1, 1803. He was born in Kentucky in 1782.

Floyd was highly respected by both Lewis and Clark. He was a civilian who was appointed to serve as one of the original three sergeants. The fact that he was appointed over other men who were older, had more experience as woodsmen and had military service, speaks highly of him. His cousin, Nathaniel Pryor, was also a member of the expedition and was also appointed sergeant. While at Camp Dubois, Floyd was placed in charge of the officers' quarters and stores in their absence. His diary started on May 14, 1804, and ended August 18, 1804, two days before he died. On August 18, while at a council with the Oto and Missouri Indians, it was noticed that he was looking pale. On the 19th he was severely ill. Lewis tried to assist him, but nothing helped.

On August 20, the expedition left the council site. John Ordway recorded the events:

we Sailed on verry well til noon when we came too on S.S. Sergt. Charles Floyd Expired directly after we halted a little past the middle of the day. He was laid out in the Best Manner possible. We proceeded on to the first hills N.S. there we dug the Grave on a handsome Slightly Round knob close to the bank. We buried him with the honours of war. the usual Serrymony performed. . .we put a red cedar post, hughn &

branded his name date& C.- we named those Bluffs Sergeant Charles Floyds Bluff. . . .we then proceeded on a short distance to a creek which we call Floyds Creek.

Today it is thought that Floyd died of appendicitis. He was the first American soldier to die west of the Mississippi.

Floyd's grave is south of present-day Sioux City, Iowa. On the return journey the Corps visited his grave. It had been opened so he was reburied. In 1857, the river flooded and nearly washed the grave out so it was moved back a little on the bluff. In 1895, he was reburied again, and finally, in 1901, his remains were placed under the shaft that stands today. His journal, brief as it is, has been published.

JOSEPH FIELDS AND REUBIN FIELD(S) were probably born sometime after 1774. Their parents moved to Kentucky in 1783. Clark enlisted the brothers on August 1, 1803. Both were held in high esteem by their captains. After the return Lewis wrote "two of the most active and enterprising young men who accompanied us. It was their peculiar fate to have been engaged in all the most dangerous and difficult scenes of the voyage, in which they acquitted themselves with much honor."

Some believe that Joseph, and perhaps Reubin, may have worked for their older brother Ezkial, in the salt business before the expedition. Clark knew of them and their family. Reubin did have some problems with discipline early in the expedition, but he was able to overcome them. After the return Clark recommended Reubin for a promotion as a lieutenant. Joseph was credited with killing the first buffalo on August 23, 1804. He was one of the men who made salt during the winter on the Pacific. Both brothers were considered excellent shots and good hunters. They were with Lewis when they encountered the Shoshoni and later the Blackfeet while exploring the northern reaches of the Marias River in 1806. Their encounter with the Blackfeet left one or two Indians dead. After the Corps' return, the two went back to Kentucky. It seems that Joseph met a violent death by October 1807, as recorded by Clark. Reubin married Mary Myrtle in 1808 and settled down to farming. Records indicate that he died in 1822.

GEORGE GIBSON was born outside of Pittsburgh, but his family later moved to Kentucky. He was one of the two men known to have brought their fiddles. He was also considered one of the better hunters, horsemen, and interpreters. After their return Gibson married and moved to Missouri. He may have served in the failed attempt to return Chief Sheheke's party to the Mandan villages. Gibson died in 1809 in St. Louis.

JOHN SHIELDS was born sometime in 1769 near Harrisonburg, Virginia. By 1784 his parents moved their family to the Smoky Mountains where he learned his skills as a blacksmith and miller. He moved to Kentucky, married, and continued to develop his skills.

One could theorize that Shields impressed the captains with his numerous skills before the expedition. Shields was married and was thirty-four years old, the oldest member when he enlisted as a private. It was his expertise as a blacksmith, gunsmith, mechanic, hunter, and his familiarity with medical knowledge that made him respected by the Corps. Shields performed his smithing skills in trade for food. That helped the Corps to survive the winter at Fort Mandan and later at Fort Clatsop. When William Bratton hurt his back, it was Shields who suggested and made the sweat lodge and herbal drink.

Lewis's report about Shields noted that *Nothing was more peculiarly useful to us, in various situation, then the skill and ingenuity of this man as an artist, in repairing guns, accroutements, &c.* After the Corps returned, Shields stayed in Missouri and trapped with Daniel Boone. The following year he returned to the Falls of the Ohio area. He died in 1809. It is believed that he is buried in Corydon, Indiana.

NATHANIEL PRYOR was born on April 2, 1772 near the Falls of the Ohio in Kentucky. He was Charles Floyd's cousin. He served as one of the three original sergeants during the expedition. He remained in the army after his return and was in command of the military escort that attempted to return Chief Sheheke and his party to his Mandan village. That attempt failed. By 1808 Pryor was a lieutenant and performed some duties for Clark. Pryor left the army in 1810 and became a licensed Indian trader. He rejoined the army during the War of 1812 served as captain and fought at the Battle of New Orleans. After the war he returned to his prior occupation as Indian trader, married an Osage woman and lived near Fort Smith. He died on June 11, 1831 and is buried in Pryor, Oklahoma the town named for him.

GEORGE SHANNON was eighteen years old when he joined the expedition. He was the youngest man to serve. Shannon was born in Pennsylvania in 1785 and his family had moved to Ohio by 1800. He was one of the earliest members to join. He is thought to have been one of the men selected by Lewis in Pittsburgh and then signed on formally when they stopped at Maysville, Kentucky. He was not considered to be the best woodsman, and some writers have stressed those situations in which he was lost or separated. However, Lewis and Clark respected his great courage, perseverance and loyalty.

Early in the journey Shannon was "lost" for sixteen days. He went hunting and thought he had fallen behind and tried to catch up. He used up all his bullets and nearly starved. He had to rely on berries for food. He did manage to kill a rabbit with a stick he shot from his rifle. With all hope gone, he finally decided to give up trying to catch up to the expedition. He sat down on the riverbank hoping some Indians or trappers would come along and take him down river. However, around the bend came the expedition. In reality he was not lost, but he had been ahead of and not behind the rest of the Corps.

The high regard that Lewis and Clark had for Shannon was shown by their actions. They selected him to be part of the expedition that returned to Washington along with some Indian chiefs to meet with Jefferson. In 1807, he was part of the party that attempted to return the chiefs to their villages. The return party got into a fight with the Arikaras, and Shannon was severely wounded. As a result his leg was amputated. After that he became known as "Peg Leg" Shannon.

In 1809, Clark asked Shannon to assist Nicholas Biddle in preparing the first edition of the Lewis and Clark journals. In 1810, he went to Philadelphia to start working on them. The journals were finally published in 1814. Clark asked him to join him in the fur trade business, but Shannon had other plans. He went to the university, studied law and became a lawyer practicing in Lexington, Kentucky and a legislator. Later, he also served as senator for Missouri and as a judge. He died in 1836, at the age of fifty-one, and was buried in a cemetery in Palmyra, Missouri. His specific gravesite is not presently known.

Other members of the Corps of Discovery.

JOHN BOLEY was the only member of the Corps to serve on three of the four expeditions of exploration in the Louisiana Territory. First he served as a private with Lewis and Clark. He was not one of the permanent members, and he returned to St. Louis in April 1805 with the keelboat. Shortly after he returned he served under Zebulon Pike on his two expeditions. The first was up the Mississippi to determine its source and the second was along the Arkansas River to the Rocky Mountains to determine its source. Pike divided his command and Boley was in the return party sent down the Arkansas and was not with Pike when he was captured. After Boley's return he married and settled outside of St. Louis.

JOHN COLLINS was born in Maryland. He officially joined the Corps at Camp Dubois on January 1, 1804, but may have been transferred from Fort Massac. He was involved in a number of disciplinary actions while at Camp Dubois and on the journey. He was accused of drinking while on sentry duty. He was found guilty and received 100 lashes. However, the captains kept him as one of the permanent party. He was assigned as the cook for Sergeant Nathaniel Pryor's squad, and was often referred to as one of the hunters. After the return he was another of the Corps members involved with other groups that went west. He joined William Ashley's party. Collins died in a fight with the Arikaras in 1823.

PIERRE CRUZATTE served as a private in the army on the expedition, officially joining it in St. Charles on May 16, 1804. His father was French and his mother was an Omaha Indian. He had lost one eye and was nearsighted in the other, but this rarely seemed to act as a handicap. He had been employed in the fur trade with the Chouteau family prior to his joining Lewis and Clark. He had frequently traveled and wintered along the Missouri as far north as the Platte River. He knew Indian sign language and also spoke the Omaha language. Knowledge of both proved to be valuable along the lower Missouri. He helped to set up a council with the Missouri and Oto Indians in July 1804, and then again, with the Teton Sioux in September. He was instrumental in helping to regain possession of the white pirogue from the Sioux after they took it.

Cruzatte was considered to be one of the best boatmen on the expedition and his knowledge of the lower Missouri River made him even more valuable. It seemed he was able to "read" the river and was often assigned to the position of bowman in the keelboat. He, along with Sacagawea, was instrumental in saving valuable supplies and equipment when the winds came up nearly swamping one of the canoes. However, he is remembered the most for two other reasons. He brought his fiddle along and he entertained both the Corps and the Indians all along the journey. He is also believed to have been the person who shot Lewis in the upper thigh or buttocks. The two had gone elk hunting along the Missouri in some willow thickets. Perhaps it was Lewis's buckskin outfit and Cruzatte's use of only one eye that caused him to think that he had shot and wounded an elk. However, the reality was that Lewis was shot and there were no one else around who might have done it.

After the expedition was over, he was thought to have returned to the West to explore and trap just as many other members of the Corps did. Some historians believe he was with John McClellan's 1807 expedition to the Rockies, but little is known. Some think he died in the mid-1820s as a result of a fight with the Blackfeet as had Corps members John Potts in 1808 and George Drouillard in 1810.

JOHN DAME was born in Pallingham, New Hampshire. He joined the army in 1801. He was recruited while serving in Captain Stoddard's artillery company at Fort Kaskaskia. He served as a private. It seems he was one of the men who killed a pelican on August 8, 1804 near Pelican Island. However, it was not the one measured and described in detail by Lewis. Dame was not a member of the permanent party, but was assigned to the return party of 1805. Little else is known about him.

ROBERT FRAZER was probably born in Virginia. He was originally designated as a member of the return party, but as a result of Moses Reed's court martial and discharge, Frazer replaced him as a member of the permanent party. He was one of the few privates to keep a journal. After the Corps was disbanded in St. Louis, he remained in the party with Lewis that continued to Washington in 1806. It seems that he got permission to have his journal published, but unfortunately, it never was, and it seems to have been lost. His map, however, was published in 1807, but does not compare with Clark's maps. Frazer returned to Missouri and settled west of St. Louis and lived there until he died in 1837.

PATRICK GASS was born on June 12, 1771, in Falling Springs, Pennsylvania. He joined the local militia in 1792 to protect the local inhabitants from Indian attacks, but he saw no action. In 1794, he served as an apprentice carpenter until 1799. Then, when war with France threatened he joined the army. He served under General Alexander Hamilton, Major Jonathan Cass, and then Captain Russell Bissell. In 1803, when Lewis came to Fort Kaskaskia to look for recruits, Gass wanted to join. He was finally granted permission to join the Corps of Discovery. He initially signed on as a private with the expedition. However, on August 22, two days after the death of Sergeant Charles Floyd, Gass was elected sergeant by the men. On August 26, 1804, Lewis issued general orders giving him the rank of sergeant in "the corps of volunteers for North Western Discovery." Sergeants were expected to keep a journal, and his journal was the first published about the Lewis and Clark Expedition.

Gass was the master carpenter for the expedition. He was in charge of the construction at Camp Dubois, Fort Mandan and Fort Clatsop. He was also a boatman and later was placed in charge of one of the canoes. He built the canoes the expedition used after leaving Fort Mandan as well as the iron frame boat called *Experiment* at Great Falls. After crossing the mountains on the Nez Perce Trail he built the canoes used when the Corps left the Nez Perce and headed down the Clearwater, Snake and Columbia rivers. On the return journey he was placed in charge of the party that was left at the mouth of the Marias River while Lewis and three other men went to explore the river.

After the expedition returned, Gass worked on publishing his journal. There were some hard feelings and words with Lewis that resulted from his publishing effort. His journal was first published in 1807 and had a number of later editions. By 1814, it had been published in both French and German. When the War of 1812 broke out he enlisted in the military, lost an eye during his service and was discharged in 1815. He settled in Wellsburg in what is now West Virginia. In 1831, he married Maria Hamilton, and they had seven children, one of which died in infancy. Maria died in 1847. He died in 1870 having another distinction besides being one of the oldest members of the Corps, in that he was the last known member to die. He was almost ninety-nine. His grave is located in the Brooke Cemetery in Wellsburg, West Virginia.

SILAS GOODRICH was born in Massachusetts. He may have enlisted in the army before the expedition, but he was officially entered on its roster on January 1, 1804. Goodrich seems to be best known for his fishing skills. On August 24, 1805, Lewis referred to him as "our principal fisherman." After the corps returned, he re-enlisted in the army. Little else is known of him.

HUGH HALL was another man from Massachusetts, but may have been born in Carlisle, Pennsylvania. He was born about 1774. He first joined the army in 1798. He was serving with Captain John Campbell's infantry regiment in Tennessee before being assigned to the Corps. He was one of four to come from Captain Campbell's company. Hall, along with Collins, was court-martialed for stealing whiskey and getting drunk. Even though Hall had problems with alcohol, he was an original member of the permanent party and remained so. He was referred to as a hunter in the journals. He injured his foot during an accident while at Fort Clatsop. He was in the St. Louis area in 1809. Little else is known about him.

THOMAS HOWARD was also from Massachusetts. He had joined the army and was serving in Captain Campbell's Second Infantry Regiment in Tennessee when Lewis and Clark passed. He was transferred and officially entered the Corps on January 1, 1804. Howard had some disciplinary problems. While at Camp Dubois Clark noted that Howard "never Drinks water."

Howard had the distinction of being the last member of the Corps to be court-martialed. On February 9, 1805 Howard returned to the fort after the gate was closed. Instead of calling to the guard to open the gate, he scaled the stockade in the presence of an Indian. The Indian followed suit and came in behind Howard. Lewis had the guard take charge of Howard, and then he had a serious talk with the Indian. Lewis noted the danger in which Howard had now placed the whole Corps and fort. The next day Howard was court-martialed, found guilty and sentenced to fifty lashes. It is interesting to note that Lewis forgave him. Later while at Fort Clatsop, Lewis noted of Werner and Howard that "neither of them are very good woodsmen." There must have been other useful qualities that the captains saw that were never mentioned. After the expedition was over Howard remained in the army.

FRANCOIS LABICHE was recruited at Fort Kaskaskia, but his official enlistment was on May 16, 1804 in St. Charles along with Pierre Cruzatte. Labiche was appointed to the permanent party. He was recruited as an experienced boatman, interpreter and Indian trader. He played important roles when it came time to speak to the different Indians along the way and during formal councils. Lewis had Labriche return with him and the Indians to Washington during the winter of 1806-7. He returned to St. Louis and seems to have lived there until at least 1834.

JEAN BAPTISTE LEPAGE was a Frenchman living with the Mandans in 1804. He joined the Corps that winter and replaced John Newman who had been court-martialed and was sent back. Lepage's official enlistment was on November 3, 1804. There is some indication that he had previously traveled on the Missouri and Little Missouri west of the Mandan villages. He may have even helped to provide information used in the preparation of Clark's maps during that winter.

HUGH MCNEAL was born in Pennsylvania. He may have been in the army before he enlisted in the Corps. He was assigned to serve as a member of the permanent party and was in the second squad under Sergeant Floyd. On August 12, 1805, McNeal was with Lewis when they went ahead of the main party to find the Shoshoni. They climbed towards Lemhi Pass. Lewis wrote that below him McNeal *stood with a foot on each side of this rivulet. . . to bestride the mighty & heretofore deemed endless Missouri.* It seems that he remained in the army after his return.

JOHN NEWMAN was born in 1785. He was already serving in the army when Lewis and Clark came to Fort Kaskaskia. He was in

Captain Bissell's company of the First Infantry Regiment. In October, 1804, Newman faced a court-martial for "expressions of criminal and mutinous nature." He was found guilty and sentenced to seventy-five lashes and expelled from the party. The reality of the situation caused him to remain with the Corps until the spring when he was sent back to St. Louis in the spring of 1805. He worked hard to redeem himself so he could finish the journey. The captains, however, would not change his punishment. It seems that he settled in Missouri and married. By the 1830s Newman was trapping along the Missouri. He was killed in a fight with the Yankton Sioux in 1832.

JOHN ORDWAY was born in New Hampshire in about 1775. He was serving in the military in Captain Russell Bissell's infantry company in Kaskaskia, Illinois, in November 1803, when Lewis came to select members for the expedition. He was one of the few who were chosen from the many who volunteered there. He was officially placed on the expedition's roll on January 1, 1804. Lewis picked him to serve as one of the sergeants. Lewis considered him to be the most reliable of his noncommissioned officers. He was trusted by his men and was often placed in command when Lewis and Clark were not present. This happened frequently while at Camp Dubois, also known as Camp Wood. He was responsible for making sure that the sawyers, sugar makers, blacksmiths and hunters were fulfilling their duties. He also was in charge of Lewis's "practicing party" and of rewarding the best marksman. As a sergeant he was expected to keep a journal. While not as detailed as the captains' journals, he has an entry for every day of the journey from the day they left Wood River until they returned to St. Louis.

Ordway performed his duties well during the expedition. Most of the entries in Lewis and Clark's journals refer to him in the capacity of carrying out his duties or requests that he performed faithfully. On the return journey when the party was first divided in two, he was with Captain Clark's party. When the party reached Three Forks Clark divided his party. Ordway was placed in command of nine other men to take the canoes down to the Great Falls, make the portage, and join with Lewis and his party who had taken the overland route to explore the Marias River. Clark and the others cut over to the Yellowstone River.

After their successful return to St. Louis, Ordway was part of the Corps that returned along the old Wilderness Road to Washington with Lewis and the Mandan Chief Big White in 1806. Later that year, he was discharged from the army, and he returned to New Hampshire. Then, in 1809, he married, moved to Missouri, and became a successful farmer. He died around 1817. His journal was first published in 1916, nearly one century later.

JOHN POTTS was born in Dillenburg, Germany in 1776. Before enlisting in the army, he had been employed as a miller. He joined the army in 1800 and was serving in Captain John Campbell's company of the Second Infantry Regiment. He was reassigned to the Corps in November 1803 and arrived at Camp Dubois on December 22, 1803. He was selected by the captains to serve as a member of the permanent party. Potts was often noted as a hunter. After their return Potts returned to the mountains like many other members of the Corps. He joined Manuel Lisa's fur trading company. He was with John Colter in the Three Forks area when they got into a fight with the Blackfeet. Potts was killed in the encounter, but Colter was able to escape.

MOSES REED was originally assigned to the permanent party by the captains. He had some early discipline problems while at Camp Dubois. Under the guise of returning to look for a knife he lost, Reed deserted on August 4, 1804, was apprehended and brought back to camp on the 17th, court-martialed and sentenced on the 18th. He was dishonorably discharged, had to run the gauntlet, and given hard labor for the duration of his stay. Later, in October, he may have been involved in another disciplinary incident involving Newman, but Reed received no additional punishment. In the spring Reed was sent back to St. Louis with the keelboat. Little or nothing is known of him after that.

JOHN ROBINSON (Robertson) may have been born about 1780 in Streatham, New Hampshire. He enlisted and was serving at Fort Kaskaskia with Captain Amos Stoddard's company before he joined the Corps. There appears to be some confusion about his service. Robinson is first referred to as a corporal by Clark, but later after some problems occurred, he is listed as a private. There is no specific explanation. Robinson did have some other disciplinary problems before the journey started in the spring. The captains assigned him to the return party. There is also some question concerning his return. There is some evidence he may have returned in June 1804 not in the spring of 1805 as is more widely held. There is not enough information to exactly determine the truth.

JOHN THOMPSON enlisted in 1801 and was serving in Captain Amos Stoddard's Artillery Company. He was assigned to the permanent party and was later assigned to serve as the cook for Sergeant Floyd's squad. He may have had some experience as a surveyor, and that could account for Clark's comments about him as "a valuable member of the party." His services would have been useful in relation to mapping. By the late 1820s he had reportedly been killed.

EBENEZER TUTTLE was born in New Haven, Connecticut in 1773. He was one of the older members of the Corps. He had been a farmer before he joined the army in 1803. He was serving under Captain Stoddard at Fort Kaskaskia before becoming a member of the Corps. He was assigned to the return party under Corporal Richard Warfington. As with John Robertson there is little information about him in the journals and some question about his return. He may have been the person who returned in June, not Robinson.

CORPORAL RICHARD WARFINGTON was born in Louisburg, North Carolina in 1777. He had joined the army in 1799. In 1803 he was serving in the command of Captain John Campbell's company of the Second Infantry Regiment at South West Point, Tennessee. He was reassigned to the Corps on November 24, 1804. The captains placed him in charge of the return party. It seems that the initial plan was that the party would return sometime in the late summer with some of the captains' reports. However, it was changed so the party remained at Fort Mandan through the winter.

Warfington's enlistment ended, but the captains asked that he remain so that he could take the keelboat back under his military authority. Warfington accepted. When the permanent party continued west on April 7, 1805, the return party headed back down the Missouri with Warfington in command. They returned successfully to St. Louis and the reports, artifacts and specimens were shipped successfully back to the president. Lewis recommended a bonus for Warfington. Little else is known about him after his return.

WILLIAM WERNER may have been in the army prior to his enlistment with the Corps. During the winter months Werner was involved in some disciplinary incidents and then again in St. Charles. He was assigned to be a member of the permanent party and retained that position. He was also assigned as the cook for Sergeant Ordway's squad. Sometime after the return Werner moved to Virginia and settled there.

ISAAC WHITE was born in Holiston, Massachusetts around 1775. He was serving in the military before enlisting with Lewis and Clark, having joined in 1801. He was recruited from Captain Stoddard's artillery company at Fort Kaskaskia. He was a member of Corporal Warfington's mess and assigned to his return party that brought the

Captains' reports, plant and animal specimens, and artifacts back. Little else is known about him

JOSEPH WHITEHOUSE was another of the privates who kept a journal of the expedition, however, it was not published during that time. He is believed to have been born in Virginia in 1775, and in 1784 moved to Kentucky. He became skilled at dressing hides. He was already serving in the army when he was recruited from Captain Daniel Bissell's infantry regiment at Fort Massac. It seems he was in and out of trouble during his life. He was transferred to the Corps on January 1, 1804. While at Camp Dubois he faced disciplinary action, but was kept as a member of the permanent party. He was one of the men who was reported lost for a few days while out hunting, suffered from frostbite, and later hurt his leg in a boat mishap. He was mentioned as a hunter and often used his tailoring skills to repair clothing. After his return he lived in Missouri where he was arrested for debt in 1807. When the war of 1812 broke out, he re-enlisted in the army. However, he was reported as deserting in 1817.

ALEXANDER WILLARD was born on August 24, 1778, in Charlestown, New Hampshire. By 1800, he was living in Kentucky. He enlisted in the army and served in Captain Amos Stoddard's artillery company as a private. He was considered to be one of the two physically strongest members of the expedition, York being the other one. Willard, along with John Shields, was a blacksmith. He made and kept the metal equipment in good condition. He also made items for the Indians. That was important when bartering for food and other items needed from the Indians. However, he was one of the few members court-martialed for misconduct. On July 11, 1804, during the early part of the expedition, he had been found sleeping while on sentry duty. That was considered a very serious offense that endangered the lives of the entire Corps. He was punished with 100 lashes. He served faithfully for the rest of the journey.

In 1808, Willard was appointed by Lewis to serve as the government's blacksmith for the Sauk and Fox Indians and later for the Delawares and Shawnees. In 1807, he married. He and his wife had twelve children. He served in the military during the War of 1812. He settled in Missouri, Wisconsin, and then, in 1852, he went to California by covered wagon with his family to look for gold. He died on March 6, 1865, in Franklin, California and was buried there. A photograph of him in his later years is known to exist. The only other member known to be photographed was Patrick Gass.

RICHARD WINDSOR apparently was a member of Captain Russell Bissell's First Infantry Regiment stationed at Fort Kaskaskia. He was transferred to the Corps officially on January 1, 1804. He was a member of the permanent party. He was frequently mentioned as one of the men assigned as a hunter and Ordway included him as one of the "best" hunters. He fell and nearly slipped off a cliff while exploring the Marias River. After he returned he re-enlisted in the army and served until 1819. He lived in Missouri for a few years and then moved to an area on the Sangamon River in Illinois.

CHIEF SHEHEKE (Big White) was born in the Mandan village known today as Village on a Slant. By the time of Lewis and Clark he was chief of the lower Mandan village, which was located on the west side of the Missouri River near present-day Washburn, North Dakota. Lewis and Clark first met Big White on October 24, 1804. During the long cold winter, Chief Big White and other chiefs of the neighboring Mandans, Hidatsa, and Arikaras were in constant contact with the Corps.

Big White provided both food and information that would prove invaluable for Lewis and Clark, helping them survive that winter and later when they resumed their journey west. It was decided to build their winter quarters, Fort Mandan, on the east bank of the Missouri near Big White's village. Clark recorded Big White's reaction to their decision, *We were Sorry when we heard of your going up, but now you are going down (by Big White's village), we are glad, if we eat you Shall eat, if we Starve you must Starve also, our village is too far to bring the Corn to you, but we hope you will Call on us as you pass the place you intend to stop.* He kept his word. Trade for corn and other foods became constant occurrences. Less than two weeks later Big White brought 100 pounds of buffalo meat to the Corps. A few weeks later the Corps was invited to go buffalo hunting. Shortly thereafter, the explorers were invited to participate in one of the Mandan buffalo ceremonies. At a meeting on January 7, 1805, Big White provided Clark with a sketch of the rivers, especially the Yellowstone, west to the Rocky Mountains.

When the Corps returned to the Mandans in August 1806, the captains persuaded Big White to return to Washington to meet the president. Big White took his wife, Yellow Corn, and their child, White Painted Horse. They departed on August 17. On December 31, 1806, he met President Jefferson. His stay in the East was supposed to only last a few months, but it would last three years. In 1807, former Sergeant Pryor, led a party to return Big White and his family, but

Arikaras attacked the return party. They forced the expedition to return. In 1809, another expedition successfully returned Big White home.

CAMEAHWAIT (One Who Never Walks) was the chief of the Lemhi Shoshoni band that inhabited the area near the headwaters of the Missouri. His warrior name was Too-et'-te-con'-e, the Black Gun. The Shoshoni traditionally camped on both sides of the continental divide near the Lemhi Pass. When Lewis met them they were camped west of the divide on the east bank of the Lemhi River. The Shoshoni were nearly starving when the Corps arrived. Cameahwait's band was comprised of about 100 warriors, 300 women and children, and a herd of 400-700 horses. Their plans to return to the plains to hunt buffalo were interrupted by Lewis and Clark's arrival.

Lewis and Clark could not have been much luckier because Sacagawea was with them. Cameahwait was the chief of the Shoshoni band from which Sacagawea had been captured. He also was Sacagawea's brother. So, when Lewis and Clark brought her back they helped re-unite a family and also met a brother who became indebted to them. Cameahwait told the captains of the only safe ways across the mountains. The river they camped on was not navigable. There was one route to the far south across the present-day lava plains of Idaho and the other route to the north over the Nez Perce Trail. The latter trail was used by the Indians to get from the west side of the mountains to the plains near Great Falls. He suggested that that was the best route to use. He also told them that the Nez Perce lived on a river that ran into a lake that tasted salty.

After much negotiation Cameahwait agreed to help provide the Corps with enough horses to take them over the mountains. He provided an old man who knew the route. "Old Toby," as referred to by the captains, was the guide. On September 1, 1805, the Corps of Discovery left Cameahwait and the Shoshoni Indians. They headed north along the route that they were told would bring them to the Nez Perce Trail.

Lewis had promised that the U.S. would bring peace to the plains and stop the Hidatsa Indians and others from raiding the Shoshoni. He had also said that trade would increase and they would be able to get the rifles needed to protect themselves and make them safer and stronger. However, within a few years, Cameahwait was killed by the Hidatsa who were once again raiding and stealing as they had done before Lewis and Clark ventured west.

TWISTED HAIR was a chief of the Nez Perce band on the Clearwater River in western Idaho. It was his band that the expedition met after crossing the Lolo Trail. The crossing was a terrible hardship on the members of the Corps. They were cold, weak, sick, and nearly starving. They recuperated at Twisted Hair's camp where they were given dried salmon and the flour of the camas to eat.

The explorers also needed canoes for the rest of the trip down the rivers to the Pacific. The Nez Perce helped them construct five dugout canoes and taught them how to make them by "burning out the holler of our canoes." Twisted Hair drew a map of the area and rivers to the west that Lewis and Clark took with them. He agreed to have the Nez Perce watch over the Corps' thirty-eight horses, saddles, and other equipment until they returned the following year. Chiefs Twisted Hair and Tetoharsky even agreed to go ahead of the Corps to tell the Indians farther west along the rivers that the explorers came in peace. They were also able to help interpret because they knew the languages of the Indians as far west as The Dalles.

When the Corps returned in June of 1806, Twisted Hair returned their horses as promised. He told Lewis and Clark that the trail over the mountains was not yet open and they should remain in the camp until the river level changed and the snow on the mountains melted. They remained for a couple of weeks, but grew more and more impatient. Against the chief's advice they decided to attempt a crossing. One week after leaving the Nez Perce the Corps was forced to return. The Lolo Trail was still deep in snow. They had difficulty in finding and following the trail. Twisted Hair had been correct. On June 24, 1806, when told the conditions were right, the Corps set off again with three guides provided by Twisted Hair to lead them over the Lolo Trail to Travelers Rest.

SEAMAN was the Newfoundland dog that Lewis acquired in 1803 for $20.00. Little is actually known about the life of Seaman except for the few passages about him in the journals of Lewis, Clark, and others, and a few references after the journey.

Until recently there had been some controversy about his name. For a number of years he had been called Scannon, but recent historians now agree that his name was Seaman. It appears the mix-up was based on the interpretation of the handwritten entries. Journal entries suggest Seaman was a male dog.

From the journals it seems that Seaman was with Lewis when he left Pittsburgh. Seaman played the important roles as early warning system, hunter, retriever, guard dog, and beloved companion to all the members of the expedition. After leaving Fort Mandan the party began to encounter grizzly bears. Seaman was able to warn the party of their presence. He was very useful in catching and retrieving squirrels, antelope, deer, fowl, beaver and other animals. On May 19, 1805, Seaman was bitten by a wounded beaver, which he was retrieving. It nearly killed him, but fortunately, Lewis's medical skills helped to save him. Ten days later, on May 29, 1805, Seaman had recovered sufficiently to save Lewis and others by chasing off a charging Buffalo that had entered the camp that evening.

Like other members of the Corps, Seaman suffered from the prickly pear cactus and mosquitoes. On April 11, 1806, he may have again escaped death. Three Chinook Indians tried to steal Seaman. Fortunately, during the chase the Indians dropped the rope and Seaman was freed. Dogs were pets, but they were also used as food by some of the tribes. Seaman's stature is shown by the fact that on several occasions members of the expedition ate horses or Indian dogs when supplies were short. But there was apparently never any thought of eating Seaman

The journals of Lewis, Clark and others don't mention the fate of Seaman. The last direct entry about him by Lewis was on July 15, 1806. Some historians don't think he returned. However, some secondary evidence does seem to indicate that he did complete the journey safely. One account holds that Seaman was with Lewis on his fateful journey to Washington. After Lewis died and was buried Seaman remained at his grave until he also died. His collar was later sent to Clark. An entry in a book of epitaphs by Timothy Allen published in 1814 describes a collar worn by Seaman after the expedition's return. On it was written "The greatest traveller of my species. My name is SEAMAN, the dog of captain Meriwether Lewis, whom I accompanied to the Pacifick ocean through the interior of the continent of North America." The collar was reported to have been in the Alexandria Museum. In 1812 Clark was sent a note of thanks for the "truly valuable present." The letter did not, however, specify what the gift was. Unfortunately, a fire destroyed the museum in 1871, and with it, the collar.

CHAPTER THREE
History of the trail

The mouth of the River Dubois is to be considered as the point of departure. – Meriwether Lewis

On May 14, 1804, the Corps of Discovery set out from Camp Dubois, and so began the journey that would change and shape the United States of America. The journey ended on September 23, 1806, when they returned to St. Louis. The captains' journals, and those of other Corps members, are the recorded descriptions of the major and daily events that occurred as the Corps moved up the Missouri, across the continent, over the mountains to the Pacific Ocean and then back. But the history of the journey is more than just those recorded events.

A major historical event does not occur in a vacuum, political or otherwise. It usually has a history much longer and more complicated than the event itself. This was especially true of the Lewis and Clark Expedition and the Louisiana Purchase with which it is associated. Long before its purchase, and even before there was a United States, the upper Louisiana or what later became the Louisiana Territory was the center of the dreams of one man—that man was Thomas Jefferson. The fulfillment of part of his dreams was made possible by the actions of two other men—Meriwether Lewis and William Clark. For the United States, the Louisiana Purchase was a milestone in its formation, but in terms of the larger world environment into which it fit, it was only a sideshow in the intrigue and theater of Napoleon's European politics that involved France, Great Britain, Spain and also the United States. It is in this larger more complex context that this brief history of the Lewis and Clark Trail will be surveyed.

It is also very important to remember that our concept of time and distance is very different than that of Jefferson's and Lewis and Clark's world. We live in a world of multi-media and satellite communications that allows us to see and hear things from around the world almost instantaneously. Our systems of transportation are hundreds of times faster. In the time of Jefferson and Lewis and Clark, communications over large distances was based primarily on the transportation systems. Events could happen in one part of a country or the world and not be known in the other for many months or years, sometimes making the decision-making process difficult and the actions of others of little relevance to the actual outcome.

1743

On April 13 Thomas Jefferson was born at Shadwell, the family farm in what became Albemarle County, Virginia. His family had been one of the earliest families to move west into that part of Virginia. His father, Peter, had also been an early explorer, a proponent of westward expansion and made one of the earliest accurate maps of the area. Jefferson was always proud of his family's part in the westward movement in Virginia, and it became a major influence on his life.

1763

The French and Indian War, known as the Seven Years War in Europe, ended with the Treaty of Paris. Britain and her allies won, and France was defeated. France lost most of her colonies in North America with the exception of some islands in the Caribbean and off Newfoundland. Canada and the French lands east of the Mississippi went to England. In 1762 France had signed the Treaty of Fontainebleau with Spain. It gave Spain the Louisiana area west of the Mississippi and New Orleans, and thus kept Britain from obtaining them.

1770

William Clark was born August 1 in Caroline County a few miles from Jefferson's home. The Jefferson and Clark families knew each other. The Clark family moved to their new home, called Mulberry Hill, at the Falls of the Ohio in Kentucky in 1784.

1774

Meriwether Lewis was born August 18 at Locust Hill in Albemarle County, Virginia. The Lewis and Jefferson families were good friends and neighbors. It was even reported that in later years Jefferson would use mirrors to signal Lewis when he wanted him.

1776-1783

The Declaration of Independence, written by Jefferson, was signed in Phildelphia. Both Meriwether Lewis and William Clark were too young to fight in the war. William's older brother, George Rogers Clark, because of his victories in the west, became a war hero both in Virginia and the United States.

1778

Jonathan Carver's book *Travels through the Interior Parts of North America in the years 1766, 1767, 1768* was published. Jefferson was fascinated by it. His map of North America showed the interior of Upper Louisiana and a "central pyramid" of land from which the major western rivers flowed, including the Missouri which flowed east to the Mississippi and also the Oregon River which flowed west to the Pacific. It also indicated that the continent was about 3,000 miles wide.

1779

Thomas Jefferson became governor of Virginia. Jefferson's Virginia was larger than the Virginia of today. It included West Virginia, and land claims in the Ohio over to the Mississippi, and some felt, all the way to the Pacific.

1783

The Treaty of Paris was negotiated with Great Britain ending the American Revolution. Independence was granted to the United States. The western border of the United States was set at the Mississippi River. However, the northernmost part of the Mississippi River had not yet been explored, nor had the location of its source been determined. The British and Americans agreed that navigation of the Mississippi River would be open to both the British and Americans. The southern border was agreed to be Spanish Florida. The exact position of that border, however, was in question with the Spanish.

Although the western boundary of the United States was the Mississippi River, in 1783 Jefferson discussed plans for sending an expedition west of the Mississippi to the Pacific. He tried to persuade George Rogers Clark to head the expedition, but he refused, and Congress did not seem to support it either.

John Ledyard's *A Journal of Captain Cook's Last Voyage in the Pacific* was published giving the longitude of the Pacific/Oregon Coast. This helped to confirm the width of the North American continent. Jefferson added this book to his library and studied it.

1783-1800
Jefferson was active in the government under the Articles of Confederation serving as a delegate to Congress from Virginia. Under President Washington, Jefferson served for a time as head of the Department of Foreign Affairs (Secretary of State). When John Adams was elected president in 1796, Jefferson was elected vice-president.

As more Americans moved west of the Appalachian Mountains into Kentucky, Tennessee, and Georgia, and into Ohio and the rest of the old Northwest Territory, river navigation down the Ohio and Mississippi rivers became more important. Control of the Mississippi and Louisiana-New Orleans was rapidly becoming a vital interest for the United States. It increasingly played a major role in national politics.

Political factions (parties) were developing in the United States at this time. The Federalists, of which Alexander Hamilton was one of its major leaders, tended to support a stronger more centralized government, encouraged business expansion and were more pro-British. On the other side were the anti-Federalists, they became known as the Democrat-Republicans. Thomas Jefferson became its leader. They favored a weaker and less centralized form of government, envisioned a more rural society, and were pro-French. As these two groups vied for power in the government, and the differences became more pronounced, conflicts arose between individuals and even within and between the states.

1785
Jefferson met John Ledyard in Paris. They discussed Ledyard's plan to explore North America and to travel across it from west to east. He hoped to arrange passage on a ship to the Pacific coast and then start his overland journey. Jefferson

encouraged Ledyard's plan, but could offer no real support. Still lacking in funding, support, and with no passage on a ship, Ledyard left London in late 1787 intent on making a land crossing of Europe and Russia. Once at the Pacific he hoped to arrange for passage from Russia to North America where he would start his exploration. However, in February of 1788, the Russians stopped him in eastern Siberia, sent him back, and his plan of exploration ended. He died a year later while starting a trip to explore the interior of Africa.

1792

Robert Gray sailed along the Pacific Coast and in May discovered the mouth of the Columbia River, Carver's Oregon River. Gray named the river after his ship and traveled up it for about thirty miles. He fixed the location of the mouth of the Columbia River, the main river that appeared to drain the lands in the far Northwest west of the Rocky Mountains—the Oregon Country. By knowing both the latitude and longitude of the mouth of the Columbia, one was able to determine more precisely the width of the unexplored part of the continent.

By the end of the year the subject of an expedition to the West had resurfaced. The young eighteen year-old Meriwether Lewis requested that Jefferson allow him to participate in the expedition to explore the lands west of the Mississippi. Jefferson rejected his request.

1793

In January Jefferson, vice-president of the America Philosophical Society, recommended that the society send an expedition under the leadership of the French Botanist André Michaux to explore the lands along the Missouri to the Pacific and study the nature of the vegetation. He warned Michaux not to be captured by the Spanish or the British. However, political complications developed that shortly ended the plan. Edmond Genet, a new French ambassador had come to the United States. Jefferson was a strong supporter of France and its continuing revolution at home. As George Washington's Secretary of State Jefferson met with Genet. They engaged in discussions concerning Louisiana. Genet wanted to foster rebellions in Canada against the British and in Louisiana against the Spanish. It soon became evident that Genet planned to use André Michaux as the conduit for revolution and to engage Kentuckians, including George Rogers Clark, in a war against Great Britain and Spain. Jefferson finally realized there would be political problems for him and the country. He was forced to drop plans for the expedition, his support for Michaux and to request that Genet be recalled. However, Jefferson's series of instruction first given to Michaux would be repeated with minor changes a decade later to Lewis.

Alexander MacKenzie, a Scottish fur trader and an employee of the North West Company, and nine other men completed their journey of exploration across the Canadian Rocky Mountains of North America on July 20. They had headed up river from Fort Fork on the Peace River. As they climbed higher their troubles increased. They crossed over to the Bad (Frazer) River where their problems got worse. They lost their canoe and most of their supplies. They were forced to go overland. Finally, they met some Indians and with their assistance arrived at the Pacific Ocean. MacKenzie found no easy water route, but he did encourage the British to expand their hold and control over trade with the Indians. He wrote a book, *Voyages From Montreal*, recounting both his 1789 journey to the Artic Ocean and his 1793 trek to the Pacific.

1794
The Whiskey Rebellion broke out. Both Lewis and Clark served in the military under General "Mad" Anthony Wayne.

1795
Lewis was transferred to Captain Clark's elite rifle unit. For about six months they served together. The two men learned to trust each other and formed a bond of respect which would never be broken.

In October the United States and Spain signed the Pinckney Treaty, negotiated by Thomas Pinckney. The boundary of Florida was set and Spain agreed to ensure the "freedom of navigation" on the Mississippi River and the "right of deposit" for American goods in New Orleans near the mouth of the Mississippi River.

1796
Toussaint Charbonneau, a trapper for the North West Company moved to the Knife River Indian villages of the Hidatsa and Mandans along the Missouri in the upper Great Plains in present-day North Dakota.

1799

Napoleon became First Consul of France. He planned the expansion of the French Empire in Europe and in the Americas, including the Caribbean Islands and the mainland.

1800

Sacagawea, a member of the Lemhi Shoshoni band, was kidnapped by the Hidatsa. The Shoshonis were camped near Three Forks in present-day Montana. She was taken back to the Hidatsa villages on the Knife River. Later she became the wife/property of Toussaint Charbonneau.

Napoleon expanded his power in France and in Europe. On September 30 the two republics, France and the United States, established formal relations and agreed to end the informal war at sea caused by the French's naval harassment of American merchant vessels.

On October 1 the French signed the secretly negotiated Treaty of San Ildefonso with Spain, also known as the Treaty of Montefontaine in France. It gave France control of Louisiana, the land west of the Mississippi River including the great Missouri River's watershed in exchange for Tuscany. Napoleon also promised not to sell it to any third nation should he ever change his mind about controlling it. However, the French temporarily left the administration of the territory in the hands of the Spanish. Publicly both nations denied the change, but rumors soon surfaced, and continued to spread. Spain also soon realized that the Kingdom of Tuscany was not all that Napoleon represented it to be.

Thomas Jefferson was elected third president of the United States. While industry was expanding in New England and becoming more important to America's economy, Jefferson's vision of the United States was still one of an agrarian society. Agricultural production continued to expand along the Ohio River Valley and in the Northwest Territories north of the Ohio River. The free flow of produce and goods down the Ohio River and then down the Mississippi River to the Gulf of Mexico had become a vital interest for the United States. For some it was an issue worth fighting for. Jefferson was intent on getting control of the area without becoming drawn into a war, especially with France.

1801
Before Jefferson took office as president he began to think seriously about exploring the west and started to develop a program of exploration. His plans became more extensive than that of any president until perhaps those of recent years and our space program. The new president had yet to discuss his plans with Congress. The rumors of the French control of Louisiana had already reached Jefferson.

On February 23 Jefferson wrote his young friend Meriwether Lewis asking him to become his private secretary. Jefferson wanted more than a secretary. He wanted an aide, someone he could trust, one who could talk to members of Congress, and one who shared his ideas about the west. Lewis continued in his military service and retained his rank of captain. Jefferson took the oath of office on March 4.

Alexander MacKenzie's *Voyages from Montreal* was published. Jefferson eagerly read about the journey. It served to reinforce his desire to explore the West and his hope that a easy water route to the Pacific could still be discovered. A copy of the book was given to Lewis and Clark before they began their journey.

Negotiations to purchase New Orleans and west Florida with France and Spain. Success would ensure the United States with control of the mouth of the Mississippi River, the port city of New Orleans, and, additionally, the mouths of some other rivers that emptied into the Gulf of Mexico. Jefferson learned about the transfer of Louisiana to France. He instructed the American ambassadors Robert Livingston and Thomas Pinckney, respectively, to France and Spain to intensify their diplomatic negotiations.

1802
Napoleon faced setbacks in Europe, in Egypt, and then in the Caribbean Island of Santo Domingo (Haiti). A slave revolt led by Toussaint-L'Ouverture in 1791 resulted in a crushing defeat of the French troops. Napoleon's forces now became engaged in a very costly re-conquest of Santo Domingo. He had hoped to retake it, and then to use it as a base to re-establish control over Louisiana. In June Toussaint was captured, but fighting continued. By the end of the year the French had sustained tremendous casualties from both fighting and disease,

especially yellow fever. Napoleon was forced to give up his hope of re-establishing control over Santo Domingo and, therefore, his plans for a French Empire in the Americas. Now, he had to plot a way to minimize his losses without benefiting the other European states, especially England and Spain. He knew it would be difficult to protect an overseas empire without control of Santo Domingo and a strong navy. He also knew he needed money for his future war against Great Britain.

After discussions, the U.S. Congress authorized two million dollars for the purchase of New Orleans and the east bank of the Mississippi (west Florida). Jefferson again urged Livingston to press the issue.

Jefferson asked Meriwether Lewis to lead an expedition to the Pacific Ocean. Jefferson's elaborate plan began to unfold. Secrecy was still a major concern. They wanted to keep the plans from the French, Spanish and British, and also from possible opposition in Congress and the government.

On October 15, in Barcelona, Spain, Louisiana was formally transferred from Spain to France. But the Spanish officials still administered the area, and, coincidentally, on October 16, the Spanish officials in New Orleans suspended the "right of deposit" for Americans. It seems to have been done without the consent of Napoleon and France. If the situation prohibiting Americans from safely storing their goods awaiting transport lasted for a prolonged period, the economy of the western lands would suffer greatly. It would also increase political problems in both Washington and the West. In December, Jefferson told Congress of the French acquisition of Louisiana, but not the Spanish action in New Orleans.

1803
On January 18, Jefferson sent Congress a secret request "for the purpose of extending the external commerce of the U.S." for $2,500 for a small expedition of ten to twelve men to the West. He still did not tell Congress of the action of the Spanish in New Orleans.

In March, Jefferson sent James Monroe to France to move negotiations for New Orleans and West Florida along, with a new authorization to spend up to ten million dollars.

Lewis left Washington his journey to obtain the equipment and supplies needed for the expedition and to improve his knowledge and skills in navigation, mathematics, medicine, botany and natural history. He traveled to Harpers Ferry, Virginia to order arms and supplies for fifteen men and a "dismantiable" iron framed boat, next to Lancaster, Pennsylvania to study, and then to Philadelphia for additional studies and more supplies. He returned to Washington in late June.

In April communications from the Spanish King arrived in New Orleans ordering the Spanish officials there to rescind the closure of the port. American ships and Americans began to flood into New Orleans. Neither the Spanish officials nor the French officials in New Orleans were aware of the secret negotiations in Paris to sell New Orleans and Louisiana.

In April Napoleon told Charles Maurice de Talleyrand-Perigord, first minister, and Marquis de Barbé-Marbois, minister of finance, of his decision to sell Louisiana. He instructed Barbé to meet with Livingston to present his offer of "all or nothing" regarding Louisiana. However, on April 11, Talleyrand presented it. It was unofficially accepted except for the price. Monroe arrived in Paris on April 12. He soon entered into the discussions and also agreed. The document was presented on the April 27. It was signed May 2 by Livingston and Monroe, but dated April 30. Acting for the United States they agreed to buy all of the Louisiana Territory in cash and claims for the equivalent of about $15,000,000. They did this knowing the price was five million more than Monroe was authorized to pay, and also that they had not been authorized to buy all of Louisiana. Napoleon was now free to pursue his European design. On May 18 he declared war on Great Britain.

On June 19 Lewis wrote William Clark asking that he join the expedition as his co-commander with the rank of captain and explaining the still secret nature of their expedition. In early July Lewis was off to Pittsburgh. He stopped at Harpers Ferry again and arranged for the iron boat to be shipped by wagon to Wheeling with other additional supplies.

On the eve of July 4 Jefferson received news of the purchase of all of Louisiana. Congress approved the purchase a few months later. All this happened before the Spanish governments in New Orleans and St. Louis transferred authority of Louisiana to France.

On July 26 not having heard from Clark regarding his offer, Lewis began the process of selecting an alternate, Lieutenant Moses Hooke. Clark had not received Lewis's offer until July 16, four weeks after Lewis's letter was sent. Lewis received Clark's July 19 letter of acceptance on August 3.

Lewis left Pittsburgh on August 31 when the keelboat's construction was finally completed. The selection process of the members of the Corps of Discovery started in Pittsburgh. Seaman, Lewis's Newfoundland was aboard. The trip down the Ohio was harder than anticipated. The river level was very low and the boats frequently had to be pulled over sandbars by the men or by oxen from local farmers.

On October 19, the Senate approved the treaty and purchase of Louisiana. On October 31 Congress approved additional related legislation.

Lewis stopped at a variety of places on the trip: first at Wheeling to pickup the additional supplies that were shipped there; next at present-day Moundsville, West Virginia to visit the Indian Mounds; then a brief halt at Marietta, Ohio, next at Maysville, Kentucky, where John Colter was recruited; then in the Cincinnati, Ohio area and Big Bone Lick, Kentucky; and next to the Falls of the Ohio in mid-October. At the falls Lewis met Clark, and additional men who came to be known as the "nine young men from Kentucky" were selected. In November more men were selected at Fort Massac, including George Drouillard; then a short stay at Cape Girardeau; and finally to Fort Kaskaskia where additional members were added.

On November 30 a ceremony was held in New Orleans transferring control of Lower Louisiana from Spain to France. Then on December 20 in a ceremony in the Place d'Armes, sovereignty was transferred from France to the United States.

Lewis arrived in St. Louis on December 5. On December 13 the site for Camp Dubois had been selected and construction of their winter camp got underway.

1804
During the winter months the members of the Corps of Discovery were busy preparing for the expedition. In addition

to their activities related to daily living, they drilled, practiced their marksmanship, packed their equipment, practiced their water skills, learned to work with their fellow Corps members, and became molded into a unit. Clark handled more of the responsibilities concerning the camp, while Lewis dealt more with the official responsibilities in Cahokia, St. Louis, and Washington.

On March 9-10 a second ceremony was held in St. Louis with the Spanish and the French. It officially transferred sovereignty of the Upper Louisiana Territory to the France and then to the United States on the next day. Lewis was present at the ceremony. President Jefferson later appointed General James Wilkinson Governor of the Louisiana Territory. He shared Jefferson's view of making the new territory primarily into a new homeland for the eastern Indians as they became displaced. The unrealistic nature of this plan would soon become evident. While in New Orleans, Wilkinson told the Spanish that the expedition was more than just scientific. Spain feared that Lewis and Clark might secretly explore into the Spanish lands that could later result in mass migrations of Americans into their territory. Wilkinson also suggested that they try to intercept and stop Lewis and Clark. Over the next two years, four attempts were made. Fortunately, none succeeded. It was later discovered that Wilkinson served as an agent for Spain.

On March 26 Congress made the first division of the Louisiana Territory. The District of Orleans (similar to the present state of Louisiana) and the District of Louisiana were created. This was done even before the exact size, location, and boundaries of the Louisiana Purchase were agreed upon.

On April 14 Jefferson appointed surveyor Thomas Freeman to lead an expedition to explore the Arkansas and Red rivers to their headwaters. Freeman had surveyed the U.S.-Spanish border in Florida in 1796. Freeman chose Peter Custis to assist him. Captain Richard Sparks was in charge of the military. The expedition was to obtain similar information to that requested of Lewis and Clark. However, the expedition was postponed. It would be two years before it finally got under way.

On May 14 preparations for the expedition were about complete. Clark and the Corps officially set sail from Camp Dubois at 4 p.m. Lewis had gone to St. Louis to finish last minute details. He traveled overland to meet the expedition at St. Charles. The pattern for travel during the journey included the practice whereby the majority of the expedition worked the boats, a few members hunted on shore, while one of the captains often walked on the shore to do a little more exploring.

The boats arrived in St. Charles on May 16 and waited for Captain Lewis to join them. A local celebration was held and the party left on May 21.

May 25 they passed La Charette (St. John), the last "outpost" of civilization.

[See the journal section for a more complete reading of the events as recorded in the journals between June 26 and September 7, 1804.]

On June 26-28 the Corps camped at the junction of the Kansas & Missouri rivers. Exploring, hunting, making needed repairs, drying and re-packing their goods and equipment occupied the men.

Brief Independence Day celebrations were held in the morning and evening. One creek was named July 4th and another, where they camped, Independence Creek.

On July 21 the Corps passed the great Platte River.

From July 30-August 3 the Corps camped at a place they named Council Bluffs. The captains' first official council was held with the Oto & Missouri Indians. The officers and men put on their uniforms or best clothing. The council area was prepared complete with an awning made from the keelboat Discovery's sail. The council included parades speeches from the captains, more speeches from the Indians and finally gift giving. This would be the basic pattern used by the captains in their future councils with the other Indian groups.

The Corps passed Blackbird Hill on August 11. A great chief of the Omaha Indians had died four years earlier and was buried on the hill.

A council was held with the Omaha Indians on August 19.

Sergeant Charles Floyd died August 20. He was buried with military honors on a high bluff above the Missouri. His name was given to that bluff and a nearby river.

On August 23 Joseph Field shot and killed the first buffalo. Lewis and eleven men went to dress it and bring it back to the boats. The Corps had long heard about them, most had not seen them or eaten any before. That day Sergeant John Ordway recorded them "as great a curiousity to me." Buffalo soon became a staple. (It is interesting to note that in colonial times the eastern or woodland buffalo, sometimes called wild cattle, once abundant as far east of the Mississippi River as Pennsylvania, had been hunted to near extinction by the time of the expedition.)

On August 25 the captains and other members of the Corps hiked six miles to visit Spirit Mound. They found no trace of the mythical little people the Indians said inhabited the hill.

The Corps established a camp on the south side of the river near some high bluffs from August 30 - September 1. A successful council was held with the Yankton Sioux. The bluff where they camped was named Calumet (peace pipe) Bluff.

One purpose of the expedition was to collect information about and specimens of the animals discovered. On September 7 the Corps spent a good part of the day and night in pursuit of this task. The captains discovered a large prairie dog town at the base of a conical shaped hill they had climbed. The decision was made to capture some. The men had to dig in the hard soil and dug down six feet, but had no success. Then they carried five barrels of water from the river to the prairie dog village. There they poured the water down a hole to force the animals out. The result—one live prairie dog captured. The next spring it was sent back to Jefferson along with other specimens, artifacts, and reports.

Contact was finally made with the Teton Sioux near a river the captains called "Bad River." The Teton Sioux were the strongest and most feared Indians in the region. A council was held on September 25. Actions, possibly some personal Indian rivalries, perceptions held by both parties, and difficulty with communications made this conference most difficult. Hostilities almost broke out, but fortunately for both sides, an altercation was averted. The Corps left, but remained suspicious and on guard.

In mid-October the Corps met the Arikara as they continued up the Missouri. The first council was held on the 10 and 11. Clark wrote, *we Delivered a Similar Speech to those delivered the Ottoes & Sioux, made three Chiefs, one for each Village and gave them Clothes & flags. . . .after the council was over we Shot the Air gun. . . .the Inds. Much astonished at my black Servent. . . .* Clark noted some "jealousy" between chiefs and another council was held farther up river at a different village.

On October 24 the Corps met the Mandans. They spent the winter with them and their neighbors, the Hidatsa. The captains learned much about the general course of the Missouri to the west and its major tributaries. Time was also spent writing reports and preparing plant and animal specimens that would be sent back in the spring.

Construction on Fort Mandan began November 2. The men started to move in on November 17. The captains moved in on the November 20. It was completed in late December. It was a very cold winter, but the fort served them well.

Toussaint Charbonneau offered his services as interpreter to the captains on November 4. His wives were Shoshoni, and one of them was pregnant. The captains agreed to hire him and allowed Charbonneau to bring one wife, Sacagawea.

Back in the "old" United States, Jefferson defeated Charles Pinckney and was re-elected president. This was unknown to the Corps of Discovery.

1805

Jean Baptiste Charbonneau was born on February 11 to Sacagawea. Clark noted Sacagawea had a difficult labor, but shortly after having been given an Indian medicine made from the rattle of a rattlesnake she gave birth to a baby boy. He became the youngest member of the Corps of Discovery.

The captains continued to use the winter and early spring to organize and write reports, to learn about the local Indian cultures, to learn more about the route and land ahead of them, and to make the physical preparations for the journey still facing them. The experience with the Mandan and the Hidatsa had been a very positive one for the Corps.

On April 7 the Corps left Fort Mandan and headed up the Missouri. The keelboat commanded by Corporal Warfington headed back to St. Louis. It was loaded with specimens, artifacts, reports, and Clark's map for Jefferson. Also onboard was one of the Arikara chiefs who was to go to Washington. Once back, the information contained in the reports was published and interest in the West and the expedition increased.

On April 25, while hiking, Lewis reached the confluence of the Yellowstone River with the Missouri River. Clark arrived the next day. Measurements of the confluence were taken and a short exploration up the Yellowstone River was made.

A little farther up the Missouri River Lewis came face to face with the "white bear" or grizzly bear that the men had heard so much about from the Indians. On April 29, Lewis and another man shot two grizzly bears. Lewis recorded his description and observations about one of them. More encounters with the bears ensued. They were ferocious and hard to kill. Later Lewis recorded that he'd rather fight two Indians than one bear, and the captains required men to hunt in pairs instead of alone.

On the evening of June 2 the Corps arrived at the confluence of two rivers. The Indians had not told the captains of this river junction. The Corps camped until June 11 trying to determine which river was the Missouri. One was cold and clear and the other was muddy. Lewis and some men explored up the muddy northwestern fork, while Clark and some men went up the clear southwestern fork. After much discussion, and even though all of the Corps except the captains felt the Missouri was the muddy river, the captains decided to follow the clear river. Lewis named the other river the Marias River after his cousin. The captains decided to cache the red pirogue, the animal and plant specimens, and some of their supplies. They planned to pick these up on their return journey.

Lewis, hiking ahead of the boats, reached the Great Falls of the Missouri on June 13. The Indians had told the captains of the existence of the falls, so its presence confirmed that the captains had elected the right river to follow. The Great Falls was not just one falls but a series of them and other minor rapids. Since there was no way to continue by water the decision was made to portage around the falls. The white pirogue was cached there. Lewis had the men prepare the iron boat, but after initially floating, it sank. They decided to cache it there and build two new canoes to replace the pirogue and iron boat. The portage was just over eighteen miles, and the total time delay was nearly one month.

Farther up the Missouri the river entered a narrow canyon area that the Corps passed through on July 19-20. Lewis named the area "Gates of the Rocky Mountains."

Again Lewis walked ahead and arrived at Three Forks on July 25. The rest of the expedition arrived the next day. They measured and explored the different rivers. The three forks were named the Gallatin River, after Albert Gallatin Secretary of the Treasury, the Madison River after James Madison, Secretary of State, and the third river that flowed from the west, the Jefferson River, for the president. The Corps camped in the same place where Sacagawea was taken captive in 1800. The explorers now knew that they were close to the Shoshoni and the horses they needed.

On August 8, Sacagawea recognized Beaverhead Rock. She told the captains that her people lived in the mountains farther upstream on another branch that entered from the west.

On August 9, under orders from General Wilkinson, Zebulon Pike left St. Louis with twenty men, including John Boley, to explore the Upper Mississippi River and to locate its source.

Lewis had gone on ahead of the main group with three men George Drouillard, Hugh McNeal, and John Shields. On August 12, Lewis recorded *at a distance of 4 miles further the road took us to the most distant fountain of the waters of the mighty Missouri in surch of which we have spent so many toilsome days and wristless nights. thus far I have accomplished one of those great objects on which my mind has been unalterably fixed for so many years. . . .we proceeded on to the top of the dividing ridge. . . .I now decended the mountain about _ of a mile. . .to a handsome bold running Creek of cold Clear water. here I first tasted the water of the great Columbia river.*

On that day one of the goals set by President Jefferson had been accomplished. When Lewis walked down the far side of the dividing ridge he crossed the Continental Divide and walked out of the Louisiana Territory. They camped there and finally met the Shoshoni, under Chief Cameahwait on August 13. Lewis persuaded the Shoshonis to return with him back over the divide to meet Clark who was coming up the river. From August 17-23 the Corps camped and had a council with the Shoshonis. It was here that Sacagawea discovered that the chief was her brother Cameahwait. The captains arranged to buy some horses, and obtained the services of a Shoshoni guide whom they called Old Toby. He would guide them north to the Bitterroot Mountains and across them. The captains named the camp "Camp Fortunate."

The Corps camped at Travelers Rest on September 9 and 10. Here they recruited and prepared for the journey across the mountains on the (Nez Perce) Lolo Trail.

From September 11 until September 22, the expedition crossed the Bitterroot Mountains on the Lolo Trail, reaching the Nez Perce villages on Weippe Prairie. The journey was not easy. The trail followed the crests of the steep mountains; it was encumbered by fallen timbers; the weather was cold; the snow was deep; the men and animals slipped and fell; and food was scarce—they used their emergence rations of potable soup and even killed some their colts, But they proceeded on.

The travelers stayed with the Nez Perce for two weeks. They recuperated, arranged for the care of their horses, obtained needed food, recorded information about the Nez Perce culture, learned about the rivers ahead of them, and even learned how to make the canoes using the Indian's method of burning. On October 7 they proceeded on down the Clearwater River from Canoe Camp.

On October 10 the Corps reached the Snake River. By October 16 they camped at its junction with the Columbia.

On October 23 the Corps came to the most dangerous part of the Columbia. Within a fifty-five mile section, the expedition had to overcome four major falls and chutes. The first was Celilo Falls, the Great Falls of the Columbia below the Deschutes River. Next were the Short Narrows and Long Narrows at The Dalles, and finally, the Great Cascades of the Columbia, a four-mile series of rapids and falls. While some items and canoes were sometimes portaged, the Corps successfully took most of the canoes through most of the rapids with relatively little loss of goods and supplies.

On November 2 they passed Beacon Rock, first referred to as "Beaten Rock." Here the impact of the tide was observed. The Corps realized that they were near the Pacific Ocean and were close to accomplishing another of their goals.

On November 7 Clark wrote "Ocian in view! O! the joy." In reality they were still in the estuary of the Columbia. The Pacific was still about twenty miles west. By the November 15 the Pacific was in view of the main camp. The weather was terrible. Lewis and a few men went on ahead. It wasn't until on the 18th that all of the expedition had finally reached the Pacific. Most did it by foot.

Finding a place to camp for the winter was imperative. Winter weather, constant rain and a damp cold, was rapidly setting in. They needed a site that provided both protection and good hunting. For a few days they camped on a sandy beach near Cape Disappointment. On November 24 a polling or vote by all the members of the expedition was taken to determine where they would set up their winter camp. The vote was for the south side of the Columbia. The site was selected and on December 7 the men started construction of Fort Clatsop. The fort served as their base of operations until they left the following spring.

1806

During the winter months the captains continued meeting with the local Indians, collecting information about their cultures, collecting local plants and animals, and preparing their reports. On January 5 a camp was also established on the Pacific shore to extract salt from the ocean water. The men spent most of their time hunting, making clothing, visiting with the Indians, or working at the salt works.

On March 23 after final preparations and packing the Corps began their return journey back to St. Louis. Fort Clatsop was presented to Coboway, a chief of the Clatsops on March 22 in return for his hospitality that winter.

In April the Freeman-Custis Expedition finally got under way, two years late. It was comprised of less than thirty men, including twenty-four soldiers in two flatboats. Jefferson's instructions now included only the exploration of the Red River to its headwaters. They were to make astrolnomical observations, measure distances, record information about the geography, the minerals, and the types of plants and animals in the area. Unfortunately, only three months out, near the present Arkansas-Texas-Oklahoma border, the expedition was intercepted by the Spanish. They were forced to return, but allowed to keep the records. Far short of their goal and limited in their accomplishments, the journals still provided valuable new information about a small portion of the Louisiana Territory. The source of the Red River was finally mapped in 1852 by Captain Randolph B. Marcy.

On April 30, Pike returned from his expedition up the Mississippi. He brought much information, but had failed to find the true source of the Mississippi River. It finally was discovered July 13, 1832 by ethnologist Henry R. Schoolcraft.

The Corps arrived back at the first Nez Perce camps in early May. They picked up their horses and the supplies previously left there for safekeeping. They were anxious to proceed, but the Nez Perce warned them that the snow would still be too deep and it was too early to cross the mountains. The Corps stayed and heeded the words of the Nez Perce for a few weeks. On June 15, still anxious to get under way, the Captains decided to disregard the advice and to move ahead. Within two days they were stopped by the deep snows on the trail and were forced to return. They waited again and listened to the Nez Perce. They finally left on June 24 with three Nez Perce as guides. Where the snow had been ten to fifteen feet deep, now they found it no more than seven. The party even stopped to bathe in the hot waters of Lolo Hot Springs. They had spent twenty-seven days waiting in various camps. They called the area "Long Camp" or "Camp Chopunnish" after the Nez Perce.

On June 30 the Corps completed its return trip over the Bitterroot Mountains using the Lolo Trail. It had not been easy, but it was not as difficult as their first trip. They arrived at Travelers Rest and remained there until July 2. There the captains decided to split the Corps. Lewis took a smaller group and would head north and then east along the route the Indians told them would take only a few days to get to the Great Falls. Then they would head north to explore along the Marias hoping that it reached the fiftieth parallel north.

Clark, along with Charbonneau's family and most of the men, would retrace much of their route to Three Forks. There, Clark's group was split. Some of the men continued down the Missouri with the canoes to meet Lewis and his party. Clark's party then crossed over to the Yellowstone, using what later became known as the Bozeman Pass, and explored the Yellowstone on his return. The two parties were supposed to re-unite at the junction of the Yellowstone and the Missouri.

Pike, under orders from James Wilkinson, left St. Louis on July 15 on his second journey of exploration with a party of fifteen. They went west from the St. Louis area to explore the central plains and then the southern areas of the Louisiana Territory. They explored the area near the headwaters of the Arkansas River and then moved south. Pike did identify a mountain peak that he thought was the highest in the Rockies, known today as Pike's Peak. They traveled into Spanish territory and set up camp on a tributary of the Rio Grande. In February 1807 they were met by Spanish troops who "escorted" them to Santa Fe and then to Chihuahua where they were detained for a few months. The Spanish kept most of his records. The men were released, and they returned to the United States by way of Mexico. Pike's reports helped to spur interest in trade with Santa Fe and Mexico. The records that had been taken and kept by the Spanish were re-discovered and returned to the United States about a century later.

Clark's party traveled down the Yellowstone River. On July 25 they arrived at a large sandstone formation well known to the Indians. Clark wrote his name and date on the formation and named it Pompys Tower.

About that same time, Lewis entered Blackfeet country and was exploring the northern portion of the Marias River. At a place Lewis recorded as Camp Disappointment he was finally able to take measurements and readings and realized the Marias did not reach the fiftieth parallel. Lewis, the Field brothers and Drouillard had successfully evaded contact with the Indians, but on July 26 their luck turned. They met and camped with a group of eight Indians Lewis identified as Gros Ventres of the Prairie, but Clark later described as Blackfeet. The next morning the Indians attempted to overpower the explorers and to steal their rifles and horses. A fight ensued, one Indian was killed and possibly another. The other Indians fled and so did Lewis's party. They rode almost without rest the 100 miles to the Missouri where the rest of their party was waiting. They quickly packed up and headed down river.

Clark's party arrived at the confluence of the Yellowstone first, but finding the mosquitoes terrible and game scarce he left a note and continued down river. Lewis's party arrived, found the note and followed. On August 12 the two parties were reunited (Camp Reunion). Unfortunately, a day earlier Lewis was accidentally shot by Cruzatte who mistook him for an elk.

The Mandan villages came into sight on August 14. The explorers received a hearty welcome from the Mandans, a celebration and council was held. The Corps remained there until August 17. Charbonneau, Sacagawea, and Pomp chose not to go to Washington and instead remained with the Mandans. Clark told them of his desire to take Pomp and educate him as if he were his own son. Sacagawea turned the request down, but indicated that when Pomp was older they would consider it. Clark finally was able to get Chief Sheheke and his family to return to Washington with the captains.

John Colter requested permission to accompany two traders, Joseph Dickson and Forrest Hancock who were on their way up to the Yellowstone country to trap. Permission was granted on the condition that no other member would ask to leave. The Corps then resumed its journey home. Lewis continued to recover slowly from the gunshot wound. Farther down river they encountered some French trappers and learned that the Arikara chief who had gone to Washington had died back East. The captains did not tell the Arikara about the chief's death when they stopped at their villages. That news was brought to the Arikara a few weeks later by Joseph Graveline. After hearing the news, the Arikara became hostile to white traders.

In Washington, Jefferson was able to have Wilkinson's appointment as governor rescinded. Jefferson considered giving the appointment to James Monroe as his replacement but later decided on Lewis.

By September 9 the Corps had passed the Platte River. Lewis had recovered and was able to walk again. On September 15 they passed their old camp at the Kansas. When the Corps arrived at La Charette the members were given a small celebration, and the following day a larger one at St. Charles.

Lewis and Clark returned to St. Louis on September 23. The journey was officially over, but the celebrations continued. On September 25 a dinner and ball was held at William Christy's Tavern. The two captains, along with Pierre Chouteau and the Mandan and Osage Indian delegations, began their trip to Washington. They arrived at the Clarksville/Louisville area in early November. There they again agreed to split up. In mid-November Lewis resumed his trip to Washington with the Indian delegation. In Frankfurt, Lewis and the Mandans took the Wilderness Road by way of the Cumberland Gap to his home at Locust Hill, to Monticello, and then arriving by the end of December in Washington. Chouteau took the Osage on a more easterly route and arrived in Washington a few days before Lewis. Clark followed in mid-December, also by the Wilderness Road, and arrived later in January.

On December 30 President Jefferson formally met the Mandan Chief Sheheke and the Osage chiefs.

1807

The first formal ball and celebration hosted by Washington officals was held on January 15 for Lewis and Clark. Neither Jefferson nor Clark was able to attend.

On February 28 Lewis was appointed governor of the Louisiana Territory. Congress confirmed Clark's appointment as Superintendent of Indian Affairs for the Louisiana Territory and as brigadier general of the militia for the Louisiana Territory on March 7. By the beginning of July Clark had moved to St Louis. To the Indians who would visit St. Louis, and for many years to come, the city was known as "Red Head's (Clark's) Town." One of Lewis and Clark's first duties was to return the visiting Indians back to their homes.

In April, Lewis announced plans for the publication of three volumes and a map. The volumes would be organized as: a narrative of the journey; a description of the geography and the ethnology of the Indians encountered; and the scientific findings and results of the expedition. Volume I was to be published by the end of the year. However, Lewis's new duties and other problems diverted his attention from this very important task. It was one that he failed to complete.

On July 7 Patrick Gass's *Journal of the Voyages and Travels of a Corps of Discovery, under the command of Capt Lewis and Capt Clarke of the Army of the United States from the mouth of the River Missouri through the interior parts of North America to the Pacific Ocean, during the years 1804, 1805, & 1806* was published. This was the first journal by a member of the expedition to be published. The first editions had no illustrations. Within a year it was published in England, by 1810 in France and then in 1814 in Germany. It was re-published three times in the United States before Lewis and Clark's journal finally became available.

1808
On March 8 Lewis finally moved to St. Louis. He tried to handle the politics and problems associated with governing the vast Louisiana Territory, but they seemed overwhelming.

John Potts became the second member of the Corps of Discovery to die. Potts was killed by the Blackfeet near Three Forks. John Colter was captured but escaped.

Fort Osage was established by William Clark. The post was first called Clark in honor of him, but the name soon was changed to reflect the Indians it served. The post was part of the factory system to control Indian trade. Although it was not a military fort, soldiers were stationed there. The fort became associated with the Santa Fe trade that developed in the 1820s. By 1827 the fort was abandoned.

James Madison was elected president. Lewis lost some of his support as new men occupied other powerful positions.

1809
Charbonneau and Sacagawea visited Clark in St. Louis. They took Clark up on his earlier offer to educate Pomp. Pomp stayed with Clark and his formal schooling began. A new life and the world were soon opened to Pomp.

Conditions on the Missouri had deteriorated. The Sioux joined the Arikara to stop any expeditions going up river. Pierre Chouteau, a wealthy, powerful, and respected fur trader was selected to lead a large well-armed party to return Chief

Sheheke and his family home. They succeeded in returning the Mandans, but the financial bill was high.

Problems continued to mount for Lewis. Many were financial. Most were related to his position as Governor, or resulted from his role as leader of the expedition and his responsibilities for the safe return of the Indians who returned with the expedition. Lewis decided to return to Washington, in hopes of explaining and settling the matters. However, when traveling on the Natchez Trace he died from gun shot wounds on October 11 while staying over night at an inn, Grinders Stand. He was believed to have committed suicide, perhaps during a period of depression stemming from his problems. However, some scholars today question that. Lewis was buried nearby.

1810
Pike published his *An Account of the Expedition to the Sources of the Mississippi and through the West Part of Louisiana.* Just as Gass's journal had been devoured by the public so was Pike's. In 1811 it was published in England. Then editions were published in 1812 in French and in 1813 Dutch and German editions. But, still nothing from Lewis and Clark.

Jefferson expected Clark to take over the task of organizing and publishing the official journal of the expedition. Clark turned to Nicholas Biddle, a well-known literary figure of Philadelphia, to oversee the job of preparing the manuscript. By the early spring of 1810 Biddle had started on it. Besides the captains' journals, Biddle had Sergeant John Ordway's journal and also the assistance of George Shannon, another member of the expedition, to help prepare the publication.

John Colter had another run in with the Blackfeet at Three Forks. He survived, but decided to leave the mountains. George Drouillard, however, decided to remain there. He was not as lucky. In May, he was killed by the Blackfeet.

1811-13
John Jacob Astor, one of the wealthiest men in the United States, started in the fur business in 1787. As head of the American Fur Company, he decided to establish a fur trading post in Oregon. This venture was a fulfillment of Jefferson's dream and a natural outgrowth of the Lewis and Clark Expedition. American traders had gone up the Missouri in increasing numbers since Lewis and Clark, but Astor had

Oregon and the Pacific as the goal. The area was rich in furs. The British had been expanding in the area. In May of 1811 Fort Astoria was built near old Fort Clatsop. It was the first American settlement west of the Rockies, but problems beset Astor from almost the beginning. In the War of 1812, the British captured the fort and forced Astor to give up the post. A party of returning Astorians, led by Robert Stuart, returned to St. Louis by land. Much of the route they used would later be incorporated into the Oregon Trail.

1812
On April 30 the Territory of Orleans entered the union as the Louisiana, the 18th state. The Territory of Louisiana became the Missouri Territory.

Sacagawea reportedly died December 20 of "putrid fever" at Fort Manuel. Carbonneau was away. Their baby daughter, Lizette, was later sent to live with Clark in St. Louis.

1813
Clark was appointed governor of the Missouri Territory.

1814
The official journal, *History of the Expedition under the Command of Captains Lewis and Clark*, was finally published. It was not the three-volume publication initially planned, but more like volume I with some materials that would have been included in volume II. Little of the scientific material was included. Only 2,000 copies were published. Unfortunately, the publisher went bankrupt, and Clark still was trying to get a copy in 1816. The original journals, maps, and related materials were finally turned over to the American Philosophical Society in 1817 and 1818. It would be nearly ninety years before most of Lewis and Clark's journals and findings were finally made public with Rueben Gold Thwaites's *Original Journals of the Lewis and Clark Expedition, 1804-1806*. And, it would be another century before Gary E. Moulton's thirteen-volume publication, *The Journals of the Lewis and Clark Expedition*, was completed and published. It included not only all the original materials, but also all the journals by other members and other related materials available at that time.

1818

On October 20, the United States and Great Britain signed the Convention of 1818. The 49th Parallel from near Lake of the Woods in Minnesota to the Rocky Mountains and Continental Divide was established as the border. The Oregon Territory would be jointly occupied. The Oregon border would not be settled until 1848 when the 49th Parallel was continued on to the Pacific Ocean.

1819
Spain signed the Adams-Onis Treaty on February 22. It gave up its claim to Oregon, ceded Florida to the United States. The boundaries for the old Louisiana Territory used portions of both the Red River and the Arkansas River.

1821
On August 10, Missouri became a state. It was the second area originally part of the Louisiana Purchase to enter the union. William Clark ran for governor, but was not elected. He still retained his position with Indian Affairs.

1823
Jean Baptiste "Pomp" Charbonneau met Prince Paul of Wurttemberg (Germany). He traveled with him and later that year went to Europe. There he remained with Paul's family. Pomp returned to the United States in 1829. Like his father, he would spend most of the rest of his life as a guide and interpreter. He finally settled in California and became the magistrate of San Luis Rey Mission in California, until he was bitten by gold fever and left for Montana in 1866.

1826
On July 4, the fiftieth anniversary of the Declaration of Independence, Thomas Jefferson, Father of the Declaration of Independence, third President of the United States, and the great visionary of westward expansion, died at Monticello.

1832-34
In 1832 George Catlin traveled up the Missouri and painted the Indians and the area. The following year Prince Maximilian of Weid-Neuweid (Germany) and his Swiss artist, Karl Bodmer, started their two-year journey to the West. Bodmer sketched and painted the Indians and scenes along the Ohio, Mississippi and Missouri rivers. For part of the journey Charbonneau acted as interpreter for Maximilian.

1837

Smallpox was carried up the Missouri river by steamboat. It quickly spread among the Indians. It was estimated that about ninety percent of the Mandans and Hidatsa died. The Indians who had befriended the Corps of Discovery, and their way of life that had dominated that area of the Missouri and northern plains only a few decades before now almost disappeared. Even the Blackfeet, farther out on the plains, suffered greatly from smallpox within a few years. The west of Lewis and Clark was rapidly disappearing. (One can also only speculate on what the history of the West would have been if the captains had been able to successfully inoculate the Indians for smallpox as had initially been discussed by Lewis and Jefferson. The outbreaks that occurred after the time of the expedition would have been much less devastating.)

1838

William Clark, co-captain of the Corps of Discovery, Superintendent of Indian Affairs, fondly known as the "Red-Headed Chief," Governor of the Missouri Territory, died on September 1. He was buried in what is now the Bellefontaine Cemetery in St. Louis, Missouri.

Post-1838

Few members of the Corps of Discovery were still alive. It would be more than another thirty years before the last member died. In 1866 Pomp died and was buried near Danner, Oregon, while on his way to the Montana gold fields, leaving only Patrick Gass. He died four years later in 1870 at the age of ninety-nine and was buried in Wellsburg, West Virginia.

CHAPTER FOUR

The maps of Lewis and Clark

T he mapping of the North American continent began with its dis-covery. While some explorers went inland, it was the coastal areas that were first mapped and settled. Most of the early explorations were driven by economic and religious reasons. Many of the earliest explorers were hoping for riches, looking for gold and sil-ver, hoping to discover the elusive northwest passage, or were mis-sionaries trying to bring new converts to their faiths. During the early colonial period the Dutch were forced out while the French and the British began moving west into the interior of North America. By the eighteenth century the quest for gold was replaced by ventures com-peting for control of the lucrative fur trade with the Indians. In the South and West, Spain was still trying to both consolidate its control and expand northward.

In the eighteenth century the French and British began a struggle for the control of North America. The French established forts and some villages in Canada and west of the Appalachians in the Ohio and Mississippi river basins and on the Great Lakes. They also pushed into the northern interior plains expanding their fur trade area. The British likewise expanded and countered every French move. The Russians were moving down the Pacific coast from Alaska towards Oregon and California, while the Spanish moved up the west coast into California. By the signing of the Treaty of Fontainebleau in 1762 with Spain and the Treaty of Paris in 1763 with Britain, France lost almost all of her lands in North America, yet French traders, culture and influence remained dominant in some areas. The British contin-ued to expand their influence, trying to replace the French in their for-mer areas in Canada and west of the Appalachians. After the

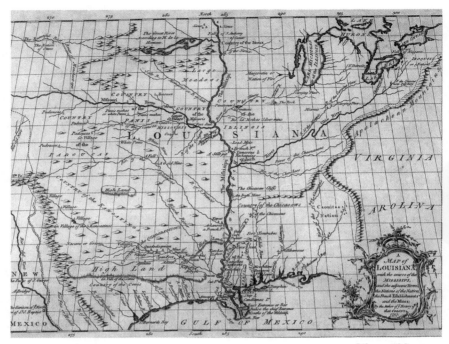

LE PAGE/DU PRATZ MAP 1763 —
"A Map of Louisiana, with the course of the Mississippi."

American Revolution, the Americans began to push into British and
Spanish areas and hoped to replace them. Some even dreamed of a
country from coast to coast.

Knowledge of the deep interior of the North American continent
was limited. There were very few maps available to Lewis and Clark
when they began their expedition, and the reliability of many of them
was questionable. Most of the lands east of the Mississippi had been
explored, but there had been limited exploration into the Great Plains
and Rocky Mountains. The newly formed government of the United
States was just beginning to survey and map its lands west of the
Appalachian Mountains. With the acquisition of the Louisiana
Territory, the size of the United States doubled, but as noted earlier,
the knowledge of exactly what it encompassed was limited.

Thomas Jefferson was a man of the Intellectual Revolution. He had
a natural curiosity about the unknown and a desire to learn about the
west and to have it explored. As a result, he tried to keep up with the
most recent information available. Jefferson was an avid reader, and

his library collection reflected this. It was considered to be one of the most extensive in the United States. As a friend of Jefferson, and later his secretary, Lewis studied at Monticello, and Jefferson's books were available to him. When the expedition finally got under way, Jefferson made sure that Lewis and Clark had some of the most recent maps available, including those of Antoine-Simeon Le Page du Pratz, Alexander Mackenzie, George Vancouver, Aaron Arrowsmith, David Thompson, and Nicholas King. Other maps were also known to Jefferson and Lewis and Clark and later were obtained and played a role in their perceptions and knowledge of the interior of North America.

One of the maps with information on the interior of the continent was by the Antoine Simon Le Page du Pratz, a French military engineer and Louisiana planter. He lived in Louisiana in the early 1700s and explored parts of the area. His first book and map were published in 1758, and his second in 1763. His publication was in Jefferson's library, and Lewis had acquired an English version.

Another of the earlier maps that Jefferson studied was Jonathan Carver's map that accompanied his *Travels in the Interior Parts of North America in the Year 1766, 1767, & 1768*. It was published in 1778. In 1766 the British Crown offered a reward for any private party that discovered the Northwest Passage. Carver joined with Robert Rogers in an exploring venture. They ran into financial problems and Carver was forced to end his exploration. Carver had explored much of the area now part of Minnesota and Wisconsin, but had not made it farther west. On his map much of the information about the land west of the Mississippi River to the Pacific was apparently based on limited information and conjecture. It showed a central area where the five great rivers of the west began: the Oregon River (later the Columbia) flowed west into the Pacific; the Colorado flowed south into the Gulf of California; the Red River of the North into Lake Winnipeg and Hudson Bay; the St. Louis east into Lake Superior; and the Mississippi south into the Gulf of Mexico. It indicated a single major mountain range running north and south starting in Mexico, but not continuing through modern Canada. Most significantly was the aspect of the map that showed the continent to be about 3,000 miles wide at the latitude of the mouth of the Oregon River.

In 1783, *A Journal of Captain Cook's Last Voyage in the Pacific* by John Ledyard was published. Ledyard had served on Cook's ship *Resolution*. In 1784 James Cook's book, *A Voyage to the Pacific Ocean*, was published. Cook had explored the Pacific Northwest. Cook's map,

CARVER — "A New Map of North America From the Latest Discoveries."

Chart of the NW Coast of America and the NE Coast of Asia explored in the years 1778 and 1779 provided the best information on the Pacific coast available at his time. Unfortunately, Cook missed seeing the mouth of the Oregon/Columbia River, thought that Vancouver Island was the mainland and missed Puget Sound. However, included on his chart was the longitude reading for the Oregon coast. Using it with the known longitude of New York, the width of the continent could be determined, and Carver's figure was confirmed. A later map by Nicholas King relied heavily on Cook's map. Jefferson had a copy of Ledyard's book. He was even acquainted with John Ledyard and tried to get him to explore North America. The shortcomings of Cook's map were shortly remedied.

Another map that played a small but significant role in the early mapping of North America was compiled by the American Robert Gray's exploration of the Pacific Coast in May 1792. Gray succeeded in

VANCOUVER' CHART — "A Chart Shewing Part of the Coast of N.W. America,"

finding the mouth of the Oregon River and sailed up it about twenty miles and traded with the Indians. He made a chart of the area and named the river the Columbia River after his ship, and determined the latitude of the mouth. Now both the latitude and the longitude of the mouth of the Columbia River were known, 46° 18′ N Lat. 123° 26′

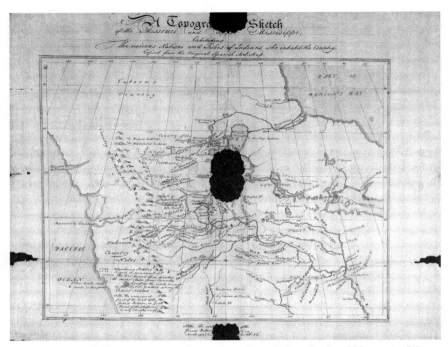

Yale Collection of Western Americana, Beinecke Rare Book and Manuscript Library
SOULARD MAP

W Long. This became even more significant later because Lewis and Clark hoped to portage from the Missouri to a tributary of the Columbia and then follow it to the Pacific. In 1804 Lewis measured the latitude and longitude of St. Louis, Camp Dubois, and the confluence of the Missouri and Mississippi. , 38° 40′ Lat. 92° 30′ W Long. Now they knew the beginning and ending point of their journey.

George Vancouver was another explorer who had originally accompanied James Cook on his trip around the world and his exploration of the Northwest coast of North America. In October 1792 Vancouver explored the Pacific coast and learned of Gray's accomplishments. Vancouver's ship, *Discovery*, was too large to pass the Columbia River sandbar, but Robert Broughton sailed his smaller ship, the *Chatham* about 100 miles up the Columbia to near the future site of Fort Vancouver. Vancouver's account of exploration was published as *A Voyage of discovery to the North Pacific ocean, and Round the World* in 1798. The chart "A Chart Shewing Part of the Coast of N.W. America," which included a detailed insert of the lower Columbia, was used by Nicholas King in preparation of his map. Lewis also made a

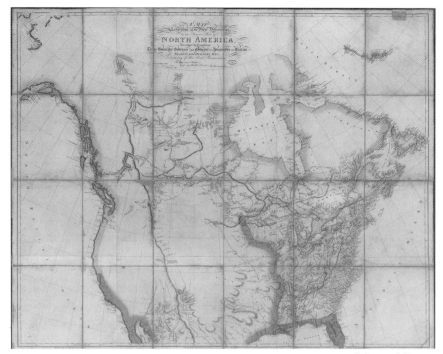

ARROWSMITH — "A Map Exhibiting all the New Discoveries
in the Interior Parts of North America."

copy of the Broughton portion of the lower Columbia and took it with
him.

There was still a vast unknown area between the Pacific coast and
the Mississippi River. One of the maps that was available to Jefferson
and Lewis and Clark was one by Antoine Soulard, *A Topographical
Sketch of the Upper Missouri and Upper Mississippi.* There are some
similarities with Carver's map, such as the narrow width of the Rocky
Mountains, but it did include what appeared to be a lot of details
about the rivers and locations of the various Indian groups. The relative order of the rivers joining the Missouri is basically correct, but
most of the details about the locations of the rivers are inaccurate,
especially those farther from the mouth of the Missouri. The Grand
Detour is greatly overestimated when compared with the Arrowsmith
and Evans/MacKay maps.

Alexander Mackenzie traveled to the Arctic and then to the Pacific
through northern Canada. His map "A Map of America between

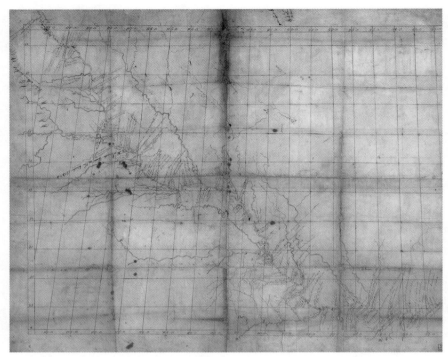

EVANS/MCKAY MAP

Latitudes 40 and 70 North and Longitudes 45 and 180 West, Exhibiting Mackenzie's Track" was published in his *Voyages from Montreal, on the River St. Laurence, through the Continent of North America to the Frozen and Pacific Oceans*; In the Years 1789 and 1793. The book was published in 1801 and Thomas Jefferson devoured it. He gave a copy of the map to Lewis and Clark.

Two other maps also available and more accurate were the Aaron Arrowsmith map and John Evans/James MacKay map. The Arrowsmith map included the route explored by McKenzie across Canada. The eastern portion of North America is quite accurate, but little of the central and western portions of North America are filled in. Again, the Rocky Mountains appear to be a fairly narrow range of mountains. His first edition was published in 1795 and a second in 1802, which Lewis obtained. There had been some exploration of the area west of the Mississippi. That was best represented by the work of John Evan and James Mackay. They had traveled up the Missouri and reached the Mandan villages on September 23, 1795. MacKay also

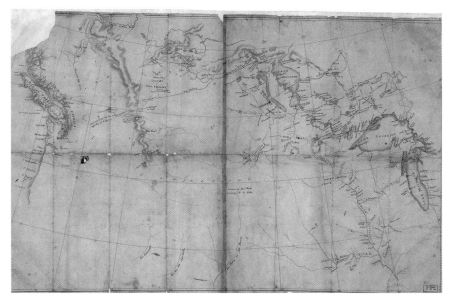

Library of Congress
KING — Map of the Western part of North America.

traveled into the interior of Nebraska. The map provided other traders, and finally, Lewis and Clark, with extensive information about the route up the Missouri River and its various tributaries along that section of the river. Nicholas King used the Arrowsmith in the production of his map.

David Thompson was a surveyor and employee of the North West Company. He mapped the trade route from Lake Superior to Lake Winnipeg via the Assiniboine River, the Mandan villages on the Missouri, the Red River, and headwaters area of the Mississippi. His map was the first to indicate the Great Bend of the Missouri where it turns west. This information was also used by Nicholas King in making his map.

The Nicholas King map was taken by Lewis and Clark. It had been made specifically for the expedition. The Secretary of the Treasurer asked Nicholas King, a well-known cartographer and Washington's surveyor, to prepare a map using the most reliable information available. It was Lewis and Clark's task to fill in the blank area and hopefully to confirm the accuracy of the rest.

Lewis and Clark had very good information about their route down the Ohio and up the Mississippi to St. Louis in 1803. For the section of their journey from their start at Camp Dubois up the Missouri to the Mandan village area they had some basic knowledge provided by their maps and also from those in the Corps who had traveled parts of the route before. Their own exploration and continual readings and calculations provided even more accurate information. During the winter of 1804-05 Clark worked on a map of the Missouri up to the Mandan villages. That map was part of the reports sent to Jefferson in the spring of 1805.

While the Corps wintered at Fort Mandan, the captains continued to collect information from the Mandans and Hidatsas about the Missouri River's route west to the mountains. They learned about the

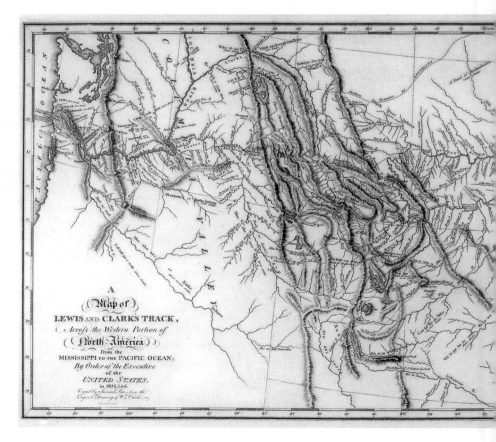

CLARK MAP — A Map of Lewis and Clark's Track Across the Western

major tributaries and the existence of the Great Falls of the Missouri. Armed with this information the journey west was a little easier.

The last map in this section is the Clark Map that was completed after the journey. Considering the time, the conditions and the equipment, the accuracy of the Clark map is almost unbelievable. The interior of the Great Plains to the Pacific now had a face. Note that the preconceived idea of a single mountain range was replaced by a wide maze of mountains. Clark kept revising his map in the years following their journey as new information was brought back by trappers, explorers, and travelers. Prince Maximilian even used copies of Clark's maps during his journey up the Missouri in 1833-4. One method of evaluating the success of the journey is to compare the

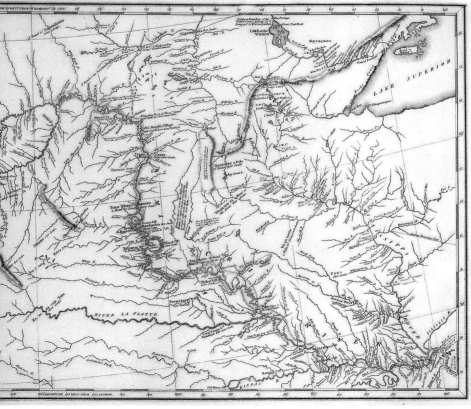

Library of Congress / American Philosophical Society

Portion of North America from the Mississippi to the Pacific Ocean.

Clark and King maps. Using only that standard, the success of the expedition is more than evident. By adding the information derived from the Pike and the Custis-Freeman expeditions and others, the interior of the Louisiana Territory was rapidly becoming known.

CHAPTER FIVE
Chronicle

O ne of the best ways to learn about the expedition and to find out what the journey was like is to read the journals of the members of the Corps. Firsthand accounts are usually excellent sources of information. They are also better than reminiscences that are sometimes blurred by the passage of time. Letters from those involved are also very helpful. It appears that there may have been seven journals kept by members of the expedition, perhaps more. This is based largely on a letter to Jefferson from Lewis in April of 1805 in which he refers to them, but it is also substantiated from other materials.

The journals known to presently exist are those by Meriwether Lewis, William Clark, Charles Floyd, John Ordway, Joseph Whitehouse, and Patrick Gass. It is thought that Nathaniel Pryor, Alexander Willard, and Robert Frazer may have also kept some form of journal. Jefferson had instructed the captains to keep two copies of their journals during their journey. While generally the captains did this, there seems to be lapses in their journals that now exist. While it is possible that during or since the expedition pages or parts were lost, there is some circumstantial evidence that the captains did not always keep daily accounts. There was no single book in which everything was kept. The journey was just too long, and it would have been very cumbersome. There are a number of bound journal books, skin bound journals and separate sheets and pages. In addition to the daily entries there are extensive field notes that include information on the varied subjects they were instructed to obtain. There are also the charts and maps and other summary reports and letters.

At first, the captains only encouraged the members of the Corps to keep records, but shortly after embarking on the journey up the Missouri they decided to do more than that. On May 26, 1804, they recorded in their own journals the *Detachment Orders" given to the sergeants and men of the expedition. Lewis noted the following, "The sergts. in addition to those duties are directed each to keep a separate journal from day today of all passing occurrences, and such other observations on the country &c. as shall appear to them worthy of notice-* The original sergeants were John Ordway, Charles Floyd, and Nathaniel Pryor. Ordway's journal exists, as well as Floyd's. Ordway's journal is the only journal with an entry for every single day of the journey. However, because Floyd died a little more than three months into the journey, his diary is incomplete. Patrick Gass replaced Floyd as the third sergeant after Floyd died. Gass's journal was the first to be published. He had started his journal even before he replaced Floyd. Whitehouse was a private and his journal was known. It was published but only in the past century. Because Pryor was one of the original sergeants, he should have kept a daily record based on the captains' orders. However, his records have not been found. It is thought that Willard and Frazer also kept records, but their journals are not known to exist. In 1806 Frazer announced plans to publish his journal, but there is no record of its publication. However, his manuscript map of the journey was published in 1807. Perhaps the journals of these last three men are stashed away in an old chest or box, in someone's attic or basement in the home of a descendant or relative, or in some file in a governmental office, all just waiting to be rediscovered. Ordway's journal had been in the possession of Nicholas Biddle and was used for reference in the preparation of the 1814 publication of Lewis and Clark's journals. It was not published and was put away by Biddle with other Clark papers and remained lost until 1913 when it was rediscovered and subsequently first published a few years later.

There are still some disagreements or questions about exactly when the captains made their different journal entries. Some appear to have been recorded at the end of the day or perhaps the following day and others much later. They may have been based on the daily field notes that were taken. Then when time availed the captains, entries were made. The captains kept more than one daily journal during parts of the journey. Parts of the second copy were sometimes only slightly different, but in others there was additional material in the entries. The second copy may also have been kept for safety reasons in case one was lost or destroyed. The men may have even written theirs together or copied from one another since some sections of the different diaries are the same. When compared to the captains' journals, the others typically contain much less information and appear to be recorded within a day or two of the happenings.

The daily entries that are used in this chapter come from portions of the official Lewis and Clark 1814 publication. The entries from Lewis and Clark are used because their accounts were the most extensive and the official ones that were finally first published in 1814. Lewis originally was responsible for the publication of the account. However, he never was able to organize the works, and his death in 1809 further slowed the publication process. Clark was then given the task of preparing the account. He sought the assistance of Nicolas Biddle.

Biddle was given the journals and papers of both Lewis and Clark and also the journal of John Ordway. George Shannon, a member of the Corps of Discovery, was asked by Clark to assist Biddle. New troubles with the printing company slowed publication further. Paul Allen was asked to do the final revisions and editing. The official account, *History of the Expedition under the Command of Captains Lewis and Clark*, was finally published in 1814. Two thousand copies were published. The segments here appear as their descriptive daily accounts, but they are not direct quotations from their individual journals, nor from their field notes, charts, drawings, or scientific and ethnic recordings. They are composites written in the style of daily entries with Clark's knowledge.

Much of the scientific material and discoveries were not included in the two volume edition because that material was to be published separately, but, unfortunately, it wasn't published. The portion that is included here is the version of what the public read nearly 200 years ago. Thus, our readers today will get a chance to learn about the expedition in the very manner in which earlier people did by reading one of the two printed accounts that were available. It would be another century before the original journals, field notes and other papers were published for people to read. Today, various kinds of editions of the original journals are available for those who want to read everything they wrote.

So, come follow along as the Corps makes its way 695 miles up the Missouri from near present-day Independence/Kansas City, Missouri, north to the area east of the Fort Randall Dam, South Dakota. The journey took about two and a half months, from June 26, 1804 to September 7, 1804. They left their June 25 camp near the mouth of the Big Blue, north of present-day Independence on the north side of the Missouri River about three mile east of the I-435 bridge or about three miles southwest of the State Road 291 Liberty Bend Bridge. The journey ends at their camp of September 7, 1804, about eight miles east of today's Fort Randall Dam.

Present-day name locations have been added in brackets, ie [Sioux City] at the end of some entries. This will help to identify the corresponding area today. Many of the daily entries also have related material in both the pictorial journey and museum chapters.

CHAPTER SIX

Journal

Official 1814 publication, History of the Expedition under the Command of Captains Lewis and Clark

26th. At one mile we passed at the end of a small island, Blue Water creek, which is about thirty yards wide at its entrance from the south. Here the Missouri is confined within a narrow bed, and the current still more so by counter currents or whirls on one side and a high bank on the other. We passed a small island and a sandbar, where our tow rope broke twice, and we rowed round with great exertions. We saw a number of parroquets, and killed some deer; after nine and three quarter miles we encamped at the upper point of the mouth of the river Kanzas: here we remained two days, during which we made the necessary observations, recruited the party, and repaired the boat. The river Kanzas takes its rise in the plains between the Arkansas and Platte rivers, and pursues a course generally east till its junction with the Missouri which is in Latitude 38° 31' 13"; here it is three hundred and forty and a quarter yards wide, though it is wider a short distance above the mouth. The Missouri itself is about five hundred yards in width; the point of union is low and subject to inundations for two hundred and fifty yards, it then rises a little above high water mark, and continues so as far back as the hills. On the south of the Kanzas the hills or highlands come within one mile and a half of the rivers; on the north of the Missouri they do not approach nearer than several miles; but on all sides the country is fine. The comparative specific gravities of the two rivers is, for the Missouri seventy-eight, the Kanzas seventy-two degrees; the water of the latter have a very disagreeable taste; the former has risen during yesterday and to day about two feet. On the banks of the Kanzas reside the Indians of the same name, consisting of two villages, one at about twenty, the other forty leagues from its mouth, and amounting to about three hundred men. They once lived twenty-four leagues higher than the Kanzas, on the south bank of the Missouri, and were then more numerous, but they have been reduced and banished by the Sauks and Ayauways, who being better supplied with arms have an advantage over the Kanzas, though the latter are not less fierce or warlike than themselves. This nation is now hunting in the plains for buffaloe which our hunters have seen for the first time. [Kansas City area]

On the 29th, we set out late in the afternoon, and having passed a sandbar, near which the boat almost lost, and a large island on the north, we encamped at seven and a quarter miles on the same side in the low lands, where the rushes are so thick that it is troublesome to walk through them. Early the next morning, 30th, we reached, at five miles distance, the mouth of a river coming in from the north, and called by the French, Petite Riviere Platte, or Little Shallow river; it is about sixty yards wide at its mouth. A few of the party who ascended informed us, that the lands on both sides are good, and that there are several falls well calculated for mills; the wind was from the south west, and the weather oppressively warm, the thermometer standing at 96 above 0 at three o'clock P. M. One mile beyond this is a small creek on the south, at five miles from which we encamped on the same side, opposite the lower point of an island called Diamond island. The land on the north between the Little Shallow river, and the Missouri is not good and subject to overflow-on the south it is higher and better timbered.

July 1st. We proceeded along the north side of Diamond island, where a small creek called Biscuit creek empties itself. One and a half miles above the island is a large sandbar in the middle of the river, beyond which we stopped to refresh the men, who suffered very much from the heat. Here we observed great quantities of grapes and raspberries. Between one and two miles further are three islands and a creek on the south known by the French name of Remore. The main current which is now on the south side of the largest of the three islands, ran three years, as we were told on the north, and there was then no appearance of the two smaller islands. At the distance of four and a half miles we reached the lower point of a cluster of small islands, two large and two small, called Isles des Parcs or Field Island. Paccaun trees were this day seen, and large quantities of deer and turkies on the banks. We had advanced twelve miles.

July 2d. We left our encampment, opposite to which is a high and beautiful prairie on the southern side, and passed up the south of the islands, which are high meadows, and a creek on the north called Parc creek. Here for half an hour the river became covered with drift wood, which rendered the navigation dangerous, and was probably caused by giving way of some sandbar, which had detained the wood. After making five miles we passed a stream on the south called Turky creek, near a sandbar, where we would scarcely stem the current with twenty oars, and all the poles we had. On the north at two miles further is a large island called by the Indians, Wan-car-da-war-card-da, or the Bear Medicine island. Here we landed and replaced our mast, which had broken three days ago, by running against a tree, overhanging the river. Thence we proceeded, and after night stopped on the north side, above the island, having come eleven and a half miles. Opposite our camp is a valley, in which was situated an old village of the Kanzas, between two high points of land, and on the bank of the river. About a mile in the rear of the village was a small fort, built by the French on an elevation. There are now no traces of the villages, but the situation of the fort may be recognized by some remains of chimnies, and the general outline of the fortification, as well as by the fine spring which supplied it with water. The party, who were stationed here, were probably cut off by the Indians, as there are no accounts of them.

July3d. A gentle breeze from the south carried us eleven and a quarter miles this day, past two islands, one small willow island, the other large, and called by the French Isle des Vaches, or Cow island. At the head of this island, on the northern shore, is a large pond containing beaver, and fowls of different kinds. After passing a bad sandbar, we stopped on the south side at an old trading house, which is now deserted, and half a mile beyond it encamped on the south. The land is fine along the rivers, and some distance back. We observed the black walnut and oak, among the timber; and the honeysuckle and the buck's-eye, with the nuts on them. [Lewis & Clark State Park, Missouri]

The morning of the 4th July was announced by the discharge of our gun. At one mile we reached the mouth of a bayeau or creek, coming from a large lake on the north side, which appears as if it had once been the bed of the river, to which it runs parallel for several miles. The water of it clear and supplied by a small creek and several springs, and the number of goslins which we saw on it, induced us to call it Gosling lake. It is about three quarters of a mile wide, and seven or eight miles long. One of our men was bitten by a snake, but a poultice of bark and gunpowder was sufficient to cure the wound. At ten and a quarter miles we reached a creek on the south about twelve yards wide and coming from an extensive prairie, which approached the borders of the river. To this creek which had no name, we gave that of Fourth of July creek; above it is a high mound, where three Indian paths centre, from which is a very extensive prospect. After fifteen miles sail we came to on the north a little above a creek on the southern side, about thirty yards wide, which we called Independence creek, in honour of the day, which we could celebrate only by an evening gun, and a additional gill of whiskey to the men. [Atchison, Kansas]

The next day, 5th, we crossed over to the south and came along the bank of an extensive and beautiful prairie, interspersed with copses of timber, and watered by Independence creek. On this bank formerly stood the second village of the Kanzas; from the remains it must have been once a large town. We passed several bad sandbars, and a small creek to the south, which we called Yellow Ochre creek, from a bank of the mineral a little above it. The river continues to fall. On the shores are great quantities of summer and fall grapes, berries and wild roses. Deer is not so abundant as usual, but there are numerous tracks of elk around us. We encamped at ten miles distance on the south side under a high bank, opposite to which was a low land covered with tall rushes, and some timber.

July 6. We set sail, and at one mile passed a sandbar, three miles further an island, a prairie to the north, at the distance of four miles called Reevey's prairie, after a man who was killed there; at which place the river is confined to a very narrow channel, and by a sandbar from the south. Four miles beyond is another sandbar terminated by a small willow island, and forming a very considerable bend in the river towards the north The sand of the bar is light, intermixed with small pebbles and some pit coal. The river falls slowly, and owing either to the muddiness of its water, or the extreme heat of the weather, the men perspire profusely. We encamped on the south having made twelve miles. The bird called whip-poor-will sat on the boat for some time.

In the morning, July 7th, the rapidity of the water obliged us to draw the boat along with ropes. At six and three quarters miles, we came to a sandbar, at a point oppositie a fine rich prairie on the north, called St. Michael's. The prairies of this neighbourhood have the appearance of distinct farms, divided by narrow strips of woodland, which follow the borders of the small runs leading to the river. Above this, about a mile, is a cliff of yellow clay on the north. At four o'clock we passed a narrow part of the channel, where the water is confined within a bed of two hundred yards wide, the current running directly against the southern bank with no sand on the north to confine it or break its force. We made fourteen miles, and halted on the north, after which we had a violent gust about seven o'clock. One of the hunters saw in a pond to the north which we passed yesterday a number of young swans. We saw a large rat, and killed a wolf. Another of our men had a stroke of the sun; he was bled, and took a preparation of nitre which relieved him considerably. [St. Joseph, Missouri]

July 8. We set out early, and soon passed a small creek on the north, which we called Ordway's creek, from our sergeant of that name who had been sent on a shore with the horses, and went up it. On the same side are three small islands, one of which is the Little Nodawa, and a large island called the Great Nowada extending more than fiver miles containing seven or eight thousand acres of high good land, rarely over-flowed, and one of the largest islands of the Missouri. It is separated from the northern shore by a small channel of from forty-five to eighty yards wide, up which we passed, and found near the western extremity of the island the mouth of the river Nodawa. The river persues nearly a southern course, is navigable for boats to some distance, and about seventy yards wide above the mouth, though no so wide immediately there, as the mud from the Missouri contracts its channel. At twelve and a quarter miles, we encamped on the north side, near the head of

Nodawa island, and opposite a smaller one in the middle of the river. Five of the men were this day sick with violent headaches. The river continues to fall.

July 9th. We passed the island opposite to which we last night camped, and saw near the head of it a creek falling in from a pond on the north, to which we gave the name of Pike ponds, from the numbers of that animal which some of our party saw from the shore. The wind changed at eight from N.E. to S.W. and brought rain. At six miles we passed the mouth a Monter's creek on the south, and two miles above a few cabins, where one of our party had encamped with some Frenchmen about two years ago. Further on we passed an island on the north, opposite some cliffs on the south side, near which Loup or Wolf river falls into the Missouri. This river is about sixty yards wide, it head near the same sources as the Kanzas, and is navigable for boats, at some distance up. At fourteen miles we encamped on the south side.

Tuesday 10th. We proceeded on by a prairie on the upper side of Wolf river, and at four miles passed a creek fifteen yards wide on the south called Pape's creek after a Spaniard of that name, who killed himself there. At six mile we dined on an island called by the French Isle de Salomon, or Solomon's island, opposite to which on the south is a beautiful plain covered with grass, intermixed with wild rye and a kind of wild potatoe. After making ten miles we stopped for the night on the northern side, opposite a cliff of yellow clay. The river has neither risen or fallen to day. On the north the low land is very extensive, and covered with vines; and the south, the hills approach nearer the river, and back of them commence the plains. There are a great many goslins along the banks. [White Cloud, Kansas]

Wednesday 11th. After three miles sailing we came to a willow island on the north side, behind which enters a creek called by the Indians Tarkio. Above this creek on the north the low lands are subject to overflow, and further back the undergrowth of vines particularly, is so abundant that they can scarcely be passed. Three miles from Tarkio we encamped on a large sand island on the north, immediately opposite the river Nemahaw.

Thursday 12th. We remained here to day for the purpose of refreshing the party, and making lunar observations. The Nemahaw empties itself into the Missouri from the south, and is eighty yards wide at the confluence, which is in lat.3° 55´ 56´´. Capt Clarke ascended it in the perioque about two miles to the mouth of a small creek on the lower side. On going ashore he found in the level plain several artificial mounds or graves, and the adjoining hills others of a larger size. The appearance indicated sufficiently the former population of this country, the mounds being certainly intended as tombs; the Indians of the Missouri still preserving the custom of interring the dead on high ground. From the top of the highest mound a delightful prospect presented itself-the level and extensive meadows watered by the Nemahaw, and enlivened by the few trees and shrubs skirting the borders of the river and its tributary streams-the lowland of the Missouri covered with undulating grass, nearly five feet high, gradually rising into a second plain, where rich weeds and flowers are interspersed with copses of Osage plum; further back are seen small groves of trees; an abundance of grapes; the wild cherry of Missouri, resembling our own, but larger, and growing on a small bush; and the chokecherry, which we observed for the first time. Some of the grapes gathered to-day are nearly ripe. On the south of the Nemahaw, and about a quarter of a mile from its mouth, is a cliff of freestone, in which are various inscriptions and marks made by the Indians. The sand island where we encamped, is covered with two species of willow, broad and narrow leaf.

July 13th. We proceeded at sunrise with a fair wind from the south, and at two miles, passed the moth of a small river on the north, called Big Tarkio. A channel from the bed of the Missouri once ran into this river, and formed an island called St. Joseph's, but the channel is now filled up, and the island is added to the north shore. Further on to the south, is situated an extensive plain, covered with a grass resembling timothy in its general appearance, except the seed which is like a flaxseed, and also a number of grape-vines. At twelve miles, we passed an island on the north, above which is a large sandbar covered with willows: and at twenty and a half miles, stopped on a large sandbar, in the middle of the river opposite a high handsome prairie, which extends to the hills four or five miles distant, though near the bank the land is low, and subject to be overflowed. This day was exceedingly fine and pleasant, a storm of wind and rain from north-northeast, last night, having cooled the air. [Corning, Missouri]

July 14. We had some hard showers of rain before seven o'clock, when we set out. We had just reached the end of the sand island, and seen the opposite banks falling in, and so lined with timber that we could not approach it without danger, when a sudden squall, from the northeast, struck the boat on the starboard quarter, and would have certainly dashed her to pieces on the sand island, if the party had not leaped into the river, and with the aid of the anchor and cable kept her off: the waves dashing over her for the space of forty minutes; after which, the river became almost instantaneously calm and smooth. The two periogues were ahead, in a situation nearly similar, but fortunately no damage was done to the boats or the loading. The wind having shifted to the southeast, we came at the distance of two miles, to an island on the north, where we dined. One mile above, on the same side of the river, is a small factory, where a merchant of St. Louis traded with the Ottoes and Pawness two years ago. Near this is an extensive lowland, part of which is overflowed occasionally, the rest is rich and well timbered. The wind again changed to northwest by north. At seven and a half miles, we reached the lower point of a large island, on the north side. A small distance above this point, is a river, called by the Maha Indians, Nishnahbatona. This is a considerable creek, nearly as large as the Mine river, and runs parallel to the Missouri the greater part of its course, being fifty yards wide at the mouth. In the prairies or glades, we saw wild-timothy, lambsquarter, cuckleberries, and on the edges of the river, summer-grapes, plums, and gosseberries. We also saw to-day, for the first time, some elk, at which some of the party shot, but at too great a distance. We encamped on the north side of the island, a little above Nishnahbatona, having made nine miles. The river fell a little.

July 15. A thick fog prevented our leaving the encampment before seven. At about four miles, we reached the extremity of a large island, and crossing to the south, at the distance of seven miles, arrived at the Little Nemaha, a small river from the south, forty yards wide a little above its mouth, but contracting, as do almost all the rivers emptying into the Missouri, at its confluence. At nine and three quarters miles, we encamped on a woody point, on the south. Along the southern bank, is a rich lowland covered with peavine, and rich weeds, and watered by small streams rising in the adjoining prairies. They too, are rich, and though with abundance of grass, have no timber except what grows near the water: interspersed through both are grapevines, plums of two kinds, two species of wild-cherries, hazelnuts, and gosseberries. On the south there is one unbroken plain; on the north the river is skirted with some timber, behind which the plain extends four or five miles to the hills, which seem to have little wood.

July 16. We continued our route between a large island opposite to our last night's encampment, and an extensive prairie on the south. About six miles, we came to another large island, called Fairsun island, on the same side; above which is a spot, where about twenty acres of the hill have fallen into the river. Near this, is a cliff of sandstone for two miles, which is much frequented by birds. At this place the river is about one mile wide, but not deep; as the timber, or sawyers, may be seen, scattered across the whole of its bottom. At twenty miles distance, we saw on the south, an island called by the French, l'Isle Chance, or Bald island, opposite to a large prairie, which we called Baldpated prairie, from a ridge of naked hills which bound it, running parallel with the river as far as we could see, and from three to six miles distance. To the south the hills touch the river. We encamped a quarter of a mile beyond this, in a point of woods on the north side. The river continues to fall. [Brownsville, Nebraska area]

Tuesday, July 17. We remained here this day, in order to make observations and correct the chronometer, which ran down Sunday. The latitude we found to be 40° 27′ 5″ 4/10. The observation of the time proved our chronometer too slow, by 6″ 51″ 6/10. The highlands bear from our camp, north 25° west, up the river. Captain Lewis rode up the country, and saw the Nishnahbatona, about ten or twelve miles from its mouth, at a place not more than three hundred yards from the Missouri, and a little above our camp. It then passes near the foot of the Baldhills, and is at least six feet below the level of the Missouri. On its banks are oak, walnut, and mulberry. The common current of the Missouri, taken with the log, is 50 fathoms in 40″, at some places, and even 20″.

Wednesday, July 18. The morning was fair, and a gentle wind from the southeast by south, carried us along between the prairie on the north, and Bald island to the south; opposite the middle of which, the Nishnahbatona approaches the nearest to the Missouri. The current here ran fifty fathoms in 41″. At thirteen and a half miles, we reached an island on the north, near to which the banks overflow; while on the south, the hills project over the river and form high cliffs. At one point a part of the cliff, nearly three quarters of a mile in length, and about two hundred feet in height, has fallen into the river. It is composed chiefly of sandstone intermixed with an iron ore of bad quality; near the bottom is a soft slatestone with pebbles. We passed several bad sandbars in the course of the day, and made eighteen miles, and encamped on the south, opposite to the lower point of the Oven islands. The country around is generally divided into prairies, with little timber, except on low points, islands, and near creeks, and that consisting of cottonwood, mulberry, elm, and sycamore. The river falls fast. An Indian dog came to the bank; he appeared to have been lost and was nearly starved: we gave him some food, but he would not follow us.

Thursday, July 19. The Oven islands are small, and two in number; one near the south shore, the other in the middle of the river. Opposite to them is the prairie called Terrien's Oven, from a traders of that name. At four and a half miles, we reached some high cliffs of a yellow earth, on the south, near which are two beautiful runs of water, rising in the adjacent prairies, and one of them with a deerlick, about two hundred yards from its mouth. In this neighbourhood we observed some iron ore in the bank. At two and a half miles above the runs, a large portion of the hill, for nearly three quarters of a mile, has fallen into the river. We encamped on the western extremity of an island, in the middle of the river, having ten and three quarter miles. The river falls little. The sandbars which we passed to-day, are more numerous, and the rolling sands more frequent and dangerous, than any we have seen; these obstacles increasing as we approach the river Platte. The Missouri here is wider also than below, where the timber on the banks resists the current; while here the prairies which approach, are more easily washed and underminded. The hunters have brought for the last few days, no quadruped, but deer: great quantities of young geese are seen to-day: one of them brought calamus, which he had gathered opposite our encampment, and a larger quantity of sweetflag. [Nebraska City, Nebraska]

Friday, July 20. There was a heavy dew last night, and this morning was foggy and cool. We passed at about three miles distance, a small willow island to the north, and a creek on the south, about twenty-five yards wide, called by the French,

L'eau qui Pleure, or Weeping Water, and emptying itself just above a cliff of brown clay. Thence we made two and a half miles to another island; three miles further to a third: six miles beyond which is a fourth island; at the head of which we encamped on the southern shore; in all eighteen miles. The party, who walked on the shore to-day, found the plains to the south, rich, but much parched with frequent fires, and with no timber, except the scattering trees about the sources of the runs, which are numerous and fine. On the north, is a small prairie country. The river continues to fall. A large yellow wolf was this day killed. For a month past the party have been troubled with biles, and occasionally with dysentery. These biles were large tumours which broke out under the arms, on the legs, and, generally, in the parts most exposed to action, which sometimes became too painful to permit the men to work. After remaining some days, they disappeared without any assistance, except a poultice of the bark of the elm, or Indian meal. This disorder, which we ascribe to the muddiness of the river water, has not affected the general health of the party, which is quite good, if not better, than the health of the same number of men in any other situation.

Saturday, July 21. We had a breeze from the southeast, by the aid of which we passed, at about ten miles, a willow island on the south, near high lands covered with timber, at the bank, and formed of limestone with cemented shells: on the opposite side is a bad sandbar, and the land near it is cut through at high water, by small channels forming a number of islands. The wind lulled at seven o'clock, and we reached, in the rain, the mouth of the great Platte, at the distance of fourteen miles. The highlands which had accompanied us on the south, for the last eight or ten miles, stopped at about three quarters of a mile from the entrance of the Platte. Captains Lewis and Clarke ascended the river in a periogue, for about one mile, and found the current very rapid; rolling over sands, and divided into a number of channels; none of which appeared deeper than five or six feet. One of our Frenchmen, who spent two winters on it says that it spreads much more at some distance from the mouth; that its depth is generally not more than five or six feet; that there are many small islands scattered through it, and that from its rapidity and the quantity of its sand, it cannot be navigated by boats or periogues, though the Indians pass it in small flat canoes made of hides. That the

Saline or Salt river, which in some seasons is too brackish to be drank, falls into it from the south about thirty miles up, and a little above it Elkhorn river from the north, running nearly parallel with the Missouri. The river is, in fact, much more rapid than the Missouri, the bed of which it fills with moving sands, and drives the current on the northern shore, on which it is constantly encroaching. At its junction the Platte is about six hundred yards wide, and the same number of miles from the Mississippi. With much difficulty we worked round the sandbars near the mouth, and came to above the point, having made fifteen miles. A number of wolves were seen and heard around us in the evening. [Bellevue, Nebraska]

July 22. The next morning we set sail, and having found at the distance of ten miles from the Platte, a high and shaded situation on the north, we encamped there, intending to make requisite observations, and to send for the neighbouring tribes, for the purpose of making known the recent change in government, and the wish of the United States to cultivate their friendship.

OUR camp is by observation latitude 41° 3′ 11″. Immediately behind it is a plain about five miles wide, one half covered with wood, the other dry and elevated. The low grounds on the south near the junction of the two rivers, are rich, but subject to be overflowed. Farther up, the banks are higher, and opposite our camp the first hills approach the river, and are covered with timber, such as oak, walnut, and elm. The intermediate country is watered by the Papillon, or Butterfly creek, of about eighteen yards wide, and three miles from the Platte; on the north are high open plains and prairies, and at nine miles from the Platte, the Musquitoe creek, and two or three small willow islands. We stayed here several days, during which we dried our provisions, made new oars, and prepared our dispatches and maps of the country we had passed, for the president of the United States, to whom we intend to send them by a perigue from this place. The hunters have found game scarce in this neighbourhood; they have seen deer, turkies, and grouse; we have also an abundance of ripe grapes; and one of our men caught a white catfish, the eyes of which were small, and its tail resembling that of a dolphin. The present season is that in which the Indians go out into the prairies to hunt buffaloe; but as we discovered some hunter's tracks, and observed the plains on fire in the direction of their villages, we hoped that they might have returned to gather the green Indian corn, and therefore dispatched two men to the Ottoes, or Pawnee villages with a present of tobacco, and an invitation to the chiefs to visit us. They returned after two days absence. Their first course was through an open prairie to the south, in which they crossed Butterfly creek. They then reached a small beautiful river, called Come de Cerf, or Elkhorn river, about one hundred yards wide, with clear water and a gravelly channel. It empties a little below the Ottoe village into the Platte, which they crossed, and arrived at the town about forty-five miles from our camp. They found no Indians there, though they saw some fresh tracks of a small party. The Ottoes were once a powerful nation, and lived about twenty miles above the Platte, on the southern bank of the Missouri. Being reduced, they migrated to the neighbourhood of the Pawnees, under whose protection they now live. Their village is on the south side of the Platte, about thirty miles from its mouth; and their number is two hundred men, including about thirty families of Missouri Indians, who are incorporated with them. Five leagues above them, on the same side of the river, resides the nation of Pawnees. This people were among the most numerous of the Missouri Indians, but have gradually been dispersed and broken, and even since the year 1797, have undergone some sensible changes. They now consist of four bands; the first is the one just mentioned, of about five hundred men, to whom of late years have been added the second band, who are called the republican Pawnees, from their having lived on the republican branch of the river Kanzas, whence they migrated to join the principal band of the Pawnees: the republican Pawnees amount to nearly two hundred and fifty men. The third, are the Pawnees Loups, or Wolf Pawnees, who reside on the Wolf fork of the Platte, about ninety miles from the principal Pawnees, and number two hundred and eighty men. The fourth branch originally resided on the Kanzas and Arkansaw, but in their wars with the Osage, they were so often defeated, that they at last retired to their present position on the Red river, where they form a tribe of four hundred men. All these tribes live in villages, and raise corn; but during the intervals of culture rove in the plains in quest of buffaloe.

Beyond them on the river, and westward of the Black mountains, are the Kaninaviesch, consisting of about four hundred men. They are supposed to have emigrated originally from the Pawnees nation; but they have degenerated from improvements of the parent tribe, and no longer live in villages, but rove through the plains.

Still further to the westward, are several tribes, who wander and hunt on the sources of the river Platte, and thence to Rock Mountain. These tribes, of which little more is known than the names and the population, are first, the Staitan, or Kite Indians, a small tribe of one hundred men. They have acquired the name of Kites, from their flying; that is, their being always on horseback; and the smallness of their numbers is to be attributed to their extreme ferocity; they are the most warlike of all western Indians; they never yield in battle; they never spare their enemies; and the retaliation of this barbarity has almost extinguished the nation. Then come the Wetapahato, and Kiawa tribes, associated together, and amounting to two hundred men; the Castahana, of three hundred men, to which are to be added the Cataka of seventy-five men, and the Dotami. These wandering tribes, are conjectured to be the remnants of the Great Padouca nation, who occupied the country between the upper parts of the river Platte, and the river Kanzas. They were visited by Bourgemont, in 1724, and then lived on the Kanzas river. The seats, which he describes as their residence, are now occupied by the Kanzas nation; and of the Padoucas, there does not now exist even the name.

July 27. Having completed the object of our stay, we set sail, with a pleasant breeze from the N.W. The two horses swam over to the southern shore, along which we went, passing by an island, at three and a half miles, formed by a pond, fed by springs: three miles further is a large sand island, in the middle of the river; the land on the south being high, and covered with timber; that on the north, a high prairie. At ten and a half miles from our encampment, we saw and examined a curious collection of graves or mounds, on the south side of the river. Not far from a low piece of land and a pond, is a tract of about two hundred acres in circumference, which is covered with mounds of different heights, shapes, and sizes: some of sand, and some of both earth and sand; the largest being nearest the river. These mounds indicate the position of the ancient village of the Ottoes, before they retired to the protection of the Pawnees. After making fifteen miles, we encamped on the south, on the bank of a high handsome prairie, with lofty cottonwood in groves, near the river. [Council Bluffs, Iowa]

July 28. At one mile, this morning we reached a bluff, on the north, being the first highlands, which approach the river on that side, since we left the Nadawa. Above this, is an island and a creek, about fifteen yards wide, which, as it has no name, we called it Indian Knob creek, from a number of round knobs bare of timber, on the highlands, to the north. A little below the bluff, on the north, is the spot where the Ayauway Indians formerly lived. They were a branch of the Ottoes, and emigrated from this place to the river Desmoines. At ten and three quarter miles, we encamped on the north side, opposite an island, in the middle of the river. The land, generally, on the north, consists of high prairie and hills, with timber: on the south, low and covered with cottonwood. Our hunter brought to us in the evening, a Missouri Indian, whom he had found, with two others, dressing an elk; they were perfectly friendly, gave him some meat, and one of them agreed to accompany him to the boat. He is one of the few remaining Missouris, who live with the Ottoes: he belongs to a small party, whose camp is four miles from the river; and he says, that the body of the nation is now hunting buffaloe in the plains: he appeared quite sprightly, and his language resembled that of the Osage, particularly in his calling a chief, inca. We sent him back with one of our party next morning,

Sunday, July 29, with an invitation to the Indians to meet us above on the river, and then proceeded. We soon came to a northern bend in the river, which runs within twenty yards of Indian Knob creek, the water of which is five feet higher than that of the Missouri. In less than two miles, we passed Boyer's creek on the north, of twenty-five yards width. We stopped to dine under a shade, near the highland on the south, and caught several large catfish, one of them nearly white, and all very fat. Above this highland, we observed the traces of a great hurricane, which passed up the river obliquely from the N.W. to S.E. and which tore up large trees, some of which perfectly sound, and four feet in diameter, were snapped off near the ground. We made ten miles to a wood on the north, where we camped. The Missouri is much more crooked, since we passed the river Platte, though generally speaking, not so rapid; more of prairie, with less timber, and cottonwood in the low grounds, and oak, black walnut, hickory, and elm.

July 30. We went early in the morning, three and a quarter miles, and encamped on the south side, in order to wait for the Ottoes. The land here consists of a plain, above the highwater level, the soil of which is fertile, and covered with a grass from five to eight feet high, interspersed with copses of large plums, and a currant, like those of the United States. It also furnishes two species of honeysuckle; one growing to a kind of shrub, common about Harrodsburgh (Kentucky), the other is not so high: the flowers grow in clusters, are short, and of a light pink colour; the leaves too, are distinct, and do not surround the stalks, as do those of the common honeysuckle of the United States. Back of this plain, is a woody ridge about seventy feet above it, at the end of which we formed our camp. This ridge separates the lower from a higher prairie, of a good quality, with grass, of ten or twelve inches in height, and extending back about a mile, to another elevation of eighty or ninety feet, beyond which is one continued plain. Near our camp, we enjoy from the bluffs a most beautiful view of the river, and the adjoining country. At a distance, varying from four to ten miles, and of a height between seventy and three hundred feet, two parallel ranges of highland affords a passage to the Missouri, which enriches the low grounds between them. In its winding course, it nourishes the willow islands, the scattered cottonwood, elm, sycamore, lynn, and ash, and the groves are interspersed with hickory, walnut, coffeenut, and oak. [Fort Atkinson State Historical Park, Nebraska]

July 31. The meridian altitude of this day made the latitude of our camp 41° 18' 1 4/10". The hunters supplied us with deer, turkies, geese, and beaver; one of the last was caught alive, and in a very short time perfectly tamed. Catfish are very abundant in the river, and we have also seen a buffaloefish. One of our men brought in yesterday an animal called, by the Pawnees, chocartoosh, and, by the French blaireau, or badger. The evening is cool, yet the mosquitoes are very troublesome.

We waited with much anxiety the return of our messenger to the Ottoes. The men whom we dispatched to our last encampment, returned without having seen any appearance of its having been visited. Our horses too had strayed; but we were so fortunate as to recover them at the distance of twelve miles. Our apprehensions were at length relieved by the arrival of a party of about fourteen Ottoe and Missouri Indians, who came at sunset, on the second of August, accom-

panied by a Frenchman, who resided among them, and inter-
preted for us. Captains Lewis and Clarke went out to meet
them, and told them that we would hold a council in the morning. In the mean time we sent them some roasted meat, pork,
flour, and meal; in return for which they made us present of
watermelons. We learnt that our man Liberte had set out from
their camp a day before them: we were in hopes that he had
fatigued his horse, or lost himself in the woods, and would soon
return; but we never saw him again.

August 3. The next morning the Indians, with their six
chiefs, were all assembled under an awning, formed with the
mainsail, in presence of all our party, paraded for the occasion.
A speech was then made, announcing to them the change in
government, our promises of protection, and advice as to their
future conduct. All the six chiefs replied to our speech, each in
his turn, according to rank: they expressed their joy at the
change in the government; their hopes that we would recom-
mend them to their great father (the president), that they
might obtain trade and necessaries; they wanted arms as well
for hunting as for defence, and asked our mediation between
them and the Mahas, with whom they are now at war. We
promised to do so, and wished some of them to accompany us to
that nation, which they declined, for fear of being killed by
them. We then proceeded to distribute our presents. The grand
chief of the nation not being of the party, we sent him a flag, a
medal, and some ornaments for clothing. To the six chiefs who
were present, we gave a medal of second grade to one Ottoe
chief, and one Missouri chief; a medal of the third grade to two
inferior chief of each nation: the customary mode of recogniz-
ing a chief, being to place a medal round his neck which is considered among his tribe as proof of his consideration abroad.
Each of these medals was accompanied by a present of paint,
garters, and cloth ornaments of dress; and to this we added a
canister of powder, a bottle of whiskey, and a few presents to
the whole, which appeared to make them perfectly satisfied.
The airgun too was fired, and astonished them greatly. The
absent grand chief was an Ottoe, named Weahrushhah, which,
in English, degenerates into Little Thief. The two principal
chietains present were, Shongotongo, or Big Horse; and
Wethea, or Hospitality; also Shosguscan, or White Horse, an
Ottoe, the second a Missouri. The incidents just related,
induced us to give to this place the name of the Council-bluff;

the situation of it is exceedingly favourable for a fort or trading factory, as the soil is well calculated for bricks, and there is an abundance of wood in the neighbourhood, and the air being pure and healthy. It is also central to the chief resorts of the Indians: one day's journey from the Mahas; two and a quarter from the Pawnees Loups village; convenient to the hunting grounds of the Sioux; and twenty-five days journey to Santa Fe.

The ceremonies of the council being concluded, we set sail in the afternoon, and encamped at the distance of five miles, on the south side, where we found the mosquitoes very troublesome. [DeSoto National Willife Refuge]

August 4. A violent wind, accompanied by rain, purified and cooled the atmosphere last nigh; we proceeded early, and reached a very narrow part of the river, where the channel is confined within a space of two hundred yards, by a sand point on the north, and a bend on the south; the banks in the neighbourhood washing away, the trees falling in, and the channel filled with buried logs. Above this is a trading house, on the south, where one of our party passed two years, trading with the Mahas. At nearly four miles, is a creek on the south, emptying opposite a large island of sand; between this creek and our last night's encampment, the river has changed its bed, and encroached on the southern shore. About two miles further, is another creek on the south, which like the former, is the outlet of three ponds, communicating with each other, and forming a small lake, which is fed by streams from the highlands. At fifteen miles, we encamped on the south. The hills on both sides of the river are nearly twelve or fifteen miles from each other; those of the north containing some timber, while the hills of the south are without any covering, except some scattering wood in the ravines, and near where the creeks pass into the hills; the rich plains and prairies occupying the intermediate space, and partially covered, near the water, with cottonwood. There has been a great deal of pumice stone on the shore to-day.

August 5th. We set out early, and, by means of our oars, made twenty and a half miles, though the river was crowded with sandbars. On both sides the prairies extend along the river; the banks being covered with great quantities of grapes, of which three different species are now ripe; one large and resembling the purple grape. We had some rain this morning, attended by high wind; but generally speaking, have remarked that thunder storms are less frequent than in the Atlantic states, at this season. Snakes too are less frequent, though we killed one to-day of the shape and size of the rattlesnake, but of a lighter colour. We fixed our camp on the north side. In the evening, captain Clarke, in pursuing some game, in an easterly direction, found himself at the distance of three hundred and seventy yards from camp, at a point of the river whence we had come twelve miles. When the water is high, this peninsula is overflowed, and judging from customary and notorious changes in the river, a few years will be sufficient to force the main current of the river across, and leave the great bend dry. The whole lowland between the parallel range of hills seems formed of mud and ooze of the river, at some former period, mixed with sand and clay. The sand of the neighbouring banks accumulates with the aid of that brought down the stream, and forms sandbars, projecting into the river; these drive the channel to the opposite banks, the loose texture of which it undermines, and at length deserts its ancient bed for a new and shorter passage; it is thus that the banks of the Missouri are constantly falling, and the river changing its bed.

August 6. In the morning, after a violent storm of wind and rain from N. W. we passed a large island to the north. In the channel separating it from the shore, a creek called Soldier's river enters; the island kept it from our view, but one of our men who had seen it, represents it as about forty yards wide at its mouth. At five miles, we came to a bend of the river towards the north, a sandbar, running in from the south, had turned its course so as to leave the old channel quite dry. We again saw the same appearance at our encampment, twenty and a half miles distant on the north side. Here the channel of the river had encroached south, and the old bed was without water, except for a few ponds. The sandbars are still very numerous.

August 7. We had another storm from the N. W. in the course of the last evening; in the morning we proceeded, having the wind from the north, and encamped on the northern shore, having rowed seventeen miles. The river is encumbered with sandbars, but no islands, except two small ones, one called Detachment island, and formed on the south side by a small stream.

We dispatched four men back to the Ottoes village in quest of our man Liberte, and to apprehend one of the soldiers, who left us on the 4th, under pretence of recovering a knife which he had dropped a short distance behind, and who we fear has deserted. We also sent small presents to the Ottoes and Missouris, and requested that they would join us at the Maha village, where a peace might be concluded between them.

August 8. At two miles distance, this morning we came to a part of the river, where there was concealed timber difficult to pass. The wind was from the N.W. and we proceeded in safety. At six miles, a river empties on the northern side, called the Sioux Indians, Eaneahwadepon, or Stone river; and by the Frenc, Petite Rivere des Sioux, or Little Sioux river. At its confluence it is eighty yards wide. Our interpreter, Mr. Durion, who has been to the sources of it, and knows the adjoining country, says that it rises within nine miles of the river Desmoines; that within fifteen leagues of that river it passes through a large lake nearly sixty miles in circumference, and divided into two parts by rocks which approach each other very closely: its width various: it contains many islands, and is known by the name of the Lac d'Esprit: it is near the Dogplains, and within four days march from Mahas. The country watered by it, is open and undulating, and may be visited in boats up the river for some distance. The Desmoines, he adds, is about eighty yards wide where the Little Sioux river approaches it: it is shoaly, and one of its principal branches is called Cat river. Two miles beyond this river is a long island which we called Pelican island, from the number of that animal which were feeding on it: one of these being killed, we poured into his bag five gallons of water. An elk, too, was shot, and we had again to remark that snakes are rare in this part of the Missouri. A meridian altitude near the Little Sioux river made the latitude 41° 42′ 34″. We encamped on the north, having some sixteen miles.

August 9. A thick fog detained us until past seven o'clock, after which we proceed with a gentle breeze from the southeast. After passing two sandbars we reached, at seven and a half miles, a point of highland on the left near which the river has forced itself a channel across a peninsula, leaving on the right a circuit of twelve or eighteen miles, which is now recognized by the ponds and islands it contains. At seventeen and a half miles, we reached a point on the north, where we encamped. The hills are at a great distance from the river for the last several days; the land on both sides low, and covered with cottonwood and abundance of grape vines. An elk was seen to-day, a turkey also shot, and near our camp is a beaver den: the musquitoes have been more troublesome than ever for the last two days. [Lewis & Clark State Park, Iowa]

August 10. At two and a half miles, we came to a place called Coupee a Jacques, where the river has found a new bed, and abridged a circuit of several miles: at twelve and a half miles, a yellow stone on the left. This is the first highland near the river above Council-bluff. After passing a number of sand-bars we reached a willow island at the distance of twenty-two and a half miles, which we were enabled to do with our oars and a wind from the S.W. and encamped on the north side.

August 11. After a violent wind from the N.W. attended with rain, we sailed along the right of the island. At nearly fiver miles, we halted on the south side for the purpose of examin-ing a spot where one of the great chief of the Mahas named Blackbird, who died about four years ago of smallpox, was buried. A hill of yellow soft sandstone rises from the river in bluffs of various heights, till it ends in a knoll about three hun-dred feet above the water; on the top of this is a mound, of twelve feet diameter at the base and six feet high is fixed in the center; on which we placed a white flag, bordered with red, blue, and white. The Blackbird seems to have been a personage of great consideration; for ever since his death he is supplied with provisions, from time to time, by the superstitious regard of the Mahas. We descended to the river and passed a small creek on the south, called, by the Mahas, Waucandipeeche, (Great Spirit is bad.) Near this creek and the adjoining hills the Mahas had a village, and lost four hundred of their nation by a dreadful malady which destroyed the Blackbird. The meridian altitude made the latitude 42° 1′ 3 8/10′′ north. We encamped, at seventeen miles distance, on the north side in a bend of the river. During our day's course it has been crooked; we observed a number of places in it where the old channel is filled up, or gradually becoming covered with willow and cot-tonwood; great numbers of herrons are observed to-day, and the musquitoes annoy us very much. [Badger Lake, Iowa]

August 12. A gentle breeze from the south, carried us along about ten miles, when we stopped to take a meridian altitude, and sent a man across to our place of observation: yesterday he stepped nine hundred and seventy-four yards, and the distance we had come around, was eighteen miles and three quarters.

The river is wider and shallower than usual. Four miles beyond this bend a bluff begins, and continues several miles; on the south it rises from the water at different heights, from twenty to one hundred and fifty feet, and higher as it recedes on the river" it consists of yellow and brown clay, with soft sandstone imbeded in it, and is covered with timber, among which may be observed some red cedar: the lands on the opposite side are low and subject to inundation, but contain willows, cottonwood, and many grapes. A priaire-wolf came near the bank and barked at us; we attempted unsuccessfully to take him. This part of the river abounds in beaver. We encamped on a sand-island in a bend to the north, having made twenty miles and a quarter.

August 13. Set out at daylight with a breeze from the southeast, and passed several sandbars. Between ten and eleven miles we came to a spot on the south, where a Mr. MacKay had a trading establishment in the year 1795 and 1796, which he called Fort Charles. At fourteen miles, we reached a creek on the south, on which the Mahas reside, and at seventeen miles and a quarter, formed a camp on a sandbar, to the south side of the river, opposite the lower point of a large island. From this place sergeant Ordway and four men were detached to the Maha village with a flag and present, in order to induce them to come and hold a council with us. They returned at twelve o'clock the next day, August 14. After crossing a prairie covered with high grass, they reached the Maha creek, along which they proceeded to its three forks, which join near the village: they crossed the north branch and went along the south; the walk was very fatiguing, as they were forced to break their way through grass, sunflowers and thistles, all above ten feet high, and interspersed with wild pea. Five miles from our camp they reached the position of the ancient Maha village: it had once consisted of three hundred cabins, but was burnt about four years ago, soon after the smallpox had destroyed four hundred men, and a proportion of women and children. On a hill, in the rear of the village, are the graves of the nation; to the south of which runs the fork of the Maha creek: this they crossed where it was about ten yards wide, and followed its course to the Missouri, passing along a ridge of hill for one and a half mile, and a long pond between that and the Missouri: they then recrossed the Maha creek, and arrived at the camp, having seen no tracks of Indians nor any sign of recent cultivation.

In the morning 15th, some men were sent to examine the cause of a large smoke from the northeast, and which seemed to indicate that some Indians were near; but they found that a small party, who had passed that way, had left some trees burning, and that the wind from that quarter blew the smoke directly towards us. Our camp lies about three miles northeast from the old Maha village, and is in latitude 42° 13′ 41″. The accounts we have had of the effects of the smallpox on that nation are most distressing; it is not known in what way it was first communicated to them, though probably by some war party. They had been a military and powerful people; but when these warriors saw their strength wasting before a malady which they could not resist, their phrenzy was extreme; they burnt their village, and many of them put to death their wives and children, to save them from so cruel an affliction, and that all might go together to some better country.

On the 16th, we still waited for the Indians: a party had gone out yesterday to Maha creek; which was damned up by the beaver between the camp and the village: a second went to-day. They made a kind of drag with small willows and bark, and swept the creek: the first company brought three hundred and eighteen, the second upwards of eight hundred, consisting of pike, bass, fish resembling salmon, trout, redhorse, buffaloe, one rockfish, one flatback, perch, catfish, a small species of perch called, on the Ohio, silverfish, a shrimp of the same size, shape and flavour of those about Neworleans, and the lower part of the Mississippi. We also found very fat muscles; and on the river as well as the creek, are different kinds of ducks and plover. The wind, which in the morning had been from the northwest, shifted round in the evening to the southeast, and as usual we had a breeze, which cooled the air and relieved us from the musquitoes, who generally give us great trouble.

Friday 17. The wind continued from the southeast, and the morning was fair. We observed about us a grass resembling wheat, except that the grain was like rye, also some similar to both rye and barley, and a kind of timothy, the seed of which branches from the main stock, and is more like a flaxseed than a timothy. In the evening, one of the party sent to the Ottoes, returned with the information that the rest were coming on with the deserter: they had also caught Liberte, but, by a trick, he made his escape: they were bringing three of the chiefs in order to engage our assistance in making peace with the

Mahas. This nation having left their village, that desirable purpose cannot be effected; but in order to bring in any neighbouring tribes, we set the surrounding prairies on fire. This is the customary signal made by traders to apprize the Indians of their arrival: it is also used between different nations as an indication of any event which they had previously agreed to announce in that way; and as soon as it is seen collects the neighbouring tribes, unless they apprehend that it is made by their enemies.

August 18. In the afternoon the party arrived with the Indians, consisting of the Little Thief and the Big Horse, whom we had seen on the third, together with six other chiefs, and a French interpreter. We met them under a shade, and after they had finished a repast with which we supplied them, we inquired into the origin of the war between them and the Mahas, which they related with great frankness. It seems that two of the Missouri went to the Mahas to steal horses, but were detected and killed; the Ottoes and Missouris thought themselves bound to avenge their companions, and the whole nations were at last obligated to share in the dispute; they are also in fear of a war from the Pawnees, whose village they entered this summer, while the inhabitants were hunting, and stole their corn. This ingeneous confession did not make us the less desirous of negotiating a peace for them; but no Indians have as yet been attracted by our fire. The evening was closed by a dance, and the next day,

August 19, the chiefs and warriors being assembled at ten o'clock, we explained the speech we had already sent from the Council-bluffs, and renewed our advice. They all replied in turn, and the presents were then distributed: we exchanged the small medal we had formerly given to the Big horse for one of the same size with that of Little Thief: we also gave a small medal to a third chief, and a kind of certificate or letter of acknowledgement to five of the warriors expressive of our favour and their good intentions: one of them dissatisfied, returned us the certificate; but the chief, fearful of our being offended, begged that it might be resorted to him; this we declined, and rebuked them severly for having in view mere traffic instead of peace with their neighbours. This displeases them at first; but they at length all petitioned that it should be given to the warrior, who then came forward and an apology to us; we then delivered it to the chief to be given to the most

worthy, and he bestowed it on the same warrior, whose name
was Great Blue Eyes. After a more substantial present of small
articles and tobacco, the council was ended with a dram to the
Indians. In the evening we exhibited different objects of
curiosity, and particularly the airgun, which gave them great
surprise. Those people are almost naked, having no covering,
except a sort of breechcloth round the middle, with a loose
blanket or buffaloe robe painted, thrown over them. The names
Karkarpaha, (or Crow's Head) and Nenasawa (or Black Cat)
Missouris; and Sananona (or Iron Eyes) Neswaunja (or Big Ox)
Stageaunja (or Big Blue Eyes and Wasashaco (or Brave Man)
all Ottoes. These two tribes speak very nearly the same language, they all begged us to give them whiskey.

The next morning, August 20, the Indians mounted their
horses and left us, Having received a canister of whiskey at
parting. We then set sail, and after passing two islands on the
north, came to on that side under some bluffs; the first near
the river since we left the Ayauwa village. Here we had the
misfortune to lose one of our sergeants, Charles Floyd. He was
seized with a bilious cholic, and all our care and attention
were ineffectual to relive him: a little before his death, he said
to captain Clark, "I am going to leave you," his strength failed
him as he added "I want you to write me a letter;" but he died
with a composure which justified the high opinion we had
formed of his firmness and good conduct. He was buried on the
top of the bluff with the honours due to a brave soldier; and
the place of his interment marked by a cedar post, on which
his name and the day of his death were inscribed. About a mile
beyond this place, to which we gave his name, is a small river
about thirty yards wide, on the north, which we called Floyd's
river, where we encamped. We had a breeze from the southeast, and made thirteen miles. [Sioux City, Iowa]

August 21. The same breeze from the southeast carried us
by a small willow creek on the north, about one mile and a half
above Floyd's river. Here began a range of bluffs which continued till near the mouth of the great Sioux river, three miles
beyond Floyd's. This river comes in from the north, and is
about one hundred and ten yards wide. Mr. Durion, our Sioux
interpreter, who is well acquainted with it, says that it is navigable upwards of two hundred miles to the falls, and even
beyond them; that its sources are near those of the St. Peters.
He also says, that below the falls a creek falls in from the eastward, after passing through cliffs of red rock: of this the

Indians make their pipes; and the necessity of procuring the article, has introduced a sort of law of nations, by which the banks of the creek are scared, and even tribes at war meet without hostilities at these quarries, which possess a right of asylum. Thus we find even among savages certain principles deemed sacred, by which the rigours of the merciless system of warfare are mitigated. A sense of common danger, where stronger ties are wanting, gives all the binding force of more solemn obligations. The importance of preserving the known and settled rules of warfare among civilized nations, in all their integrity, becomes strikingly evident; since even savages, with their few precarious wants, cannot exist in a state of peace or war where this faith is violated. The wind became southerly, and blew the sand from the bars in such quantities, that we could not see the channel at any distance ahead. At four and a quarter miles, we came to two willow islands, beyond which are several sandbars; and at twelve miles, a spot where the Mahas once had a village, now no longer existing. We again passed a number of sandbars, and encamped on the south; having come twenty-four and three quarter miles. The country through which we passed has the same uniform appearance ever since we left the river Platte: rich low-grounds near the river, succeeded by undulating prairies, with timber near the waters. Some wolves were seen to-day on the sandbeaches to the south; we also procured an excellent fruit, resembling a red currant, growing on a shrub like privy, and about the height of a wild plum. [Ponca State Park, Nebraska]

August 22. About three miles distance, we joined the men who had been sent from the Maha village with our horses, and who brought us two deer. The bluffs or hills which reach the river at this place, on the south, contain allum, copperas, cobalt which had the appearance of soft isinglass, pyrites, and sandstone, the two first very pure. Above this bluff comes in a small creek on the south, which we call Rologe creek. Seven miles above is another cliff, on the same side, of alum rock, of a dark brown colour, containing in its crevices great quantities of cobalt, cemented shells, and red earth. From this the river bends to the eastward, approaches the Sioux river within three or four miles. We sailed the greater part of the day, and made nineteen miles to our camp on the north side. The sandbars are as usual numerous: there are also considerable traces of elk; but none are yet seen. Captain Lewis in proving the quality of some of the substances in the first cliff, was considerably injured by the fumes and taste of the cobalt, and took some strong medicine to relieve him from its effects. The appearance of these mineral substances enable us to account for disorders of the stomach, with which the party had been affected since they left the river Sioux. We had been in the habit of dipping up the water of the river inadvertently and making use of it, till, on examination, the sickness was thought to proceed from a scum covering the surface of the water along the southern shore, and which, as we now discovered, proceeded from these bluffs. The men had been ordered, before we reached the bluffs, to agitate the water, so as to disperse the scum, and take the water, not at the surface, but at some depth. The consequence was, that these disorders ceased: the biles too which had afflicted the men, were not observed beyond the Sioux river. In order to supply the place of sergeant Floyd, we permitted the men to name three persons, and Patrick Gass having the greatest number of votes was made a sergeant. [Elk Point, South Dakota]

August 23. We set out early, and at four miles came to a small run between cliffs of yellow and blue earth: the wind, however, soon changed, and blew so hard from the west, that we proceeded very slowly; the fine sand from the bar being driven in such clouds, that we could scarcely see. Three and a quarter miles beyond this run, we came to a willow island, and a sand island opposite, and encamped on the south side, at ten and a quarter miles. On the north side is an extensive and delightful prairie, which we called Buffaloe prairie, from having here killed the first buffaloe. Two elk swam the river to-day and were fired at, but escaped: a deer was killed from the boat; one beaver killed; and several prairie wolves were seen.

August 24. It began to rain last night, and continued this morning: we proceeded, however, two and a quarter miles, to the commencement of a bluff of blue clay, about one hundred and eighty, or one hundred and ninety feet on the south side: it seems to have been lately on fire; and even now the ground is so warm that we cannot keep our hands in it at any depth: there are strong appearances of coal, and also great quantities of cobalt, or a crystalized substance resembling it. There is a fruit now ripe which looks like a currant, except that it is double the size, and grows on a bush like a privy, the size of a damson, and of a delicious flavour; its Indian name means rabbit-berries. We then passed, at the distance of about seven miles, the mouth of a creek on the north side, called by an Indian name, meaning Whitestone river. The beautiful prairie of yesterday, has changed into one of greater height, and very smooth and extensive. We encamped on the south side, at ten and a quarter miles, and found ourselves much annoyed by the musquitoes. [Vermillion, South Dakota]

August 25. CAPTAINS LEWIS and CLARKE, with ten men, went to see an objet deemed very extraordinary among all the neighborhing Indians. They dropped down to the mouth of the Whitestone river, about thirty yards wide, where they left the boat, and at the distance of two hundred yards, ascending a rising ground, from which a plain extended itself as far as the eye could discern. After walking four miles, they crossed the creek where it is twenty-three yards wide, and waters an extensive valley. The heat was so oppressive that we were obliged to send back our dog to the creek, as he was unable to bear the fatigue; and it was not till after four hours march that we reached the object of our visit. This was a large mound in the midst of the plain about N. 20° W. from the mouth of the Whitestone river, from which it is nine miles distant. The base of the mound is a regular parallelogram, the longest side being three hundred yards, the shorter sixty or seventy: from the longest side it rises with a steep ascent from the north and south to a height of sixty-five or seventy feet, leaving on the top a level plain of twelve feet in breadth and ninety in length. The north and south extremities are connected by two oval borders which serve as new bases, and divide the whole side into three steep but regular gradations from the plains. The only thing characteristic in this hill is its extreme symmetry, and this, together with its being totally detached from the other hills which are at the distance of eight or nine miles, would induce a belief that it was artificial; but, as the earth and the loose pebbles which compose it, are arranged exactly like the steep grounds on the borders of the creek, we concluded from this similarity of texture that it might be natural. But the Indians have made it a great article of their superstition: it is called the mountain of Little People, or Little Spirits, and they believe that it is the abode of little devils, in human form, of about eighteen inches high and with remarkably large heads; they are armed with sharp arrows, with which they are very skillful, and are always on the watch to kill those should have the hardihood to approach their residence. The tradition is, that many have suffered from these little evil spirits, and among others, three Maha Indians fell a sacrifice to them a few years since. This has inspired all the neighbouring nations, Sioux, Mahas, and Ottoes, with such terror, that no consideration could tempt them to visit the hill. We saw none of these wicked little spirits; nor any place for them, except some small holes scattered over the top: we were happy enough to escape their vengeance, though we remained some time on the mound to enjoy the delightful prospect of the plain, which spreads itself out till the eye rests upon the N. W. hills at a great distance, and those of the N.E. still farther off, enlivened by large herds of buffaloe feeding at a distance. The soil of these plains is exceedingly fine; there is, however, no timber except on the Missouri: all the wood of the Whitestone river not being sufficient to cover thickly one hundred acres. The plain country which surrounds this mound has contributed not a little to its bad reputation: the wind driving from every direction over the level ground obliges the insects to seek shelter on its leeward side, or be driven against us by the wind. The small birds, whose food they are, resort of course in great numbers in quest of subsistence; and the Indians always seem to discover an unusual assemblage of birds as produced by some supernatural cause: among them we observed the brown martin employed in looking for insects, and so gentle that they did not fly until we got within a few feet of them. We have also distinguished among the numerous birds of the plain, the blackbird, the wren or prairie bird, and a species of lark about the size of a partridge, with a short tail. The excessive heat and thirst forced us from the hill, about one o'clock, to the nearest water, which we found in the creek at three miles distant, and remained an hour and a half. We then went down the creek, through a lowland about one mile in width, and crossed it three times, to the spot where we first reached it in the morning. Here we gathered some delicious plums, grapes and blue currants, and afterwards arrived at the mouth of the river about sunset. To this place the course from the mound is S. twenty miles, E. nine miles; we there resumed our periogue, and on reaching our encampment of last night set the prairie on fire, to warn the Sioux of our approach. In the mean time, the boat under serjeant Pryor had proceeded in the afternoon one mile, to a bluff of blue clay on the south , and after passing a sandbar and two islands fixed their camp at the distance of six miles on the south. In the evening some rain fell. We had killed a duck and several birds: in the boat, they had caught some large cat-fish.

Sunday, August 26. We rejoined the boat at nine o'clock before she set out, and then passing by an island, and under a cliff on the south, nearly two miles in extent and composed of white and blue earth, encamped at nine miles distance, on a sandbar towards the north. Opposite to this, on the south, is a small creek called Petit Arc or Little Bow, and a short distance above it, an old village of the same name. This village, of which nothing remains but the mound of earth about four feet high surrounding it, was built by a Maha chief named Little Bow, who being displeased with Blackbird, the late king, seceded with two hundred followers and settled at this spot, which is now abandoned, as the two villages have reunited since the death of Blackbird. We have great quantities of grapes, and plums of three kinds; two of a yellow colour, and distinguished by one of the species being longer than the other; and a third round and red: all have an excellent flavour, particularly those of the yellow kind.

August 27. The morning star appeared much larger than usual. A gentle breeze from the southeast carried us by some large sandbars, on both sides and in the middle of the river, to a bluff, on the south side, at seven and a half miles distant: this bluff is of white clay or chalk, under which is much stone, like lime, incrusted with a clear substance, supposed to be cobalt, and some dark ore. Above this bluff we set the prairie on fire, to invite the Sioux. After twelve and a half miles, we had passed several other sandbars, and now reached the mouth of a river called by the French Jacque (James river) or Yankton, from the tribe which inhabits its banks. It is about ninety yards wide at the confluence: the country which it waters is a rich prairie, with little timber: it becomes deeper and wider above its mouth, and may be navigated a great dis-tance; as its sources rise near those of St. Peter's, of the Mississippi, and the red river of lake Winnipeg. As we came to the mouth of the river, an Indian swam to the boat; and, on our landing, we were met by two others, who informed us that a large body of Sioux were encamped near us: they accompanied three of our men, with an invitation to meet us at a spot above the river: the third Indian remained with us: he is a Maha boy, and says that his nation have gone to the Pawnees to make peace with them. At fourteen miles, we encamped on a sandbar to the north. The air was cool, the evening pleasant, the wind from the southeast, and light. The river has fallen gradually, and is now low. [Yankton, South Dakota]

Tuesday, 28th. We passed, with a stiff breeze from the south, several sandbars. On the south is a prairie which rises gradually from the water to the height of a bluff, which is, at four miles distance, of a whitish colour, and about seventy or eighty feet high. Further on is another bluff, of a brownish colour, on the north side; and at the distance of eight and a half miles is the beginning of Calumet bluff, on the south side, under which we formed our camp, in a beautiful plain, to wait the arrival of the Sioux. At the first bluff the young Indian left us and joined their camp. Before reaching Calumet bluff one of the periogues ran upon a log in the river, and was rendered unfit for service; so that all our loading was put into the second periogue. On both sides of the river are fine prairies, with cotton wood; and near the bluff there is more timber in the points and valleys than we have been accustomed to see.

Wednesday, 29th. We had a violet storm of wind and rain last evening; and were engaged during the day in repairing the periogue, and other necessary occupations; when, at four o'clock in the afternoon, sergeant Pryor and his party arrived on the opposite side, attended by five chiefs, and about seventy men and boys. We sent a boat for them, and they joined us, as did also Mr. Durion, the son of our interpreter, who happened to be trading with the Sioux at this time. He returned with sergeant Pryor to the Indians, with a present of tobacco, corn, and a few kettles; and told them that we would speak to their chiefs in the morning. Sergeant Pryor reported, that on reaching their village, which is at twelve miles distance from our camp, he was met by a party with a buffaloe robe, on which they desired to carry their visitors: an honour which they declined, informing the Indians that they were not the commanders of the boats: as a great mark of respect, they were then presented with a fat dog, already cooked, of which they partook heartily, and found it well flavoured. The camps of the Sioux are of a conical form, covered with buffaloe robes, painted with various figures and colours, with an aperture in the top for smoke to pass through. The lodges contain from ten to fifteen persons, and the interior arrangement is compact and handsome, each lodge having a place for cooking detached from it.

August 30th. Thursday. The fog was so thick that we could not see the Indian camp on the opposite side, but it cleared of about eight o'clock. We prepared a speech, and some presents, and then sent for the chief and warriors, whom we received, at twelve o'clock, under a large oak tree, near to which the flag of the United States was flying. Captain Lewis delivered a speech, with the usual advice and counsel for their future conduct. We then acknowledged their chiefs, by giving to the grand chief a flag, a medal, a certificate, with a string of wampum; to which we added a chief's coat; that is, a richly laced uniform of the United States artillery corps, and a cocked hat and red feather. One second chief and three inferior ones were made or recognized by medals, and a suitable present of tobacco, and articles of clothing. We then smoked the pipe of peace, and the chiefs retired to a bower, formed by bushed, by their young men, where they divided among each other the presents, and smoked and eat, and held a council on the answer which they were to make us to-morrow. The young people exercised their bows and arrows in shooting at marks for beads, which we distributed to the best marksmen; and in the evening the whole party danced until a let hour, and in the course of their amusement we threw among them some knives, tobacco, bells, tape, and binding, with which they were much pleased. Their musical instruments were the drum, and a sort of little bag made of buffaloe hide, dressed white, with small shot or pebbles in it, and a bunch of hair tied to it. This produces a sort of rattling music, with which the party was annoyed by four musicians during the council this morning.

August 31. In the morning, after breakfast, the chiefs met, and sat down in a row, with pipes of peace, highly ornamented, and all pointed towards the seats intended for captains Lewis and Clarke. When they arrived and were seated, the grand chief, whose Indian name, Weucha, is, in English Shake Hand, and in French, is called Le Liberateur (the deliverer) rose, and spoke at some length, approving what we had said, and promising to follow our advice:

"I see before me," said he, "my great father's two sons. You see me, and the rest of our chiefs and warriors. We are very poor; we have neither power or ball, nor knives; and our women and children at the village have no clothes. I wish that as my

brothers have given me a flag and a medal, they would give
something to those poor people, or let them stop and trade with
the first boat which comes up the river. I will bring chiefs of
the Pawnees and Mahas together, and make peace between
them; but it is better that I should do it than my great father's
sons, for they will listen to me more readily. I will also take
some chiefs to your country in the spring; but before that time
I cannot leave home. I went formerly to the English, and they
gave me a medal and some clothes: when I went to the Spanish
they gave me a medal, but nothing to keep it from my skin; but
now you give me a medal and clothes. But still we are poor; and
I wish, brothers, you would give us something for our squaws."

When he sat down, Mahtoree, or White Crane, rose:

"I have listened," said he, "to what our father's words were
yesterday; and I am, to-day, glad to see how you have dressed
our old chief. I am a young man, and do not wish to take much:
my fathers have made me a chief: I had much sense before, but
now I think I have more than ever. What the old chief has
declared I will confirm, and do whatever he and you please: but
I wish that you would take pity on us, for we are very poor."

Another chief, called Pawnawneahpahbe, then said: "I am a
young man, and know but little. I cannot speak well; but I have
listened to what you have told the old chief, and will do whatever you agree."

The same sentiments were then repeated by Aweawecbache.

We were surprised at the finding that the first of these
titles means "Struck by the Pawnee," and was occasioned by
some blow which the chief had received in battle, from one of
the Pawnee tribe. The second is, in English, "Half Man," which
seems a singular name for a warrior, till it was explained to
have its origin, probably, in the modesty of the chief; who, on
being told of his exploits, would say, "I am no warrior: I am
only half a man." The other chiefs spoke very little; but after
they had finished, one of the warriors delivered a speech, in
which he declared he would support them. They promised to
make peace with the Ottoes and Missouris, the only nations
with whom they are at war. All these harangues concluded by
describing the distress of the nation: they begged us to have
pity on them: to send them traders: that they wanted powder
and ball; and seemed anxious that we should supply them with
some of their great father's milk, the name by which they distinguish ardent spirits. We then gave some tobacco to each who

attended the chief. We prevailed on Mr. Durion to remain here, and accompany as many of the Sioux chiefs as he could collect, down to the seat of government. We also gave his sons a flag, some clothes, and provisions, with directions to bring about a peace between surrounding tribes, and to convey some of their chiefs to see the president. In the evening they left us, and encamped on the opposite bank, accompanied by the two Durions. During the evening and night we had much rain, and observed that the river rises a little. The Indians, who have just left us, are the Yanktons, a tribe of the great nation of Sioux. These Yanktons are about two hundred men in number; and inhabit the Jacques, Desmoines and Sioux rivers. In person they are stout, well proportioned, and have a certain air of dignity and boldness. In their dress they differ nothing from the other bands of the nation whom we saw, and will describe afterwards: they are fond of decorations, and use paint, and porcupine quills, and feathers. Some of them wore a kind of necklace of white bear's claws, three inches long, and closely strung together round their necks. They have only a few fowling pieces, being generally armed with bows and arrows, in which, however, they do not appear as expert as the more northern Indians. What struck us most was the institution, peculiar to them, and to the Kite Indians, further to the westward, from whom it is said to have been copied. It is an association of the most active and brave men, who are bound to each other by attachment, secures by a vow, never to retreat before any danger, or give way to their enemies. In war they go forward without sheltering themselves behind trees, or aiding their natural valour by any artifice. This punctilious determination, not to be turned from their course, became heroic, or ridiculous, a short time since, when the Yanktons were crossing the Missouri on the ice. A hole lay immediately in their course, which might easily have been avoided, by going round. This the foremost of the band disdained to do; but went straight forward, and lost. The others would have followed his example, but were forcibly prevented by the rest of the tribe. These young men sit, and encamp, and dance together, distinct from the rest of the nation: they are generally about thirty or thirty-five years old; and such is the deference paid to courage, that their seats in council are superior to those of the chiefs, and their persons more respected. But, as may be supposed, such indiscreet bravery will soon diminish the numbers of those who practise it; so that the band is now reduced to four warriors, who were among our visitors. These were the remains of twenty-two, who composed the society not long ago; but in a battle with the Kite Indians, of the Black Mountains, eighteen of them were killed, and these four were dragged from the field by their companions.

Whilst these Indians remained with us we made very minute inquiries relative to their situation and numbers, and trade, and manners. This we did very satisfactorily, by means of two different interpreters; and from their accounts, joined to our interviews with other bands of the same nation, and much intelligence acquired since, we enabled to understand, with some accuracy, the condition of the Sioux hitherto so little known.

The Sioux, or Dacorta Indians, originally settled on the Mississippi, and called by Carver, Madowesians, are now subdivided into tribes, as follows:

First, The Yanktons: this tribe inhabits the Sioux, Desmoines, and Jacques rivers, and number about two hundred warriors

Second, The Tetons of the burnt woods. This tribe numbers about three hundred men, who rove on both sides of the Missouri, the White and Teton rivers.

Third, The Tetons Okandandas, a tribe consisting of about one hundred fifty men, who inhabit both sides of the Missouri below the Chayenne river.

Fourth, Tetons Minnakenozzo, and nation inhabiting both sides of the Missouri, above the Chayenne river, and containing about two hundred and fifty men.

Fifth, Tetons Saone; these inhabit both sides of the Missouri below the Warreconne river, and consist of about three hundred men.

Sixth, Yanktons of the Plains, or Big Devils; who rove on the heads of the Sioux, Jacques, and Red river; the most numerous of all tribes, and number about five hundred men.

Seventh, Wahpatone; a nation residing on the St. Peter's, just above the mouth of that river, and numbering two hundred men.

Eighth, Mindawarcarton, or proper Dacorta or Sioux Indians. These possess the original seat of the Sioux; and are properly so dominated. They rove on both sides of the

Mississippi, about the falls of Saint Anthony, and consist of three hundred men.

Ninth, The Wahpatoota, or Leaf Beds. This nation inhabits both sides of the river St. Peter's, below Yellow wood river, amounting to about one hundred fifty men.

Tenth, Sistasoone: this nation number two hundred men, and reside at the head of the St. Peter's. Of these several tribes, more particular notice will be taken hereafter.

Saturday, September 1, 1804. We proceeded this morning under light southern breeze, and passed the Calumet bluffs; these are composed of a yellowish red, and brownish clay as hard as chalk, which it resembles, and are one hundred and seventy, or one hundred and eighty feet high. At this place the hills on each side come to the verge of the river, those on the south being higher than on the north. Opposite the bluffs is a large island covered with timber; above which the highlands form a cliff over the river on the north side, called White Bear cliff; an animal of that kind being killed in one of the holes in it, which are numerous and apparently deep. At six miles we came to a large sand island covered with cottonwood; the wind was high, and the weather rainy and cloudy during the day. We made fifteen miles to a place on the north side, at the lower point of a large island called Bonhomme, or Goodman's island. The country on both sides has the same character of prairies, with no timber; with occasional lowlands covered with cottonwood, elm, and oak; our hunters had killed an elk and a beaver: the catfish too are in great abundance.

September 2. It rained last night, and this morning we had a high wind from the N. W. We went three miles to the lower part of an ancient fortification on the south side, and passed the head of Bonhomme island, which is large and well timbered: after this the wind became so violent, attended by a cold rain, that we were compelled to land at four miles on the northern side, under a high bluff of yellow clay, about one hundred ten feet in height. Our hunters supplied us with four elk; and we had grapes and plums on the banks: we also saw the beargrass and rue, on the side of the bluffs. At this place there are highland on both sides of the river which become more level at some distance back, and contain but few stream of water. On the southern bank, during this day, the grounds have not been so elevated. Captain Clarke crossed the river to examine the remains of the fortification we had just passed.

This interesting object is on the south side of the Missouri, opposite the upper extremity of Bonhomme island, and is a low level plain, the hills being three miles from the river. It begins by a wall composed of earth, rising immediately from the bank of the river and running in a direct course S. 76°, W ninety six yards; the base of this wall or mound is seventy-five feet, and its height about eight. It then diverges in a course S. 84° W. and continues at the same height and depth to a distance of fifty-three yards, the angle being formed by the sloping descent; at the junction of these two is an appearance of a hornwork of the same height with the first angle: the same wall then pursues a course N. 69° W. for three hundred yards: near its western extremity is an opening or gateway at right angles to the wall, and projecting inwards; this gateway is defended by two nearly semicircular walls placed before it, lower than the large walls; and from the gateway there seems to have been a covered way of communicating with the interval between the two walls: westward of the gate, the wall becomes much larger, being about one hundred and five feet at its base, and twelve feet high: at the end of this high ground the wall extends for fifty-six yards on a course N. 32° W; it then turns N. 23° W. for seventy-three yards: these two walls seem to have had a double or covered way; they are from ten to fifteen feet eight inches in height, and from seventy-five to one hundred and five feet in width at the base; the descent inwards being steep, whilst outwards it forms a sort of glacis. At the distance of seventy-three yards, the wall end abruptly at a large hollow place much lower than the general level of the plain, and from which is some indication of a covered way to the water. The space between them is occupied by several mounds scattered promiscuously through the gorge, in the center of which is a deep round hole. From the extremity of the last wall, in a course N. 32° W. is a distance of ninety-six yards over the low ground, where the wall recommences and crosses the plain in a course N. 81° W. for eighteen hundred and thirty yards to the bank of the Missouri. In this course its height is about eight feet, till it enters, at the distance of five hundred and thirty-three yards, a deep circular pond of seventy-three yards diameter; after which it is gradually lower, towards the river: it touches the river at a muddy bar, which bears every mark of being an encroachment of the water, for a considerable distance; and a little above the junction, is a small circular redoubt. Along the bank of the river, and at eleven hundred yards distance, in a straight line from this wall, is a second, about six feet high, and of considerable width: it rises abruptly from the bank of the Missouri, at a point where the river bends, and goes straight forward, forming an acute angle with the last wall, till it enters the river again, not far from the mounds just described, towards which it is obviously tending. At the bend the Missouri is five hundred yards wide; the ground on the opposite side highlands, or low hills on the bank; and where the river passes between this fort and Bonhomme island, all the distance from the bend, it is constantly washing the banks into the stream, a large sandbank being already taken from the shore near the wall. During the whole course of this wall, or glacis, it is covered with trees, among which are many large cotton trees, two or three feet in diameter. Immediately opposite the citadel, or the part most strongly fortified, on Bonhomme island, is a small work in a circular form, with a wall surrounding it, about six feet in height. The young willows along the water, joined to the general appearance of the two shores, induce a belief that the bank of the island is encroaching, the Missouri indemnifies itself by washing away the base of the fortification. The citadel contains about twenty acres, but the parts between the long walls must embrace nearly five hundred acres.

These are the first remains of the kind which we have had an opportunity of examining; but our French interpreter assures us, that there are great numbers of them on the Platte, the Kanzas, the Jacque, &c. and some of our party say, that they observed two of those fortresses on the upper side of the Petit Arc creek, not far from its mouth; that the wall was about six feet high, and the sides of the angles one hundred yards in length

September 3. The morning was cold, and the wind from the northwest. We passed at sunrise, three large sandbars, and at the distance of ten miles reached a small creek, about twelve yards wide, coming in from the north, above a white bluff: this creek has obtained the name of Plum creek, from the number of that fruit which are in the neighbourhood, and of a delightful quality. Five miles further, we encamped on the south near the edge of a plain; the river is wide, and covered with sandbars to-day: the banks are high and of a whitish colour; the timber scarce, but an abundance of grapes. Beaver houses too have been observed in great numbers on the river, but none of the animals themselves.

September 4. We set out early, with a very cold wind from S. S. E. and at one mile and a half, reached a small creek, called Whitelime creek, on the south side. Just above this is a cliff, covered with cedar trees, and at three miles a creek, called Whitepaint creek, of about thirty yards wide: on the same side, and at four and a half miles distance from the Whitepaint creek, is the Rapid river, or, as it is called by the French, la Riverequi Court; this river empties into the Missouri, in a course S.W. by W. and is one hundred and fifty-two yards wide, and four feet deep at the confluence. It rises in the Black mountains, and passes through a hilly country, with poor soil. Captain Clarke ascended three miles to a beautiful plain, on the upper side, where the Pawnees once had a village: he found that the river widened above its mouth, and much divided by sands and islands, which, joined to the great rapidity of the current, makes navigation very difficult, even for small boats. Like the Platte its waters are of a light colour; like that river too it throw out into the Missouri, great quantities of sand, coarser even than that of the Platte, which forms sandbars and shoals near its mouth.

We encamped just above it, on the south, having made only eight miles, as the wind shifted to the south, and blew so hard that in the course of the day we broke our mast: we saw some deer, a number of geese, and shot a turkey and a duck: the place in which we halted is a fine low-ground, with much timber, such as red cedar, honeylocust, oak, arrowwood, elm, and coffeenut. [Niobrara, Nebraska]

September 5, Wednesday. The wind was again high from the south. At five miles, we came to a large island, called Pawnee island, in the middle of the river; and stopped to breakfast at a small creek on the north, which has the name of Goat creek, at eight and a half miles. Near the mouth of this creek the beaver had made a dam across so as to form a large pond, in which they built their houses. Above this island the river Poncara falls into the Missouri from the south, and is thirty yards wide at the entrance. Two men whom we dispatched to the village of the same name, returned with information that they had found it on the lower side of the creek; but as this is the hunting season, the town was so completely deserted that they had killed a buffaloe in the village itself. This tribe of

Poncaras, who are said to have once numbered four hundred men, are now reduced to about fifty, and have associated for mutual protection with the Mahas, who are about two hundred in number. These two nations are allied by a similarity of misfortune; they were once both numerous, both resided in villages, and cultivated Indian corn; their common enemies, the Sioux and small-pox, drove them from their towns, which they visit only occasionally for the purposes of trade; and they now wander over the plains on the sources of the Wolf and Quicurre rivers. Between the Pawnee island and Goat creek on the north, is a cliff of blue earth, under which are several mineral spring, impregnated with salts: near this we observed a number of goats, from which the creek derives its name. At three and a half miles from the creek, we came to a large island on the south, along which we passed to the head of it, and encamped about four o'clock. Here we replaced the mast we had lost, with a new one of cedar: some bucks and an elk were procured to-day, and a black tailed deer was seen near the Poncara's village.

Thursday, September 6. There was a storm this morning from the N. W. and though it moderated, the wind was still high, and the weather very cold; the number of sandbars too, added to the rapidity of the current, obliged us to have recourse to the towline: with all our exertions we did not make more than eight and a half miles, and encamped on the north, after passing high cliffs of soft, blue, and red coloured stone, on the southern shore. We saw some goats, and great numbers of buffaloe, in addition to which the hunters furnished us with elk, deer, turkies, geese, and one beaver: a large catfish too was caught in the evening. The ground near the camp, was a low prairie, without timber, though just below is a grove of cottonwood.

Friday, September 7. The morning was very cold and the wind southeast. At five and a half miles, we reached and encamped at the foot of a round mountain, on the south, having passed two small islands. This mountain, which is about three hundred feet at the base, forms a cone at the top, resembling a dome at a distance, and seventy feet or more above the surrounding highlands. As we descended from this dome, we arrived at a spot, on the gradual descent of the hill, nearly four acres in extent, and covered with small hole: these are the residence of a little animal, called by the French, petit chien (little dog) who sit erect near the mouth, and make whistling noise, but when alarmed take refuge in their holes. In order to bring them out, we poured into one of the hole five barrels of water without filling it, but we dislodged and caught the owner. After digging down another of the holes six feet, we found, on running a pole into it, that we had not yet dug half way to the bottom: we discovered, however, two frogs in the hole, and near it we killed a dark rattlesnake, which had swallowed a small prairie dog; we were also informed, though we never witnessed the fact, that a sort of lizard, and a snake, live habitually with these animals. The petit chien are justly named, as they resemble a small dog in some particulars, though they have also some points of similarity to the squirrel. The head resembles the squirrel in every respect, except that the ear is shorter, the tail like that of the ground-squirrel, the toe-nails are long, the fur is fine, and the long hair is gray.

Saturday, September 8. The wind still continued from the southeast, but moderately. At seven miles we reached a house on the north side, called the Pawnee house, where a trader, named Trudeau, wintered in the year 1796-7: behind this, hills, much higher than usual, appear to the north, about eight miles off. Before reaching this house, we came by three small islands, on the north side, and a small creek on the south; and after leaving it, reached another, at the end of seventeen miles, on which we encamped, and called it Boat island: we here saw herds of buffaloe, and some elk, deer, turkies, beaver, a squirrel, and a prairie dog. The party on the north represent the country through which they passed, as poor, rugged, and hilly, with the appearance of having been lately burnt by the Indians; the broken hills, indeed, approach the river on both sides, though each is bordered by a strip of woodland near the water. [Fort Randall Dam]

Chapter Seven

The artists

Oh, how exciting it must have been to see the West through the eyes of the members of the Corps of Discovery! To have been one of the first to see the wonders of the Great Plains, the Rocky Mountains, and the Pacific with all their grandeur and dangers—the great variety of plants, the vast herds of animals of many varieties, the varied cultures of the North American Indians, and to encounter the unknown—it must have been an incredible experience! Perhaps the physical exertion of the journey made it difficult for them to appreciate it every day, but certainly they knew they were seeing and experiencing things few other people in the world had seen, or ever would see.

Finding sketches, drawings, or paintings of the western portion of the route from the period of Lewis and Clark is difficult. While Lewis and Clark did make some drawings and sketches, they were almost exclusively of the river systems; only a few plants, animals and artifacts were sketched. The landscapes they explored and saw were captured in their minds and depicted only in their words. Lewis had thought of including drawings of the Great Falls of the Missouri and also of the Columbia in his official publication. A lithograph of the Great Falls on the Missouri River based on Lewis's recollection is included. However, the Celilo Falls on the Columbia included in Clark's map of the river showing more details of the falls was not. Gass's published diary of the journey had drawings added to its later editions, but they tend to reflect general or representative topics, not an actual on site drawing.

One of these is used. Therefore, we must include the works of those individuals who came later, but before there were significant changes in the landscape of the West.

The artistic works of Karl Bodmer and George Catlin are especially important to illustrate the section of the trail or route along the Ohio, Mississippi, and Missouri rivers to the Rocky Mountains. Their works provide the greatest share of the art used. For the section west of the Missouri and Rockies, Carlton E. Watkins photographed the Columbia in the 1860s before the river was tamed and A. E. Matthews sketched the area. These are the four main artists. There are others, such as John M. Stanley and Paul Kane, who painted the far West in the 1840s and 1850s and could have been used more extensively.

KARL BODMER (1809-1893) was the most prolific artist. He was born in Riesbach, Switzerland. Today he is known as "Karl" Bodmer, but when he created the original works it was "Carl." He changed the spelling of his first name from "C" to "K" in 1850. In 1815-17 Prince Maximilian of Wied (part of modern Germany) led an expedition of exploration to Brazil. He explored the region, bringing back a collection of thousands of specimens, and recorded information about the culture and languages of the Indians, including his own crude sketches. In 1830 Maximilian started planning another expedition, but this time to North America to tour, explore and study the interior regions of the Missouri. Aware of his own limitations, Maximilian realized he needed someone to record the journey. He wrote, *He must be a landscape painter but also able to depict figures correctly and accurately, especially the Indians.*

Maximilian selected Carl Bodmer, a Swiss painter who lived in nearby Koblenz, for his 1832-34 journey up the Missouri River. Bodmer's subjects were to include the Indians, animals, cultural artifacts, structures and the landscape of the area. The originals were to be the property of Maximilian, but Bodmer could make copies. After their return to Europe, the works and the desire to publish them occupied both men for many years.

There are some interesting ties and parallels to the Lewis and Clark expedition. A larger portion of Maximilian and Bodmer's journey overlapped that of Lewis and Clark. Both expeditions traveled down the Ohio from Pittsburgh, up the Mississippi to St. Louis, and then up the Missouri River to the

Marias River. Maximilian and Bodmer also stopped near the Marias where they stayed a month at Fort McKenzie that had been established a few miles beyond the junction. They, like Lewis and Clark, also had to make a crucial decision. Because of increased dangers from the Indians, especially from the Blackfeet, they decided to cut their expedition short and return. The original plan, which never came to pass, included a visit to the Great Falls and then the headwaters of the Missouri, and possibly, over to the Columbia and down it before returning.

When they first stopped in St. Louis, they met and talked with William Clark. Maximilian desired to visit the Rocky Mountains. He hoped to join a caravan under the auspices of the Rocky Mountain Fur Company. Clark explained that they'd be less likely to see friendly Indians on the plains. He also noted the difficulty in collecting and transporting the collections of fauna and flora by land transportation. Therefore, he recommended that they visit the fur trading post and Indians along the Missouri and travel via steamboat.

On April 10, 1833, Maximilian and company set off with the American Fur Company. Before they left they obtained copies of Clark's maps of the Missouri and used them extensively during their journey up the Missouri. It was fortunate that this was done because some of Clark's original maps were later lost, and Maximilian's copies are what historians rely on today. During the winter of 1833-34, Bodmer and Maximilian met Charbonneau at Fort Clark when they stayed with the Mandans. Charbonneau was acting as interpreter there at the fort. Also, just as it took many years before Lewis and Clark had their journals published, the same was true of Maximilian's journals and Bodmer's artwork. Lewis and Clark were some of the first white men to visit some of the Indian tribes and to record information about their cultures. Maximilian and Bodmer were some of the few, and also the last, to record them before the great changes and disappearance of their cultures due to the pressures from the advancing white man's culture and the impact of diseases, especially smallpox, and to a lesser extent, malaria.

GEORGE CATLIN (1796-1872) was born in Wilkes Barre, Pennsylvania. His dream was to be the first painter to capture the life and culture of the American Plains Indians before they were destroyed by the ever-expanding westward movement of the United States and the white man. After painting primarily portraits for a number of years in the east, Catlin went west in 1830. He went to St. Louis to meet and seek the aid of William Clark in pursuing his dream. Clark helped him and even took him to Fort Clark. Over the next six years Catlin moved about the west from Texas in the South, to Minnesota in the North, and Montana in the West. It is his 1832 trip up the Missouri River to Fort Union and back that corresponds to much of Lewis and Clark's Expedition. Many of his paintings and resulting lithographs were published in his *North American Indian Portfolio*. His painting of the Blackfeet, the Crow, the Mandan and the Sioux depicted not only portraits, but also the life and culture of the Indians. Catlin's paintings provide a first-hand view of what Lewis and Clark had seen thirty years earlier. Catlin was also able to paint and capture their cultures just before major disruptions came to the Plains Indians—just as he had feared it would.

ALFRED EDWARD MATHEWS (1831-1874) was born in England. He later immigrated to the United States. During the Civil War he served with the Ohio volunteers. His sketches of battle scenes, published as lithographs, were frequently used to depict the war. After the war he went west and continued to sketch. He believed that his sketches could better capture the scenery than a photograph that was too dependent on various factors such as the weather, light and the technology of photography at the time. His works focused on scenes in the Colorado gold towns, the Rocky Mountains, along the route of the Union Pacific, and also in Montana. His *Pencil Sketches of Montana* was published in 1868. Even at that time there were still few non-Indian inhabitants in most of Montana, and the views he sketched were still very similar to those seen earlier by the Corps of Discovery.

CARLETON E. WATKINS (1829-1916) was one of the most famous photographers of the old West. He went west to California around 1850. By 1857 he had his own studio in San Francisco focusing on portraits and landscapes. He is probably best known for his early photographs of Yosemite that he started taking in 1861. It was partially as a result of his photographic work that President Lincoln gave the area some legal protection in 1864. But his importance here is in his capturing of images along the Columbia River. He came to the Northwest in 1867 and began photographing Oregon, the Columbia Gorge, British Columbia, and Montana. His images of the areas were made during the period when industrialization was just beginning to impact the landscape. Twice during his life he suffered the loss of his much of photographic work, once in 1874, and later in 1906.

A comparison and close examination of the "yesterday and today" pictures indicates a number of obvious changes. While traveling today one notices a distinct lack of certain wildlife in the area. Many of the species mentioned have disappeared from the route. Most significantly are the large herds of buffalo and elk, the lone grizzly bears, and the Audubon (Bighorn) mountain sheep that is now extinct. Even the prairie dog can be found only in greatly diminished numbers. The "goats" or pronghorn antelope, however, have survived in great numbers. Large sections of the Ohio, Mississippi, Missouri, Clearwater, Snake, and Columbia rivers have been altered by man. This is primarily the result of the construction of dams and jetties. They have flooded long sections of the river valleys, tamed the seasonal changes and meandering in the rivers, and overcome the rapids and waterfalls that were both obstacles and sites of awe to the Corps. In a few sections, the river's surface may be 100 feet higher than when Lewis and Clark traveled it. Nature itself has also moved the course of the rivers since the time of the expedition. In some places the shift can be measured in feet, while in others it must be measured in miles. In some areas there are isolated oxbow lakes that serve as reminders of the rivers' old routes. Land usage has changed in various places. Urbanization has spread in many areas along the trail. Metropolitan areas such as St. Louis, Kansas City, Omaha, and Sioux City have engulfed miles of the route. Smaller cities and villages occupy some sites. In a sense they have replaced the many Indian villages that were found along the route, parts of which remain today primarily as archaeological sites or parks. Agricultural expansion and usage of the land have greatly impacted large areas. Where once prairie grasses or sagebrush and cactus flourished, now wheat, corn, soybeans and alfalfa grow. The herds of free roaming bison and elk have been replaced by ones of various breeds of cattle on fenced ranches and farms. Lands that once were treeless prairies and sparsely covered river valleys, banks, bluffs and hills with their rocky outcroppings are now covered with trees and bushes obscuring views and sites. Earlier, the constant natural flooding and prairie fires had kept the trees and bushes to a minimum.

Duplicating the old paintings, sketches, and photographs is great fun, but the process also has its problems. Once the site is determined, getting permission to enter and move around must be obtained. Many images were made from the river, and finding that same spot on a moving river is difficult. Also, the river channel very often has changed. The site and old riverbed may now be in the middle of a farmer's field. Trees frequently block the view. Hills and formations may have eroded or fallen over time. Urbanization, construction and mining have often altered the large area of the landscape or sometimes significant parts. Getting all the hills, rocks, or other items lined up takes lots of time and some luck. Usually there is only one spot or small area where everything matches. Photo sites are more often easier to locate, as the photos are more realistic. With sketches and paintings there are always the additional problems of style and "artistic license." Once one gets a feel for the artist's technique and style it becomes easier to identify sites. Sometimes, however, the artist altered existing features, added new ones, combined things, or changed the proportions to obtain the desired effect. These problems create challenges. However, once these are overcome, there is a great feeling of satisfaction in being in the same place – only years later.

But even aside from all these forces, changes, and problems with a little imagination and perseverance, it is still possible to get a feel for the trail, and fortunately, in some areas, little has changed in the passing of 200 years, and one can almost step back to the time of Lewis and Clark.

Now let's follow the Corps as it journeys west to the great unknown.

[For reference while reading the journal captions, S.S. is the starboard(right) side and L.S. or Lbd. is the larboard (port or left) side.]

CHAPTER EIGHT

Pictorial journey: the Eastern legacy

Museum of Early Southern Decorative Arts, Winston-Salem, North Carolina

MONTICELLO — This is the home of Thomas Jefferson as it appeared when Meriwether Lewis visited, studied in the library, and prepared for the journey west. Jefferson was continually working on and renovating it throughout his life. This painting by Anna M. Thornton was done about 1802.

Here is the view of Monticello today. You can walk the grounds, tour the house and library just as Lewis did so many years ago. Only a few of the planted trees shown in the painting are alive today.

Museum of Southern Decorative Arts, Winston-Salem, North Carolina

HARPERS FERRY — This view of Harpers Ferry is at the junction of the Potomac and the Shenandoah rivers. Harpers Ferry was the site of the U.S. Armory and Arsenal. This is where Lewis came to obtain some of the rifles and other equipment needed for the Corps of Discovery. This is also where the collapsible iron frame boat, the *Experiment*, was made. It was designed in ten four foot sections, each weighing twenty-two pounds. Hides would be stretched over the forty feet long, two-foot-deep and four and a half feet wide hull. The Harper's house can be seen on the hill in the lower left.

Here is a similar view of Harpers Ferry today. This area is now part of the Harpers Ferry National Historic Park. The original armory and arsenal buildings have been demolished and replaced with other structures, but the Harper House still stands.

Darlington Memorial Library, Pittsburgh, Pennsylvania

PITTSBURGH — Pittsburgh grew up around Fort Pitt. It was established at the strategic junction of the Monongahela and Allegheny rivers where they form the Ohio River. It was then called the "Gateway to the West," much as St. Louis came to be known later after Lewis and Clark's Expedition. This view of Pittsburgh was painted by George Beck in 1806. The population of Pittsburgh was probably about 3,000. Lewis came there to have the keelboat built, departing on August 30, 1803.

The population today of greater Pittsburgh has grown to more than two million. One can visit the restored Fort Pitt blockhouse and museum at Point Park. This view is from the hill where Elliot Overlook Park is located. The painting appears to have been made lower on the hill from the point or from the neighboring hill.

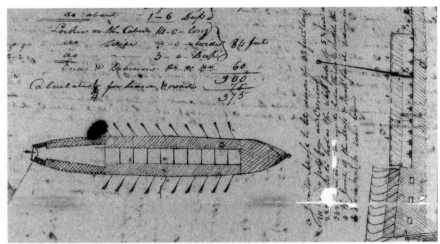

Yale Collection of Western American, Beinecke Rare Book and Manuscript Library

KEELBOAT — Today the keelboat is often called the *Discovery*. The captains often called it the barge. It was fifty-five feet long, eight feet wide, drew three feet of water, and would carry ten to twelve tons. It had twenty-two oars, a main square sail, and could be rigged with a spritsail. There was a cabin in the stern, At Camp Dubois it was outfitted with twenty-two lockers along each side. When opened up, they formed a protective wall along both sides. The boat could float with the current, be sailed, rowed, poled, or cordelled. A small cannon was also placed on the bow and two blunderbusses on the rear cabin.

This is a replica of the keelboat. It had stopped at a Lewis and Clark Trail Heritage Foundation convention in Pierre, South Dakota. It has also been used in the bicentennial celebration traveling up and down the Ohio, Mississippi, and Missouri rivers.

Paige Cruz Collection

WHEELING — On September 7 Lewis was at Wheeling picking up supplies that had been shipped there by wagon from Philadelphia and Harpers Ferry. Lewis recorded, *this is a pretty considerable Village contains about fifty houses. . . .the landing is good. . . .on a point formed by this creek and the river stands an old stockade fort, now gone to decay; this town is remarkable for being the point of embarkation for merchants and Emegrants who are about to descend the river.*

This view is of the old section of Wheeling, West Virginia, near the site of the stockade of Fort Fincastle, renamed Fort Henry in 1776. The fort is believed to have stood on the hill near South Main and 11th, behind the tall buildings in the right of the photo. The view is from the river front park.

Paige Cruz Collection

GRAVE CREEK MOUND — On the September 10 Lewis wrote, . .*went on shore to view a remarkable artificial mound of earth called by the people in this neighbourhood the Indian grave. . ..the mound is nearly a regular cone 310 yards in circumpherence at it's base & 65 feet high terminating in a blont point whose diameter is 30 feet. . .near the summit of this mound grows a white oak tree whose girth is 13 _ feet, from the aged appeance of this tree I think it's age might be resonably calculated at 300 years, . . .*

Here is the mound today, the center of Grave Creek Mound Historic Site. The Adena people built the mound in stages from about 250 to150 B.C. There is a path to the top of the mound and an excellent museum and year round visitor center at its base.

MARIETTA — Lewis stopped at Marietta on September 13 and spent the night. Lewis met with Griffin Greene, Postmaster and one of the founders of Marietta. This house, the residence of Jonathan Meig, Jr., was built in 1801-02. General Rufus Putnam's home, one of the original buildings, is located in the Campus Martius Museum.

BIG BONE LICK — Lewis spent a week in the Cincinnati area. While there he visited Big Bone Lick where mammoth bones were being excavated. In a letter to Jefferson he noted he would be sending some bones excavated by Doctor Goforth. Unfortunately, the specimens were lost at Natchez during shipment when the boat sank. This is an outside exhibit in Big Bone Lick State Park.

Thurston Collection, Filson Historical Society

MULBERRY HILL — This photo of the old Clark family home, Mulberry Hill, Louisville, was taken about 1890. The log building, built around 1785, is partially visible on the left at the top of the hill. It was the family home. The center building is part of the former slave quarters. The building in the foreground is the springhouse on a branch of the Beargrass Creek. The tree to the far right is the cypress tree reportedly planted by George Rogers Clark.

Here is the area today. It is no longer a farm but a park. Brush and smaller trees have grown on the hill. A depression in the hillside indicates the location of the old springhouse, and other depressions remain from the paths coming down the hill. The old cypress tree still grows, but it lost its single main trunk years ago and now looks quite different with its many vertical shoots.

Filson Historical Society

FALLS OF THE OHIO — This view shows the Falls of the Ohio as it appeared in 1796.

Today locks and a dam can be found at the falls. Much of the area has been altered. Here is a similar modern view from the George Rogers Clark Home Site. George Rogers Clark lived there from 1803-1809. William Clark and York probably also lived there prior to their departure with the Corps of Discovery on October 26, 1803. Just down the hill from the cabin is Lewis and Clark Plaza, commemorating the departure site of Lewis and Clark from the Falls of the Ohio. A short distance back up river is the Falls of the Ohio Interpretive Center. When the river is low, the fossil beds that formed the old falls and river bottom are clearly visible.

Bodmer, Joslyn Art Museum

ROCKPORT ON THE OHIO — Lewis and Clark passed these unusual rock formations in early November. Bodmer painted them when he traveled down the Ohio nearly thirty years later. The town of Rockport was developing when he passed. The first family moved there in 1808 and used a portion of the overhanging bluffs on the far left as their home.

Here is the same unusual rock formation today. The town of Rockport has grown up around and on top of the rock bluff. With the Ohio River dams, the river is now deeper and has eroded closer to the formation today. Vines and bushes now cover much of the rock formations. For those interested in Abraham Lincoln, this area of Indiana is rich in his history. There is an 1816-1830 replica village and Lincoln museum in the town.

FORT MASSAC — The fort was constructed by the French in 1757 on a strategic point with a commanding view of the Ohio River. In 1763 at the end of the French and Indian War the fort was ceded to the British. The following year it was abandoned by the British and then destroyed by the Chicksaw Indians. The Americans rebuilt the fort in 1794. Lewis wrote, *Arived at Massac engaged George Drewyer (Drouillard) in the public service as an Indian Interpretter, contracted to pay him 25 dollards pr. month for his service.-*

A newly reconstructed fort and visitor center can be visited today. It is located near Metropolis, Illinois. If you're a Superman fan, this is also the town for you.

Red House reconstruction, Cape Girardeau.

HANGING DOG ISLAND — After Lewis stopped in Cape Girardeau he continued north the following day. On November 24, 1803, he recorded *these rock are nearly perpendicular in many places sixty feet, and the hight of the hills apear to be about 120 feet above the bank which forms their base of perhaps 15 to 18 feet tho from appearance they never over flow,* and on November 25, he described *the coast on the Lard. qut. was higher than yesterday, the rock rising perpendicularly from the water's edge in many place & in others reather projecting than otherwise, it is the same rock discribed yesterday. . . .* Bodmer drew those rocks "rising perpendicularly."

Here is the same view today looking back down river towards Cape Girardeau from below the Apple River and Neely's Landing. Those perpendicular bluffs at the river's edge to the right of center are now part of the Trail of Tears State Park.

Bodmer, Rare Book Division, The New York Public
Library, Astor, Lenox Tilden Foundation

GRAND TOWER – On November 25, 1803 Lewis entered, *Arrived at the Grand Tower a little before sunset, passed above it and came to on the Lard. Shore for the night.* The next day Lewis climbed the rock, took measurements and also a reading on its location. Lewis noted the importance of this landmark writing, *There seems among the watermen of the Mississippi to be what the Tropics or Equinoxial Line is with regard to sailors. Those who have never passed it before are always compelled to pay or furnish some spirits to drink, or be ducked.* Bodmer passed the area and made this painting.

This landmark was first mentioned in 1673 by Jacques Marquette. The Grand Tower, now called Tower Rock, is opposite Grand Tower, Illinois. The river is higher, the tower has eroded, and more trees have grown on its top. The knob by the tower was quarried, and even the tower was threatened. Fortunately, that was averted, and it is now a protected park.

Bodmer, Joslyn Art Museum

Fire Island on the Mississippi — The captains passed this area about November 28, 1803. They were now nearing Fort Kaskaskia where more men were recruited.

Today the Mississippi River appears to have shifted its course a little here in this wide valley area southeast of Chester near Cora. A system of levies has been constructed to keep the river in its present bed and to protect the farmlands and towns. They also block the views from along the river itself. Here is a view of the area from on one of the levies looking towards the old shore and hill line. The old river bed here is now farmed. Perhaps the old trees to the right of center are all that is left of the small island.

Bodmer, Joslyn Art Museum

THE MISSISSIPPI NEAR STE. GENEVIEVE — Clark wrote on December 4, 1804, *Set out this morning before Sunrise, at _ of a mile passed the mouth of a Small Creek Called Gabia, at the mouth off this Creek is the landing place for the Trading Boats of St Genevieve, a Small town Situated on the Spurs of the high land at _ of a mile distant nearly South   This village contains (as I am informed) about 120 families, principally French,- above the mouth of this Creek the highlands approach the river. . . .at _ of a mile above Gabia Creek the high land juts into the river and form a most tremendous Clift of rocks near the Commencement of this Clift I saw a cave, the mouth of which appeared to be about 12 feet Diameter, and about 70 foot above the water."*

Bodmer's painting of the view approaching Ste. Genevieve is similar to the view described by Clark. Here is the area today. The Mississippi River has altered its course and moved away from the edge of St. Genevieve. The fertile riverbed is now farmed and protected by levies, but the view is similar.

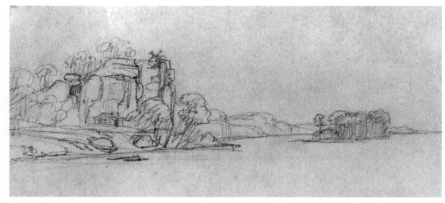

Bodmer, Joslyn Art Museum

VIEW OF ISLAND — Clark's record for December 6, 1804, noted *Passed a Small Isld. Near the middle of the river nearly opposite the point of last on the Larbd. Side of this Island the current is verry Swift, Seting imediately Against the high land, which terminates in a bluff at the river.*

This appears to be the high land and bluff that terminates at the river. They are located at Herculaneum. The island is no more, but the shallow part of the river is a hazard to barge traffic on the river today. During periods of shallow water it is said that parts of an old barge that became lodged on the old island can be seen.

CAHOKIA VILLAGE — Lewis traveled ahead of Clark and the rest of the Corps of Discovery. He first arrived at Cahokia on December 7. On December 8 he crossed the river and visited St. Louis. He returned on December 9 to rejoin Clark and the rest of the Corps who had arrived at Cahokia. Cahokia was located in Illinois which was part of the U.S. The formal transfer of land and control had not yet taken place in this area. Cahokia served as the seat of the American government in the area.

The old Cahokia Courthouse, above, stood when Lewis and Clark stayed in the area, along with the Holy Family Church below. They are located near the intersection of State Roads 3 & 156. Also in the area is the Jarrot Home.

Courtesy Eric P. Newman Collection, Missouri Historical Society

OLD ST. LOUIS — This is the earliest view of St. Louis known. It was made from the East St. Louis, Illinois, side of the Mississippi a few years after the expedition returned. It shows the homes of many of the prominent families in St. Louis. It was here the transfer of the Louisiana Territory was made from Spain to France and then from France to the United States prior to the expedition's departure. The Clark buildings are on the far right edge of the engraving.

The old docking area corresponds to the area in front of the Gateway Arch in the view today. It was on the north edge of these grounds that William Clark lived and had his own museum after he returned from the expedition. Part of the old riverfront area to the north of the arch has undergone restoration and revitalization.

Bodmer, Joslyn Art Museum

TRAPPISTS HILL — Clark and Collins visited a portion of the then extensive Cahokia Mounds area on January 9, 1804. Bodmer visited the area of the Cahokia Mounds that is now in the present park and made sketches of the mounds similar to those visited by Clark and Collins.

Most of the mounds that were in the greater St. Louis area at the time of Lewis and Clark were destroyed as the area was settled and farmed, and more recently because of urban sprawl. Fortunately, Cahokia Mounds State Park was created, and the mounds within the park area now protected. The hill, below is now called Monk's Mound. The buildings built earlier by French monks and most of the trees that had grown up have been removed. The remains of the paths running down the sides on the mound are still visible. Follow the present path and use the steps to climb to the top of the mound.

CHAPTER NINE

Camp Dubois to Fort Mandan 1804-05

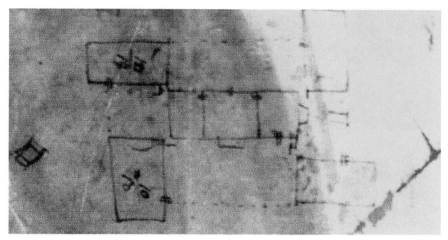

Yale Collection of Western American, Beinecke Rare Book and Manuscript Library

CAMP DUBOIS – This sketch was one of many made by Clark in designing the layout of Camp Dubois (Wood). It is also the one that the camp was based on. It is taken from his field notes. It was near here that the Corps spent the winter of 1803-4 while obtaining additional supplies, information and training.

Below is a photo of the reconstruction of Camp Dubois at the Lewis and Clark Historic Site Camp River Dubois near Hartford, Illinois. Be sure to visit the new center there. Today the Missouri River and its junction have moved between one or two miles south, the Mississippi River has shifted east, and the mouth of the Wood River is about a mile north. The historic site of Camp Dubois would now be near the west shore of the Mississippi in Missouri.

Missouri Historical Society

OLD ST. CHARLES — The Missouri River town of St. Charles was established by the French in 1769. This was where Lewis rejoined the expedition after Clark and the Corps had left Camp Dubois. The Corps was given a rousing send off by the people of St. Charles, and then in 1806, another celebration when they returned from the Pacific.. The Corps' camp was probably on the left along the river. This early view of St. Charles was painted by Ann Marie von Puhl a few years after the expedition.

The modern view is from the riverbank east of the I-70 bridge. The new building on the left is the Lewis and Clark Boathouse and Nature Center. It is home to replicas of the keelboat and pirogues. There are many old buildings in St. Charles historic area, but they date from the post Lewis and Clark period.

Bodmer, Joslyn Art Museum

CAVE AND RIVER BLUFFS — On May 23, 1804 Clark recorded, . . .*we passed a large Cave on the Lbd. Side (Called by the french the Tavern) about 120 feet wide 40 feet Deep & 20 feet high many different immages are Painted on the Rock at this place. . .Stoped about one mile above for Capt. Lewis who assended the Clifts which is (about)at the Said Cave 300 feet high. . .Capt Lewis near falling from the Pencelia of rocks 300 feet, he caught at 20 foot."*

The river has since turned away as it approaches the bluffs. Years of periodic flooding have filled much of the cave with silt and trees have over grown the area. It is located on private property and is very difficult to view. The cave area is located near the base of the bluffs towards the left side of the photo. The cliff on the right half is possibly the one that Lewis was climbing along when he fell and nearly lost his life.

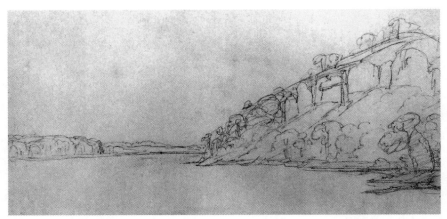

Bodmer, Joslyn Art Museum

RIVER BLUFF — Bodmer sketched this bluff after passing the cave and Tavern Creek.

The bluff is a little farther up river, about a half mile west of St. Albans towards Detters. As can be seen in the modern photo, the river has changed its course and no longer runs close to the bluffs. The photo, taken on private property, is from one of the levies that protect the area. This was probably the course taken by the steamboat *Yellowstone* when it carried Bodmer and Prince Maximilian on their tour of the West thirty years after Lewis and Clark.

Bodmer, Joslyn Art Museum

CONFLUENCE OF THE MISSOURI AND THE GASCONADE — The Corps of Discovery camped on Willow Island at the mouth of the Gasconade River May 27-29. It had rained heavily and many of their goods were wet. They remained there to dry their cargo and to hunt. Commenting on their stay, Clark recorded, *I measured the river found the Gasconnade to be 157 yds. wide and 19 foot Deep. . . .The Musquetors are verry bad."*

The location of the mouth of the Gasconade has changed very little. The mosquitoes are still in the area. The site is occupied by the U.S. Army Corps of Engineers. Willow Island is no longer an island. The Corps' campsite would be located on the north side of the Missouri at the left edge of the photo.

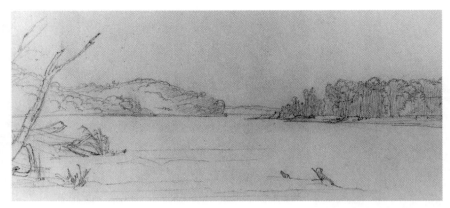

Bodmer, Joslyn Art Museum

FRANKLIN AND ARROW ROCK ON THE MISSOURI — The Corps passed this area June 8, 1804. Clark recorded, *Passed two willow Islands & a Small Creek above a Rock point on the L.S.* That "Rock point" is just to the left of center in Bodmer's sketch. Bodmer made this sketch looking up river across from present Boonville. Arrow Rock cannot actually be seen from the Franklin-Boonville area.

Below is the modern view from the bank of the Missouri River on the old Franklin side. The Corps' camp on the seventh was about one mile east of the present highway bridge on the north side of the Missouri. The abandoned old railroad bridge was built at the rock point, and its arched section obscures part of the distant hills.

Bodmer, Joslyn Art Museum

VIEW OF THE MISSOURI — On June 30, 1804, the Corps camped below Diamond Island. Clark wrote *Camped on the L.S. opsd. the Lower point of a Isd. Called diamond Island, Broke our mast."* For July 1 he wrote *a Small alarm last night   all prepared for action, Set out early this morning   passed on the North Side of Diamond Island, a Small Creek mouths opposite I call Biscuit Creek.* Bodmer's painting appears to be the area showing Diamond Island.

This view is looking up river towards what Clark called Diamond Island. The camp would have been just in from the left side of the painting. The view is on the farm grounds of the Lansing Correctional Facility. Today Diamond Island is gone and the river has meandered more than a mile away.

Bodmer, Joslyn Art Museum

BLACKSNAKE HILLS — On July 7, 1804 Clark wrote, . . .*passed a butiful Prarie on the right Side which extends back, those Praries has much the appearance from the river of farms, Divided by narrow Strips of woods* . . . The next day the Corps passed Nodaway Island which Clark recorded *is the largest I have seen. . .8 or 10000 acrs* Today the island is no more. This view of the "butiful Prarie" was painted by Bodmer when they stopped at St. Michaels Prairie. By then Joseph Robidoux of the well-known fur trading family had already settled in the area.

Today most of the prairie is gone. St. Joseph, Missouri, now occupies the area. The raised interstate highways and bridges along the river and buildings downtown make the area hard to recognize.

Bodmer, Joslyn Art Museum

THE MISSOURI BELOW THE MOUTH OF THE PLATTE — The Corps' camp of the July 20, 1804, was near the base of a point of "high land," referred to as "High Hill" on Clark's map. Today that hill is known as King Hill. The next day they passed another point of high land now known as Queen Hill and continued on past "Willow Island." Clark recorded on July 21, 1804, . . .*Some high lands covered with timber L.S. in the hill is limestone & Seminted rock of Shels &c.*

Bodmer painted the area of high lands about four or five miles south of the Platte. Note the white limestone bluff on the edge of the hill.

Here is the view today. The river is not as wide and has shifted away from the hill. The hill is north of the bridge around the bend at Plattsmouth, Nebraska.

Bodmer, Joslyn Art Museum

MOUTH OF THE PLATTE RIVER — Passing the mouth of the Platte on July 21 Lewis noted *where it enters the Missouri it's superior force changes and directs the courant of that river against it's northern bank where to compressed within a channel less than one third of the width it had just before occupyed. it does not furnish the missouri with it's colouring matter as has been asserted by some, but it throws into it immence quantities of sand and gives a celerity to its courant. . . .The sediments it deposits, consists of very fine particles of white sand while that of the Missoury is composed principally of a dark rich loam-in much greater quantity"* Maximilian had also commented on the colors of the river as they approached the junction of the two rivers.

Bodmer's painting shows the evidence of the sandbars. Catlin also painted the same area from a somewhat different perspective.

Today, the location of the mouth of the Platte is about the same. However, the width of each river is much narrower and the flow much less. The site is open to the public and has interpretive signs.

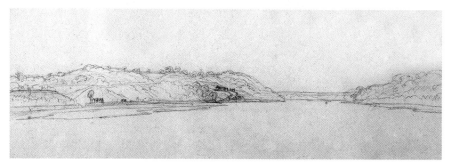

Bodmer, Joslyn Art Museum

A DISTANT VIEW OF BELLEVUE — After the leaving the Platte, Clark wrote on July 21, *at 3 miles passed a Small river on the L.S. Called Papillion or ButterflyC: 18 yds wide. . .we proceeded onto get a good place to Camp. . . .* The next day, hoping to meet the local Indians, they traveled only a short distance. Clark wrote, *Came too and formed a Camp. . .opposite the first hill which approached the river on the L.S. and covered with timbers.* Bodmer's sketch appears to be made very close to the Corps' camp on the July 21, to the left of the sketch. The hill Clark noted is the one with the Indian agency on it. "White Catfish Camp" where the Corps camped from July 22-26 would probably be behind the low hill on the right.

This similar view of the area today is from the park near the highway 370 bridge. The hill where the Indian agency was is now part of the Fontenelle Forest Preserve. Travelers can see and hike in it like it may have been when the Corps camped nearby. Parts of the stone foundation of the old trading post and agency that Bodmer visited and painted can also be seen.

Bodmer, Joslyn Art Museum

MISSOURI IN THE MORNING BELOW COUNCIL BLUFF —— The historic Council Bluff of Lewis and Clark is on the Nebraska side of the river and a few miles north of Council Bluffs, Iowa. Clark's journal entry for July 28, 1804 notes *Set out early this morning. . .at 1 me. passed a Bluff on the S.S. it being the first high land approaching the river above the Nodaway, a Island and Creek*. It seems this was the area where the Corps met a Missouri Indian who was living with the Oto. He reported that the Indians were presently out on the plains hunting buffalo. One of the Corps' men and the Indian went out to ask the Indians to return for a council. It was also only a few miles north of here that the large nearly white catfish was caught.

Bodmer made this painting of the bluff on the starboard side. The view is from the area by the intersection of I-690 and I-29, a few miles east of the present Mormon Bridge. The bluffs are presently being mined. The Corps' camp of July 27 would have been off the right edge of the painting.

Bodmer, Joslyn Art Museum

RUINS OF FORT ATKINSON — The Corps camped here from July 30-August 2 and held the famous council that gave rise to the area's name of Council Bluffs. This council with the Missouri and Otos set the pattern for the others—parades, speeches, presents, Indian speeches and promises. Reflecting on the area after the council, Clark wrote, *The Situation of our last Camp Council Bluff or Handssom Prarie appears to be verry proper place for a Tradeing establishment. . . .* In 1819 Fort Atkinson was established there. It was abandoned in 1827 when Fort Leavenworth was built closer to the white settlements and overland trails that had begun to develop.

Only the fort's stone chimneys were left on the high bank Bodmer painted. Trees have grown and now obscure the view of the bluff. You can visit the reconstructed Fort Atkinson in the town of Fort Calhoun. This view off County Road 34 is east of Fort Calhoun towards Boyer Chute National Wildlife Reserve.

Catlin, Gilcrease Museum

BLACKBIRD'S BURIAL MOUND — On August 10 the Corps camped on an island at the base of a hill. Clark recorded the events of the next morning *Capt Lewis myself & 10 men assended the Hill on the L.S. . . .to the top where the Mahars King Black Bird was buried four years ago. . . .from the tops of this Nole the river may be Seen Meandering for 60 or 70 Miles.* The burial site and pole were still prominent in Catlin's painting of a party climbing the hill. The cliff at the edge of the hill is clearly evident as is the island.

Today the river has shifted, the island is gone, but the grass area still follows the contours shown in the painting. There is no mound of earth at the top and trees have encroached and block the view of the river valley.

Catlin, Smithsonian American Art Museum, Gift of Mrs. Joseph Harrison, Jr.

FLOYD'S GRAVE — While in camp with the Mahars, Sergeant Charles Floyd took ill. He died on August 20. Clark recorded *Buried him to the top of a high round hill over looking the river & countrey Situated just below a Small river without a name to which we name & call Floyds river, the Bluffs Sergts. Floyds Bluff- we buried him with all the honors of War, and fixed a Ceeder post. . . with his name title & Day. . . month and year.*

Today it is believed that Floyd died from appendicitis. Here is a similar view of the gravesite today. The hill Catlin painted from has been terraced for cultivation. Today a 100-foot obelisk instead of a cedar post marks his gravesite.

Bodmer, Joslyn Art Museum

MOUTH OF THE BIG SIOUX RIVER — The Corps passed the mouth of the Big Sioux on August 21. The next day at a place called Elk Point Patrick Gass was elected sergeant replacing Floyd.

Bodmer painted the mouth of the Big Sioux River and the bluffs. The view is looking up the Missouri which enters from the distance left, while the Big Sioux enters from left of center. The view today is from the U.S. 20 & 77 bridge over the Missouri. Trees now cover the bluffs. The present Sioux City Welcome Center and the Lewis and Clark Center are located near the river flats shown in Catlin's painting.

SPIRIT MOUND — On August 24 Clark wrote . . .*in an imence Plain a high Hill is Situated, and appears of a Conic form and by the different nations of Indians in this quarter is Suppose to be the residence of Deavels. that they are in human form with remarkable large heads and about 18 Inches high, that they are Very watchfull, and are arm'd with Sharp arrows with which they Can Kill at a great distance; they are Said to Kill all persons who are So hardy as to attempt to approach the hill. . .So much do the Maha, Souis, Ottoes and other neighbouring nations believe this fable that no Consideration is Suffecient to induce them to approach the hill*

On August 25 Clark wrote *Capt Lewis & my Self Concluded to go and See the Mound. . . .the Countrey is leavel & open as far as Can be Seen, except Some few rises at a Great Distance, and the Mound which the Indians Call Mountain of little people or Spirits   this mound appears of a Conic form. . ., at 4 miles we Crossed the Creek 23 yards wide in an extensive Valley...at two miles further our Dog was so Heeted & fatigued we was obliged Send him back to the Creek, at 12 oClock we arrived at the hill.*

The Surrounding Plains is open void of Timber and leavel to a great extent: hence the wind from whatever quarter it may blow, drives with unusial force over the naked Plains and against the hill: the insects of various kinds are thus involuntarily driven to the mound by the force of the wind. . .the Small Bird whose food they are, Consequently resort in great numbers to this place in Surch of them. . .

One evidence which the Inds Give for believing this place to be the residence of Some unusial Spirits is that they frequently discover a large assemblage of Birds about this mound-. . .from the top of this Mound we beheld a most butifull landscape; Numerous herds of buffalow were Seen feeding in various directions.

Today a pleasant, but long hike through the restored prairie brings one to the top of the mound for a beautiful view. The wind, birds and insects are still there, but the vast herds of buffalo and elk are gone. Note that it can get very hot there in the summer.

Bodmer, Joslyn Art Museum

PONCA INDIANS ENCAMPED ON THE BANKS OF THE MISSOURI —
The Corps passed this area on September 4. They called the local
creek White Paint River, but it was called Bazile Creek when Bodmer
came through. The Corps did not meet the Poncas here but about
eleven miles up river where their village was then located. It was
about two miles west of the Missouri on Ponca Creek. The village was
uninhabited at the time because they were out hunting buffalo on the
plains.

This view in the same general area along the river is similar to
Bodmer's painting.

Bodmer, Joslyn Art Museum

GRAND TOWER OF THE MISSOURI ABOVE THE NIOBRARA — On September 7, 1804 the Corps of Discovery had this view. They camped near the tower and spent most of the day exploring the area and trying to capture a specimen of a new animal. *"we landed. . .near the foot of a round mounting. . .resembling a dome. . . .walked up, to the top which forms a Cone and is about 70 feet higher than the high lands around it, the Bass is about 300 foot in decending this Cupola, discovered a Village of Small animals that burrow in the grown   Killed one & Cought one a live by poreing a great quantity of water in his hole we attempted to dig to the beds of one of thos animals, after diging 6 feet, found by running a pole down that we were not half way to his Lodges . . . . we por'd into one of the holes 5 barrels of water without filling it. . . ."*

Their camp would have been located on the north bank on the right edge of the Bodmer painting. The Grand Tower, the "Cone" as described by Clark does not show in Bodmer's painting. The painting corresponds to the right two-thirds of the photo. The Grand Tower or "Cone" can be found near the left edge as a small light grassy bump above the trees.

Bodmer, Joslyn Art Museum

BANKS OF THE MISSOURI – On September 8, 1804, Clark noted in his entries under his Course Distance & reffurences, *7 mes. to pt. on L.S. opsd. the house of Mr. Troodo [Jean Baptiste Truteau] where he wintered in 96 & Seven Called the Pania hos. In a woo[d] to the S.S.* Clark also noted high hills in the area. Bodmer made two paintings when they passed the area. This one is of the high hills on the south side opposite the site of Truteau's house.

Today these locations can be found near the Fort Randall Dam. The photo below is from the dam itself looking at the South Shore Lakeside Recreation Area which is located on those hills. Today water from Lake Francis Case covers the lower third of the painting.

Bodmer, Joslyn Art Museum

BIJOUX HILLS OF THE MISSOURI — It was about five miles south of here that Private George Shannon rejoined the Corps. He had been "lost" or separated from the Corps for sixteen days since August 26. The Corps passed this area and could have seen these hills on September 11-13, 1804. On September 12 they only made four miles passing Troublesome Island. Clark's two entries recorded *at the upper pt of this Island the river was so crouded with Sand bars that we found great difficulty in getting the boat over, she turned on the Sand 4 times and very near turning over* and his other entry, *we found great dificuelty in passing between the Sand Bras the water Swift and Shallow,it took _ of the day to make one mile, we Camped. . . ..observed Slate & Coal mixed, Some very high hills on each Side of the river.* When Maximilian and Bodmer passed this area they faced similar conditions. Bodmer painted those "very high hills."

Today the lower bench lands, the sandbars and river bottom, including Troublesome Island, have been flooded by the Fort Randall Dam and Lake Francis Chase. The view is looking east at Twin Peaks in the Bijou Hills east of Iona, South Dakota.

Bodmer, Rare Book Division, The New York Public Library,
Astor, Lenox, Tilden Foundation

FORT PIERRE & SIOUX ENCAMPMENT — On September 24, 1804 the
Corps camped at the mouth of the Bad [Teton] River at the bend on
the far right and held their council with the Teton Sioux. Fighting
almost erupted, but tensions finally subsided. When the Corps left,
they did not trust the Teton Sioux. The inability to communicate was
a major cause. The Corps moved up river one mile or so to an island
the captains named "Bad Humored Island." The island no longer
exists, but was probably the one by the fort.

Catlin and Bodmer both sketched the area from almost the same
place. Their viewpoints are both on private property on the west side
of the Missouri. The hills used by the artists for their vantage points
have unfortunately been mined for sand and gravel and have been lev-
eled. Fort Pierre is the site of a long term archaeological project, and
the Wakpa Sica Reconciliation Center now is located on the plains
near where the Sioux camped.

Catlin, Smithsonian American Art Museum, Gift of Mrs. Joseph Harrison, Jr.

ARIKARA VILLAGES — These appear to be the two of the three villages visited by the Corps when they held their council with the Arikara. The first camp, October 8,9,10 was on an island across from the first Arikara village about five miles downstream from these two villages. The first council was held with the chiefs from all three villages. A second council was held at the camp of October 11 at the two villages on the morning of October 12. One of the Arikara chiefs accompanied the Corps up river to the Mandan and Hidatsa villages. Bodmer also painted the Arikara villages in 1833. Unfortunately, like many of the other sites along the river, these Arikara sites are now flooded by Lake Oahe formed by the Oahe Dam. The site is near the Leavenworth Monument and Historic Site north of Mobridge.

This reconstructed Arikara lodge is located at the West Whitlock Recreation Area. It is set on a river bench overlooking the Missouri River/Lake Oahe, similar to the scene depicted above.

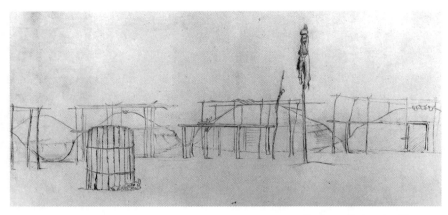

Bodmer, Joslyn Art Museum

MANDAN VILLAGE — On October 20, 1804 Clark wrote . . .*after brackfast I walked out on the L.Side to See those remarkable places pointed out by Evins, I saw an old remains of a village on the Side of a hill which the* [Arikara] *Chief with us Too ne' tells me that nation* [Mandan] *lived in a number villages on each Side of the river and the Troubleson Seauex caused them to move about forty miles higher up where they remained a fiew years & moved to the place they live now.* Clark also mentioned the old village had been fortified. The Bodmer sketch is of a different Mandan village but similar to the village Clark saw.

This reconstruction is part of the Village on a Slant at Fort Abraham Lincoln just south of Bismarck. This is the village Clark visited on October 20.

Catlin, Smithsonian American Art Museum, Gift of Mrs. Joseph Harrison, Jr.

DISTANT VIEW OF MANDAN VILLAGE — The Corps of Discovery was finally approaching the main Mandan Indian villages. On October 26, 1804 they passed this area. They noticed Indians along the river's banks. At that time Fort Clark and the Mandan village had not yet been built on the far bank of the Missouri. The Mandan villages were another day's travel north. Those sites, however, were probably similar. There was also a Mandan hunting camp nearby where later Catlin and Bodmer would make their paintings.

Today the river has moved north away from the bluffs. Where the river once flowed, cattle now feed, crops are grown and trees have reclaimed areas. The sites from where Catlin and Bodmer painted are now blocked by trees. This view is from a scenic turnout about a mile from the sites, but the view is similar.

Bodmer, Joslyn Art Museum

MANDAN EARTH LODGE — Patrick Gass described the construction of a lodge, *In a circle of a size suited to the dimensions of the intended lodge, they set up 16 forked posts five or six feet high, and they lay poles from one fork to another. Against these poles they lean other poles, slanting from the ground, and extending about four inches above the cross poles: . . . They next set up four large forks, fifteen feet high, and about ten feet apart, in the middle of the area; and poles or beams between these. The roof poles are then laid on extending from the lower poles across the beams which rest on the middle forks, of such a length as to leave a hole at the top for a chimney. The whole is then covered with willow branches, except the chimney and a hole below to pass through. On the willow branches they lay grass and lastly clay. . . This labour like every other kind is chiefly performed by the squaws.*

This replica lodge is part of the Knife River Indian Villages Historic Site.

Bodmer, Joslyn Art Museum

LODGE INTERIOR — Mandan, Hidatsa, and Arikara lodges were similar in construction as were those of the Pawnee who lived farther to the south. The Arikara and the Pawnee seem to have had a longer entrance way than the Mandan and Hidatsa. The lodges were the property of the women. Clark wrote *The houses are round and Verry large Containing Several families, as also their horses which is tied on one Side of the enterance.* Bodmer's interior painting shows much about the culture of the Mandans. Note also the horses on the side by the entrance.

Replica interiors can be seen in the lodges at both Village on a Slant and Knife River Village.

FORT MANDAN — On December 2 Lewis recorded that they had picked the location for the fort and started construction. This illustration of the building of Fort Mandan appeared in Gass's 1810 published journal. Patrick Gass, a carpenter, probably played a major part in its construction. His description of it on December 3, 1804, is also the best. *The following is the manner in which our huts and fort were built. The huts were in two rows, containing four rooms each, and joined at one end forming a triangle. When raised about 7 feet high a floor of puncheons or split planks were laid, and covered with grass and clay; which made a warm loft. The upper part projected a foot over and the roofs were made shed fashion, rising from the inner side, and making the outer wall about 18 feet high. . .*

Here is the Fort Mandan replica near Washburn, North Dakota.

Catlin, Smithsonian American Art Museum, Gift of Mrs. Joseph Harrison, Jr.

HIDATSA VILLAGE - KNIFE RIVER — This is the village where Charbonneau and Sacagawea lived when Lewis and Clark arrived. It was one of the three Hidatsa villages along with two Mandan villages that bordered the Knife River to its junction with the Missouri. Catlin painted this view in 1832. The view is from the "north" side of the river looking southwest across the Knife River.

Today the river has eroded further into the bank where some of the lodges were. The indentation or bowl shapes in the ground are still evident. Today you can walk through the village site and then down long the river's edge where the children played.

Catlin, Smithsonian American Art Museum, Gift of Mrs. Joseph Harrison, Jr

MANDAN VILLAGE — On October 27 Clark described Big White or Chief Sheheke's village, *this village is Situated on an eminance of about 50 feet above the Water in a handson Plain it Containes houses in a kind of Picket work. the houses are round and Verry large. . .* Catlin painted a similar scene of this 1832 village enclosed by a picket wall. The wooden circular structure and the tall feathered poles are related to their mythology and religion. The bullboats on some of the roofs would be used to cover the smoke holes in bad weather.

Below is the Big Hidatsa village site. The large bowl shaped depressions in the ground indicate former lodges. In 1804 the population of Indians in the Mandan and Hidatsa villages was greater than the population of St. Louis.

CHAPTER TEN

Fort Mandan to the Pacific
1805-1806

The junction of the Yellowstone with the Missouri was another milestone in the Corps of Discovery's journey west. The Indians had told the captains of this junction.

Lewis wrote, *the Indians inform that the Yellowstone river is navigable for perouges and canoes nearly to its source in the Rocky Mountains, and it's course near these mountains it passes within less than a half's day's march of a navigable part of the Missouri. it's extreme sources are adjacent to those of the Missouri, river platte, and I think probably of the South branch of the Columbia river.*

Most of this information was correct. The Missouri, Yellowstone, and the Snake rivers, but not the Platte, do have their sources near each other in northwestern Wyoming. Following the Yellowstone River would have been easier for the expedition, but Lewis and Clark were directed to follow the Missouri, and that is what they did. However, Clark would return by and explore the Yellowstone.

Lewis and a few men had ventured ahead overland and reached the Yellowstone - Missouri junction on April 25, 1805. Clark and the rest of the expedition followed the river and reached the mouth of the Yellowstone on April 26. Lewis wrote, *"found them all in good health, and much please at having arrived at this long wished for spot, and in order to add some measure to the general pleasure which seemed to pervade our little community, we ordered a dram to be issued to each person; this soon produced the fiddle, and they spent the evening with much hilarity, singing & dancing, and seemed as perfectly to forget their past toils, as they appeared regardless to those to come.*

Lewis took measurements of the two rivers at their confluence and sent one man up the Yellowstone for a few miles to explore it.

Bodmer, Joslyn Art Museum

JUNCTION OF THE YELLOWSTONE AND MISSOURI RIVERS — Bodmer's view looks almost south at the confluence. Ahead in the distance is the valley of the Yellowstone, with the Missouri coming in from the right. The actual junction is to the right of center. The Corps' April 26 campsite would probably have been located very near the center of the painting. A new interpretative center is now located near the junction. Catlin also painted the junction, but from a place on the bank of the Missouri.

Today cattle graze on the hills where antelope roamed. The view is from a few miles north of Buford off County Road 5 looking south.

Bodmer, Rare Book Division, The New York Public Library,
Astor, Lenox and Tilden Foundations

FORT UNION ON THE UPPER MISSOURI — Both Lewis and Clark thought the confluence of the Missouri and Yellowstone was a strategic location for both military and fur trading posts. The sites they recommended were about one mile apart above the flood plain on the south side of the Missouri. Later, a fur trade post and a military fort were both built in the area, but on the north side a few miles west of the confluence.

Today, the reconstructed fort is located on the same site. The river has moved about a quarter mile south from the bank where the steamboat *Yellow Stone* once docked. Bodmer painted the fort from a hill north of the fort. Today, one can visit that area and see the view nearly as Bodmer did in 1833. Two trees in the center hide much of the distant fort, and Highway 1804 cuts east and west across the plain where the Indians once camped.

Catlin, Smithsonian American Art Museum, Gift of Mrs. Joseph Harrison, Jr

DISTANT VIEW OF FORT UNION AND THE YELLOWSTONE - MISSOURI JUNCTION — Catlin visited the fort in 1832 a year earlier than Bodmer. His viewpoint is looking southeast towards the fort and the confluence. The Missouri flows in from the right side and continues to the left. Just as Lewis and Clark had predicted, once established, Fort Union became the major trading post for the Yellowstone and the upper Missouri. The flat plain on the bend at the left near the distant Missouri is the location of the 1866 military post, Fort Buford. Note the wooded bottom across the Missouri from the fort and the two wooded sections to each side, just as described by the captains in their journals.

This view on private property is taken from just inside the Montana state line northwest of Fort Union. A few decaying buildings from the old town of Mondak stand where Indian tipis once stood.

UNUSUAL ELEVATIONS – In this area the valley of the Missouri is fairly narrow. The expedition had the wind with it and traveled twenty-four miles. On April 28 Clark wrote *the Bluffs in this part as also Shew below different Staturs of Coal or carbonated wood, and Coloured earth, such as dark brown, yellow a lightish brown, & a dark red &c. . . .a high bluff point on the L. Side the river making a considerable bend. . . .* Wildlife was abundant. On the morning of April 29 a few miles from these bluffs Lewis recorded his first scientific observations and measurement of a young grizzly bear he killed.

These bluffs and distant hill are very similar to the view in the painting. A raised dirt road parallels the base of the bluffs where the river once eroded its edge into unusual shapes 200 years ago. Since the river moved away wind and rain has continued the erosion, and the old riverbed is now cultivated.

Bodmer, Joslyn Art Museum

BUFFALO HERD ON THE MISSOURI — The Corps passed this area on May 4-5, 1805. Lewis wrote *I saw imence quantities of buffaloe in every direction,* and the next day wrote *as usual saw a great quantity of game today* and added that the dead buffalo were devoured by the wolves and bears. Maximilian made similar comments in 1833. Bodmer made a sketch and later painted this similar scene.

The Corps' camp of May 4 is on the Fort Peck Indian Reservation very near this site. Today horses and cattle graze across the river where the buffalo and wolves were seen. The river moved about a mile from its old bank and trees along the present riverbank make it difficult to see the whole area.

Bodmer, Rare Book Division, The New York Public Library,
Astor, Lenox and Tilden Foundations

HILLS NEAR COW ISLAND — On the morning of May 26, 1805 the Corps passed these hills. This was also the view the expedition members had when they camped across from them on July 30, 1806 during their return journey. Their journal entries noted the bluff and the high hills.

This area is a few miles east of Cow Island on the Nez Perce Historic Trail. The river has shifted a little away from the hills and trees now block part of the view.

Bodmer, Joslyn Art Museum

BEAVER LODGE ON THE UPPER MISSOURI — Beavers were found all along the Missouri. Beaver tail was considered good eating by the Corps. Beaver lodges were seen every day along the banks and the men hunted them. On May 19, 1805, near the Musselshell River, Lewis recorded, *one of the party wounded a beaver, and my dog as usual swam in to catch it; the beaver bit him through the hind led and cut the artery; it was with great difficulty that I could stop the blood; I fear it will yet prove fatal to him.* Lewis successfully nursed him back to health.

This beaver lodge was located in the same area where the men had hunted. Beaver still seem to be abundant in the area.

MISSOURI BREAKS — Lewis' account on May 31, 1805

The expedition was passing through the section of the Missouri sometimes referred to as the Badlands and the Missouri Breaks, now part of the National Wild and Scenic River area. It looks much the same as it did when the Corps passed through. Lewis's description gives a verbal picture of much of the area. For his May 31 entry he wrote:

The hills and river Clifts which we passed today exhibit a most romantic appearance. The bluffs of the river rise to the hight of from 2 to 300 feet and in most places nearly perpendicular; they are formed of remarkable white sandstone which is sufficiently soft to give way readily to the impression of water; two or thre thin horizontal stratas of white free-stone, on which the rains or water make no impression, lie imbedded in these clifts of soft stone near the upper part of them; the earth on the top of these Clifts is a dark rich loam, which forming a graduly ascending plain extends back from _ a mile to a mile where the hills commence and rise abruptly to a hight of about 300 feet more. The water in the course of time in decending from those hills and plains on either side of the river has trickled down the soft sand clifts and woarn it into a thousand grotesque figures, which with the help of a little immagination and an oblique view at a distance, are made to represent eligant ranges of lofty freestone buildings, having their parapets well stocked with statuary; collumns of various sculpture both grooved and plain, are also seen supporting long galleries in front of those buildings; in other places on a much nearer approach and with the help of less immagination we see the remains or ruins of eligant buildings; some columns standing and almost entire with their pedestals and capitals; others retaining their pedestals but deprived by time or accident of their capital, some lying prostrate an broken others in form of vast pyramids of conic structure bearing a series of other pyramids on their tops becoming less as they ascend and finally terminating in a sharp point. nitches and alcoves of various forms and sizes are seen at different hights as we pass. . . These walls pass the river in several places, rising from the water's edge much above the sandstone bluffs, which they seem to penetrate; thence continuing their course on a straight line on either side of the river through the gradually acending plains, over which they tower to the hight of from ten to seventy feet until they reach the hills, which they finally enter and conceal themselves. these walls sometimes run parallel to each other, with several ranges near each other, and at other times intersecting each other at right angles, having the appearance of the walls of ancient houses or gardens.

Bodmer, Joslyn Art Museum

BUFFALO AND ELK ON THE UPPER MISSOURI — This view of the river is about fourteen miles below the Judith River, called the Bighorn River today, and above Dauphin Rapids. The Corps camped on May 27, 1805, a few miles downstream from this area. Lewis reported *saw a few small herds of the Bighorned anamals and two Elk only. . .*, but no buffalo. Bodmer's painting shows elk in the area with a herd of buffalo coming down to drink, but with no bighorn sheep.

This section of the river has changed little since the expedition. The view is just up from the McClelland Ferry. However, the photo today is from a slightly different angle. As with some of Bodmer's other paintings, the distant hills are out of proportion in relation to the herds of buffalo.

Bodmer, Joslyn Art Museum

REMARKABLE FORMATIONS ON THE BANKS OF THE UPPER MISSOURI — Perhaps these were what Lewis had in mind when he wrote *The water in the course of time in decending from those hills and plains. . .has trickled down the soft sand clifts and woarn it into a thousand grotesque figures. . .* or what Clark recorded when he noted the area was *well Stocked with Statuary.*

Today this formation is known as the Seven Sisters.

Bodmer, Joslyn Art Museum

UNUSUAL SANDSTONE FORMATIONS ON THE UPPER MISSOURI — Perhaps these views are what Lewis meant when he wrote *of lofty freestone buildings, having their parapets well stocked with statuary* or the *ruins of elegant buildings*

Today this formation is called Steamboat Rock. It seemed to remind the later travelers on the Missouri River of the steamboats that traveled up and down the river through here to Fort Benton. By the mid-nineteenth century it became the terminus for riverboat traffic during normal and high water conditions.

CITADEL ROCK ON THE UPPER MISSOURI — In Clark's journal, his recordings of the points and directions noted *on the Stard. Point opsd. a high Steep black rock riseing from the waters edge.* This is the view the Corps had as they moved upriver.

Today that "Steep black rock" is known as Citadel Rock. It looks much the same as it did when the expedition passed by it.

Courtesy Dan Johanssen Collection

CITADEL ROCK — This is one of the earliest known photos of Citadel Rock. The Corps had this down river view on the return journey on July 29,1806. Note the existence of some trees along both banks.

Today there are few trees in the area. During the steamboat and homesteading era of the mid and late 1800s, woodhawks and settlers cut the trees along the river and back into the hills for fuel.

Bodmer, Rare Book Division, The New York Public Library,
Astor, Lenox and Tilden Foundations

VIEW OF THE STONE WALLS — This viewpoint is looking almost directly north up the Missouri. The Corps had this view of the valley before they camped May 31, 1805. Their site is on the right about a mile past the tower on the left bank. The river then turns to the north-west. As before, wild game was abundant. They saw many Big Horned Sheep and Lewis killed one near here. Bodmer painted this view of the Missouri. One painting has bighorn mountain sheep on the hills in the right foreground and another was done without them.

The view looks much the same today, however, no bighorns were seen in the vicinity the day this photo was taken, but they had been seen on another day.

Bodmer, Joslyn Art Museum

STRANGE SANDSTONE FORMATION — In one journal Clark's May 31 entry notes *The hills and river clifts which we pass to day exhibit a most romantic appearance. The Bluffs of the river rise to the hight of from 2 to 300 feet and in most places nearly perpendicular; they are formed of remarkable white Sandstone* and later he writes of *lofty free-stone buildings. . . .remind us of Some of those large Stone buildings in the United States."*

Perhaps this was the formation he was referring to—a large stone building. It has the appearance of a strong fortress with a commanding view of the river, and today is known as Castle Rock.

Bodmer, Joslyn Art Museum

BEAR PAW MOUNTAINS — On June 2, 1805 the expedition was approaching what we know as the Marias River. The existence of that river was not known to the Corps. That caused a major problem and long delay, June 2-11, while they tried to determine which river was the Missouri. A few miles prior to reaching that river junction Clark recorded "a dark bluff." The painting appears to show that bluff.

The photo is of the dark bluffs near what is now known as Churchill Bend. It appears to match the dark bluff. The Missouri appears to have meandered some. At the time the photo was taken, the smoke and haze from the fires in northern Montana had blown into the area blocking the view of anything on the horizon. The view today is equally as grand as it was when the Corps traveled through here. On June 10 while camped at the Marias Clark noted *Sah cah gah we â our Indian woman verry sick.* Her illness grew worse until she was near death while camped at Great Falls.

Bodmer, Joslyn Art Museum

FORT MCKENZIE AT THE MOUTH OF THE MARIAS RIVER — It was at the Marias River where twenty-eight years earlier the Corps had to stop to determine which fork in the river was the Missouri. The information provided by the Hidatsa at Fort Mandan did not mention this river junction. After a few days of exploration, the captains decided that the clear river was the Missouri and named the muddy fork the Marias. They cached some supplies and the red pirogue. On June 11 Lewis and four men moved on ahead while Clark commanded the rest of the Corps.

These were the very "blackish" bluffs across from which Fort McKenzie was built by the American Fur Company in 1833. The fort, about forty-five paces square, was built on the first bench above the river. Nothing is left of the fort, and the area is sometimes cultivated.

Bodmer, Joslyn Art Museum

First chain of the Rocky Mountains above Fort McKenzie — Clark and most of the Corps passed through the river bottom shown here during the morning of June 12, 1805. Bodmer painted the area while he was at Fort McKenzie.

Climbing out of the river bottom, the broad view today is still just as inspiring as it was two hundred years ago. These are not really the Rocky Mountains, and the smoke and haze caused by the fires in northern Montana made the mountains barely visible.

Donald Peterson, Early Pictures of the Falls

GREAT FALLS OF THE MISSOURI — Lewis had this engraving of Great Falls made based on his recollection of the falls and his description of it. It was to accompany the official publication of the captains' journals.

Lewis recorded in his journal, June 13, 1805, *I proceeded on. . . whin my ears were saluted with the agreeable sound of a fall of water and advancing a little further I saw a spray arise above the plain like a column of smoke . . . .soon began to make a roaring too tremendious to be mistaken for any cause short of the great falls of the Missouri. . ."* As can be seen when compared to the photograph below, the John Barralet engraving was quite accurate.

Cascade County Historical Society Catalog #83.109.4

GREAT FALLS OF THE MISSOURI — This early photo of the Great Falls was made from the canyon wall. Lewis's description is pretty accurate.

This view really shows the dramatic changes to the area with the construction of the dam and power plant. This dam and others at the various falls have harnessed the river, and as a result the falls are not nearly as spectacular as when the Corps saw them. It appears that Lewis's viewpoint for his engraving was at the base of the left side of the rock island. It was also near here, while camped at Portage Creek, that Sacagawea was nursed back to health with the aid of laudanum and sulfur waters from the nearby Sulfur Springs.

Cascade County Historical Society Catalog #98.2.4

Handsome (Rainbow) Falls — Lewis wrote *I now thought that if a skillfull painter had been asked to make a beautifull cascade that he would almost probably have presented the precise image of this one; nor could I determine on which of those two great cataracts to bestow the palm, on this or that which I discovered yesterday; at length I determined between these two great rivals for the glory that this was pleasingly beautifull, while the other was sublimely grand.*

This view is from near the present Rainbow Falls overlook.

Cascade County Historical Society, Catalog # 949-546

GIANT SPRINGS — Imagine the photograph without the two distant homes and only the short grasses. Clark discovered the spring. On June 18 he wrote, *"we proceeded on up river. . .to the largest fountain or Spring I ever Saw, and doubt if it is not the largest in America Known, this water boils up from under th rocks near the edge of the river and falls imediately into the river 8 feet and keeps its Colour for _ a mile which is emencely Clear and of a bluish Cast.*

Immense trees and lush green grass now grow on the previous dry treeless shoreline. How the Corps would have enjoyed the cool shade! Recent estimates put the discharge at about 200 million gallons a day. The nearby dam has backed up the river and covered some of the small cascades surrounding the spring in the old photo.

A. E. Matthews, 1866, Montana Historical Society

GATES OF THE MOUNTAINS — Lewis, July 19, 1805 – *this evening we entered much the most remarkable clifts that we have yet seen. these clifts rise from the waters edge on either side perpendicularly to the hight of 1200 feet. every object here wears a dark and gloomy aspect. the towing and projecting rocks in many places seem ready to tumble on us. the river appears to have forced it's way through this immence body of solid rock for the distance of 5 _ miles and where it makes it's exit   the river appears to have woarn a passage just the width of it's channel or 150 yds. . .from the singular appearance of this place I called it the gates of the rocky mountains.*

Today, you too can experience that "crowded in" feeling. Boat trips are available into the area.

A. E. Mathews, Montana Historical Society

THREE FORKS OF THE MISSOURI — Clark was the first to arrive at the Three Forks on July 25. His journal entry notes *we proceeded on a fiew miles to the three forks of the Missouri. . . .the North fork appears to have the most water and must be Considered as the one best calculated for us to assend.* He left a note for Lewis telling him of his decision. Lewis and the majority of the party arrived on July 27.

Mathews sketched this area in 1867. It has changed very little. This view today of the Three Forks encompasses the Missouri Headwaters State Park. This is nearly the identical view and area Lewis so vividly described. It still has much of its beauty and feeling of grandeur. The immediate courses of the rivers have changed only a little. The Gallatin is the river to the immediate left. The Madison is at the distant center, and the Jefferson the distant right. The area mentioned by Lewis for the fort is the oblong low flat bluff in the center. Today it is called Fort Rock.

LEMHI PASS — Lewis, along with George Drouillard, John Shields, and Hugh McNeal, had gone on ahead of Clark, the canoes, and the main party. Lewis and his men were following an Indian road/trail. This is a portion of Lewis's entry for August 12, 1805: *at the distance of 4 miles further the road took us to the most distant fountain of the waters of the mighty Missouri in surch of which we have spent so many toilsome days and wristless nights. thus far I have accomplished one of those great objects on which my mind has been unalterably fixed for many years, judge then of the pleasure I felt in allying my thirst with this pure and ice cold water which issues from the base of a low mountain or hill of a gentle ascent for _ a mile. the mountains are high on either hand leave this gap at the head of this rivulet through which the road passes. Here I halted a few minutes and rested myself. two miles below McNeal had exultingly stood with a foot on each side of this little rivulet and thanked his god that he had lived to bestride the mighty & heretofore deemed endless Missouri. after refreshing ourselves we proceeded on to the top of the dividing ridge from which I discovered immence ranges of high mountains still to the West of us with their tops partially with snow. I now decended the mountain about _ of a mile which I found much steeper than on the opposite side, to a handsome bold running Creek of cold Clear water. here I first tasted the water of the great Columbia river. . .*

Here is the pass today and the "immence ranges of high mountains." A short walk back down the Montana side will take one to the spring Lewis thought was the source of the Missouri. A ride down the Idaho side for a few miles takes one to the spring where Lewis tasted the waters that ran to the Pacific and to their campsite.

Gustav Sohon, US Pacific Railroad Survey, XII, Plate LVII

TRAVELERS REST — It was here where the Corps camped on its way west on September 10, 1805, before Old Toby took the Corps on the Nez Perce or Lolo Trail over the Bitterroot Mountains. It was also here where the travelers rested after returning from the Pacific. They also decided to divide the Corps. Lewis would follow a short cut to the Missouri and then explore the Marias. Clark would generally return as they came, but once back near Three Forks some would cut over to explore the Yellowstone. Recent archaeological projects have located the campsite and has pinpointed the actual site of the latrine and central fire or cooking area at Travelers Rest.

The view appears not to have changed much, but it is deceptive. Homes and other buildings now nearly surround the state park. The campsite was located on the right side by the edge of the trees along Lolo Creek below the hills.

Gustav Sohon, US Pacific Railroad Survey, XII, Plate LVII

LOLO HOT SPRINGS — These springs were well known to the Indians. Clark noted in his journal on September 13, 1805, . . .*passed Several Springs. . .below one of the Indians had made a whole to bathe, I tasted this water and found it hot & not bad tasted. . .in further exa- monation I found this water nearly boiling at the places it Sprouted from the rocks. . . .as Several roads led from these Springs in different directions, my Guide took a wrong road and took us out of our rout 3 miles through intolerable rout. . . .* When the Corps returned the next year some members rested and took advantage of the springs.

Today the modern traveler can also obtain lodging in the area and enjoy the hot springs. The highway runs diagonally from near the lower left to the center right.

WEIPPE PRAIRIE — The journey over the Nez Perce or Lolo Trail took its toll on the Corps. It was cold, damp, and snowy. Food became scarce. They finally made it and met the Nez Perce at their camps on Weippe Prairie. This is a view of part of the Weippe Prairie today.

CANOE CAMP — Once the Corps had rested, they made arrangements to leave their horses with the Nez Perce and build their needed canoes. The Nez Perce taught the visitors how they built their own canoes by using fire to burn the interior of the logs instead of chopping it. The Corps quickly adopted the superior method. This is the area and park today where the canoes were built for the last leg of the journey to the Pacific Ocean.

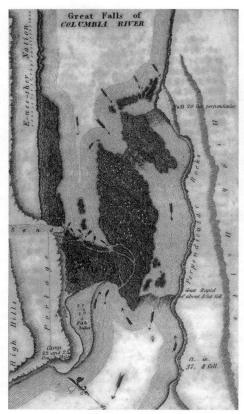

CLARK'S "MAP" OF CELILO FALLS — On October 22, 1805 the expedition arrived at the Great Falls of the Columbia – Celilo Falls—a major obstacle to river travel. The Corps used a portage on the north side of the falls to carry much of their equipment. They took their canoes over a short portage on the southern side and then shot through a narrow channel. The portage was completed on the October 23. This area was also a major fishing area for the Indians.

Today the falls have been inundated by water from The Dalles Dam which was constructed in 1957. It is hard to recognize the site. Celilo Park is located just up from the location of the now flooded falls near the short portage. The town of Celilo now occupies the former "E-nee-sher Nation" village site on Clark's map.

Oregon Historical Society, Watkins, OrHi 21583

THE DALLES — Watkins photographed the Dalles in 1867 while the river still ran free. After Celilo Falls the Corps faced the turbulent waters of the Dalles. It was the location of the Short and Long Narrows. All the water of the Columbia was forced through a narrow channel about forty-five yards wide. These were major obstacles to river transportation for many years. The Corps took two days to make the passage. After successfully passing both narrows they established Rock Fort Camp. Fort Rock Camp was used October 25-28, 1805 and again on April 15-18, 1806.

This photo is from a little upriver from where Watkins took his, but a close look of the cliffs on the far side shows the similarity. Today dams have raised the waters and flooded the rapids. Only the tops of some of the rocks now break the surface. The Dalles Dam was constructed a short distance upriver from this point and can be seen at the far right. Rock Fort is downriver a short distance from this photo. An interpretive sign marks the site in The Dalles.

Oregon Historical Society, Watkins, OrHi 21107

COLUMBIA RIVER — This view of the Columbia is just west of the Cascades and the Bridge of the Gods on the Washington side of the Columbia. The Corps passed here on November 1, 1805. Their camp was about four miles upriver. While exploring the area on October 31, 1805, Clark noted many burial vaults and Indian homes in the area. He also wrote, *at five miles I passé 4 large houses on the Stard. Side a little above the last rapid and opposite a large Island which is Situated near the Lard Side-"*

Today the rocky shoreline has been flooded by the Bonneville Dam which was built across the river just past the "large Island" in the distance on the "Lard Side." Today the shoreline here is reserved for the Umatilla and Nez Perce Indians as part of their fishing treaty area.

Oregon Historical Society, Watkins, OrHi 21101

BEACON ROCK — The Corps passed here on November 2, 1805. Clark wrote, *a remarkable high rock on the Stard. Side about 800 feet high and 400yds round, the Beaten Rock. The mountains and bottoms thickly timbered with Pine Spruce Cotton and a kind of maple* It was in this area that the Corps noticed the impact of the tide and knew they were getting near the ocean. Writing in his other journal the same day Clark noted, *proceed on down a Smoth gentle Stream of about 2 miles wide, in which the tide has its effect as high as the Beaten rock or the Last rapids at Strawberry Island.* A later journal entry refers to it as Beacon Rock. Watkins called it Castle Rock.

Here is a view of Beacon Rock today. The thick woods are still there. Beacon Rock State Park can be visited from the Washington side of the river. It is a great place to picnic.

O.H.S, Watkins, OrHi 21099

MULTNOMAH FALLS — This is one of the falls that enters the Columbia River Gorge. This picture was taken in 1868. Little had changed in this area along the Columbia by then. The Corps passed here on November 2, 1805, but they did not stop here nor mention it, yet they must have seen it.

Today it is a major stop along the Columbia for travelers. Paths lead up to the falls area. The beauty is still there, but the sounds are now different. It is located off a rest area on I-84 or can also be accessed from the historic highway.

Oregon Historical Society, Watkins, OrHi 21095

ROOSTER ROCK — On November 2, 1805 Clark was recorded *we camp under a high projecting rock on the Lard. Side, here the mountains leave the river on each Side, which from the Great Shute to this place is high and rugid. . . .The bottoms below appear extensive and thickly covered with wood. . . .The ebb tide rose here about 9 Inches,the flood tide must rise here much higher- we made 29 miles to day from the Great Shute.*

Today the area is a state park. One can picnic, camp or go boating. There is a boat ramp for pleasure boats, and a jetty which was constructed along part of the riverside to form a protected passage. A distant but similar view can be seen from a scenic turnout on the westbound side of I-84 about a mile west of Rooster Rock.

FORT CLATSOP LAYOUT — This is one of Clark's sketches of the basic plan for the Corps' winter home. They named it Fort Clatsop after one of the local Indian tribes. On November 24 the captains asked the opinions or took a vote of all expedition members, including York and Sacagawea, as to where to spend the winter. The choices included going back up the Columbia by Celilo Falls, to the Sandy River, or on the south side of the Columbia near the Pacific if a good hunting area could be found. A tally was recorded in Clark's journal and he wrote, *Proceed on to morrow & examine The*

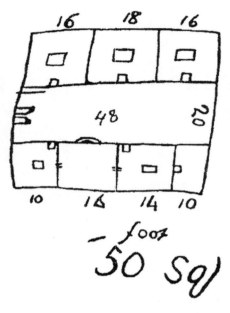

Missouri Historical Society

other side if good hunting there, as Salt is an objt. If not to proceed on to Sandy... By December 5 Lewis had picked the site for their winter camp. Within a few days the men were busy cutting logs and constructing the fort. They spent Christmas in the fort, but the fort wasn't completed until the evening of December 30.

Here is the reconstructed fort today. The lofty pines are still there.

John M. Stanley, US Pacific Railroad Survey, XII, Plate XLIV

HELLGATE — On the return journey Lewis and Clark divided the party while at Travelers Rest. Lewis and his party traveled north and then east towards Great Falls following Indian trails. They camped a few miles west of present-day Missoula. Part of Lewis's entry for July 4, 1806, reads *the first 5 miles of our rout was through a part of the extensive plain in which we were camped, we then entered the mountains with the East fork of Clark's river through a narrow confined pass on it's N. side continuing up that river 5 Ms. . . .* Here is a view of part of that "extensive plain" with the "narrow confined pass" through the mountains that they entered.

Today Missoula has spread out on the plain. The river stills flows through the plain and out of the canyon as do highways I-90 and U.S. 12. The view looks east from Reserve Street.

A. E. Mathews, Montana Historical Society

EXIT OF THE YELLOWSTONE RIVER — After leaving the Gallatin River Clark's party followed an old Indian trail over what today is known as the Bozeman Pass. Here is the view of the Yellowstone River Clark and his party would have seen on their return journey in July of 1806 as they approached the Yellowstone. It is near present-day Livingston near I-90 mile 333 on business I-90.

The view today looks almost unchanged, but that is deceiving. Fortunately, the view is protected by the local rancher who still lives on the site. Antelope can still be found on the property, but at the time of the photo the antelope moved and cattle replaced them. Houses are springing up all around the area and right across from the ranch.

CLARK'S INSCRIPTION AT POMPEY'S PILLAR — This site is on the Yellowstone River. It was during the return journey that Clark's party stopped here. It was already a landmark to the Indians in the area. Clark carved his name and date on the side of it. He named it Pompy's Tower. This is a photograph of his carving and Pompey's Pillar as it is known today. The carving is the only physical evidence of the Corps of Discovery still in its original setting. Earlier when Clark was at the Pacific he carved the phrase, "William Clark December 3rd 1805. By Land from the U.States in 1804 & 1805" on a tall pine. This was never found. Other members of the Corps also made carvings, but none were ever found and preserved. (Some people think that the carved letters "ORD" in Tavern Cave may have been made by John Ordway.)

The Academy of Natural Sciences of Philadelphia, Ewell Sale Stewart Library

NEWFOUNDLAND DOG — Nobody knows for sure what Seaman, Lewis's Newfoundland, looked like. He probably was not a solid black, but had more white on him. His head probably was not massive, and his coat not heavy. This sketch made in 1804 is one of the oldest Newfoundland images available and is probably more typical of the early Newfoundland.

Today's "Newfs" are typically black, but many have some white on their chests. Some may be brown, and others are "Landseer" or black and white, probably more like the coloring of the earlier dogs. Today, males weigh about 130-150 pounds, are big boned, with massive heads, and have a thick, full coat. Their normal life span is about eight to ten years. This modern Newfoundland, Jolly Rogers T.S. Elliot, a black and white, is owned by Peg and Ray Luomanen.

CHAPTER ELEVEN

Museums, Interpretive Centers and Historic Sites

A ll these museums, interpretive and visitor centers, and historic sites are associated with the Lewis and Clark Expedition. However, many of them have focuses on other historic periods and events. Yet, this does not diminish their importance. In fact, it only reminds us of the inter-play of historical events and how one historical period is interconnected to the next. Therefore, your visit to these places may tweak your interests in other historical events depicted and result in longer visits.

The Lewis and Clark 2003-2006 bicentennial celebration has had a major impact on the number and quality of the museums, centers, and sites. It has spurred the development of new facilities and improvements in existing ones. New research has turned up more materials that furthers our knowledge and understandings, and has sometimes caused earlier positions to be reexamined and reinterpreted.

Generally, museums house collections of original artifacts and display them with information so the visitors can better understand and appreciate them. Interpretive centers tend to use reproductions of historical artifacts and usually encourage some form of interaction and perhaps handling of the items. Information is also presented to help visitors better understand and appreciate the events. Historical sites usually refer to the actual place or close proximity to the area where an event occurred. They frequently have interpretive signs, displays, or interpretive centers. There are still more museums and centers that are in the planning stages that may not be included here at this time. Research is leading to the identification of new historic sites. Many of the small towns along the trail also have sites and museums, and these are worthy of a stop, especially for those who have more time and want to see and experience everything they can about Lewis and Clark and the Corps of Discovery. Unfortunately, not all of these small ones can be included here.

The larger museums, and centers are usually open year-round, while most of the smaller ones and some of the sites are seasonal. Be sure to check for the days and times they are open. Most of the museums and centers have sales areas where one can find a variety of Lewis and Clark books, reproduction pieces, and other items of interest, plus items reflecting the other focuses of the specific museum or center. Some of the sites included have only an interpretive panel or display. There are numerous places that are not listed here, but an observant traveler will see signs for them along the roads. The newer and larger museums and centers are making greater use of state of the art audio-visual and computer programs, life-sized displays and dioramas, and re-enactors to enhance the visitor's experience.

In addition to information about the particular museums or centers, some information will also be provided about the area as it applies to Lewis and Clark and other historical events in American history.

The National Parks Service produces pamphlets on all the historic trails including the Lewis and Clark Trail, one on the Eastern Legacy, and another on the western Historic Trail. In recent years listings of museums, visitor centers and points of interest have become available for local regions and states. Many of the pamphlets are published by the state historical societies, museum associations, state and local tourism bureaus, state parks and recreation departments, or state Lewis and Clark Bicentennial Commissions. When you are planning your trip along the Lewis and Clark Trail these would be a fine source of additional information.

The personal computer and internet have also opened up a whole new avenue for obtaining information. Many of these museums, visitor centers, parks, sites and other related organizations have websites that are very valuable.

Many of the sites of these facilities have corresponding paintings, sketches or photos in the pictorial journey section of this book.

CHARLOTTESVILLE, VIRGINIA AREA

Lewis was born in Albermarle County at Locust Hill in 1774. Near here Thomas Jefferson lived and built his home, Monticello. The two families knew each other. This is where Jefferson first dreamed of and planned for the exploration of the lands west of the Mississippi River before he became president. This is also where Lewis came to study.

Jefferson's library in Monticello was one of the best in the country. As a matter of fact, his library later became much of the basis for the Library of Congress

The Lewis home does not exist, but today you can visit Jefferson's Monticello. By studying not only the information describing Jefferson, but also by closely examining his home and grounds, one gets a better understanding of the greatness of Jefferson. Construction began on Monticello in 1770 and Jefferson was almost constantly redesigning his home. Jefferson displayed many of the items that were sent back in 1805 in his Indian Hall. Today that has been recreated with similar replica items. One item, the elk antlers, are the originals.

Monticello is located about two miles southeast of Charlottesville.

The University of Virginia, designed and laid out by Jefferson, is also in the area and can be visited.

JEFFERSON MEMORIAL, SMITHSONIAN INSTITUTE & WHITE HOUSE, WASHINGTON, DC

The nation's capital has a variety of sites surrounding the Capitol Mall that are worthy of a visit. The Jefferson Memorial is located at the tidal pool by the river, and the Smithsonian and the White House are by the mall. Jefferson was the second president to inhabit the White House.

PHILADELPHIA & LANCASTER, PENNSYLVANIA

It was in Philadelphia that Lewis was instructed in medicine, paleontology, botany and mathematics. He also bought almost two tons of supplies and a wagon to transport the supplies to Pittsburgh. Lewis was initiated into the American Philosophical Society. Today you can visit the society.

The Academy of Natural Sciences houses more than 200 of the plant specimens that were collected by Lewis and Clark during their journey. It is located at 19th & Benjamin Franklin Parkway.

While not directly related to the Lewis and Clark Expedition, Independence National Historic Park is a must stop for everyone interested in the historic founding of the United States and its early years. Independence Hall, Liberty Bell Pavilion, Declaration House, Congress Hall and New Hall Military Museum can all be visited. The visitor Center is located at 3rd & Chestnut.

Once Lewis left Philadelphia he went to Lancaster, Pennsylvania where he studied surveying and the use of the sextant at the home of Andrew Ellicott. Today, you can also visit the Ellicott's home where Lewis studied. The house is now the office of the Historic Preservation Trust of Lancaster County located at 123 N. Prince.

HARPERS FERRY NATIONAL HISTORIC PARK, HARPERS FERRY, WEST VIRGINIA

Harpers Ferry was the location of the U.S. Armory and Arsenal. It was here in 1803 that Lewis went to obtain much of the weaponry—improved rifles, powder horns, pouches, bullet molds and other equipment, that the expedition was to use. It was also here that Lewis had his "iron boat" constructed.

The park is located at the junction of the Shenandoah River and Potomac River off U.S. 340. Today the park has different museums and exhibits for each theme or "Path through History:" industry, natural history, transportation, John Brown, the Civil War, and Afro-American history. There are no original government buildings standing from the time of Lewis's visits. But the Harper Home off High Street, built in 1782, still stands

FORT PITT, PITTSBURGH, PENNSYLVANIA

Pittsburgh grew up around the site of Fort Pitt where the Ohio River is formed by the junction of the Allegheny and the Monongahela rivers. Lewis went to the area to have the keelboat constructed, and as an army officer probably would have visited the fort.

Today you can visit old Fort Pitt with its restored original block-house and newly expanded and renovated museum and visitor center. They are located in Point State Park at 101 Commonwealth Place. The old bastion blockhouse was in use when Lewis was in Pittsburgh.

STEUBENVILLE, OHIO & WELLSBURG, WEST VIRGINIA

Before reaching Wheeling, Lewis and the keelboat passed Steubenville and Charlestown, now Wellsburg. Old Fort Steuben (1787) has been reconstructed and is open seasonally. The visitor center is new. The fort had been burned before Lewis passed by and a small town had been established in 1798. The fort and town had been named in honor of German General Von Steuben who had helped to establish the Continental Army. Next to the restored fort is a cabin that was built in 1801. It was moved there from its original location a few blocks away. They are located on South Street near the river in Steubenville.

Wellsburg became the home and final resting place of Patrick Gass. He is buried in the Brooke Cemetery. Gass's diary was the first published account of the whole journey. He had replaced Charles Floyd as Sergeant after Floyd's death. Gass was the last member of the Corps of Discovery to die. The cemetery is off Pleasant Street.

INDEPENDENCE HALL & HISTORIC DISTRICT, WHEELING, WEST VIRGINIA

The town of Wheeling pre-dates the Lewis and Clark Expedition. Because river levels of the Ohio River above Wheeling were frequently low, Wheeling became an important embarking area for river travel. Lewis stayed for two days in Wheeling. He picked up the expedition's supplies that had been shipped overland by wagon from Philadelphia and Harpers Ferry.

The Wheeling Visitor Center is located at 1401 Main Street. Wheeling's early history is described including the tie to the National (Cumberland) Road. It was the first federally funded highway project and was started by Jefferson.

Independence Hall is located in the Historic district. While its focus is on the history of West Virginia and the Civil War, it does have information related to Lewis and Clark.

GRAVE CREEK MOUND HISTORIC SITE, MOUNDSVILLE, WEST VIRGINIA

Lewis visited and wrote about this site on his journey down the Ohio from Pittsburgh. This conical mound is one of the largest remaining earthen structures from the Adena Period. The mound and museum are open year-round. This fine center and museum interprets the Adena Indian Culture and the construction of the mounds. It also has some information on the Lewis and Clark Expedition.

The site is at 801 Jefferson Avenue.

MARIETTA, OHIO

Marietta is the oldest settlement in Ohio. Lewis stopped there on September 13. The river was very low, channels had to be cut and the keelboat dragged over the gravel bars. Fort Harman is not standing now, but some historic homes and shops can be seen. Within the town are more mounds from the Adena Indian culture, but Lewis did not visit them.

The Campius Martius Museum's focus is on the founding and early settlement of the town and the Northwest Territory. Inside the museum is the only surviving house of the original settlement, the General Rufus Putnam House, and related displays. There is information on Lewis and Clark in addition to the excellent exhibits on the early history of the area.

It is located at 2nd and Washington streets.

The Ohio River Museum's focus is on the types of boats that were used on the Ohio River. It also has some information on Lewis and Clark.

The museum is located on the Muskingum River on Front Street and Washington.

BLENNERHASSETT ISLAND STATE PARK, &
BLENNERHASSETT MUSEUM, PARKENBURG, WEST VIRGINIA

While not directly associated with the Lewis and Clark Expedition, these are connected to the Louisiana Territory. The large island in the middle of the Ohio was once the home of the Harman Blennerhassett family. Harman had settled there in 1798. He became prosperous, but soon became entangled with the Aaron Burr plot to separate Louisiana and the West from the United States. He was arrested in 1806 and served time in prison.

The old mansion had been destroyed in a fire in 1811. It has been reconstructed and has exhibits on the family and on the Indians who had lived there for centuries before. The mansion has living history programs. The Blennerhassett Museum is in town at 137 Juliana Street, and the mansion is on the island off Point Park.

CINCINNATI AREA, OHIO &
BIG BONE LICK STATE PARK, KENTUCKY

Lewis stayed in the area for two weeks. He picked up mail and visited with William Goforth who was involved in an archaeological dig of mammoth bones. Big Bone Lick State Park is the site of the prehistoric animal remains. The salt lick originally brought the animals to the area and some of them became mired in the bogs. The center contains some of the artifacts recovered as a result of various archaeological digs. Lewis also came to the area to examine the bones. Mammoth and mastodon bones were obtained and sent to President Jefferson, but unfortunately, they were lost in shipment down the river.

Today the museum focuses on the prehistoric animals, but there is also information on Lewis's visit. There is also a small buffalo herd in the park. It is located near Union, Kentucky off State Road 338 on Beaver Road.

East of the Cincinnati area is Maysville, Kentucky where John Colter and, possibly, George Shannon joined Lewis.

FALLS OF THE OHIO, LOUISVILLE, KENTUCKY &
CLARKSVILLE, OHIO GREATER AREA

The history of the Falls of the Ohio area and the Clark family are intertwined. George Rogers Clark, William's older brother helped to establish Louisville and Clarksville, Indiana. There are a variety of sites associated with Lewis and Clark in the greater area.

George Rogers Clark Park

In 1785 Jonathan, George's older brother also came to the Falls of the Ohio. His parents, John and Ann, and the rest of their children moved there from Virginia in 1785. Their log home became known as Mulberry Hill. In 1799 William inherited the Mulberry Hill home, lands, and slaves, including York after his father died. Today a park exists on forty-four acres of the former 300-acre home site. In 1917 the remains of the home and outbuildings were demolished for the construction of Camp Zachary Taylor, a WWI Army training camp. On the grounds of the park can be found the old family cemetery and an old cypress tree, said to be planted by George Rogers Clark, which still grows by the site of the old spring house.

The park is located off Poplar Level Road in Louisville.

Locust Grove Historic Home

Lucy Clark married William Croghan in 1789 at Mulberry Hill. Construction was started on their home, Locust Grove, in 1790. Both Mulberry Hill and Locust Grove served as social and political centers for the area. After the return of Lewis and Clark they stopped at Locust Grove on November 8, 1806 to be entertained and displayed many of the items they brought back. It seems likely that they would have also visited the home before they left on their journey, but there is no record of it. Later, from 1809 until 1818, George Rogers Clark spent the final years of his life at Locust Grove.

Today the home has been restored to the early 1800 period and many of the outbuildings have also been reconstructed. The focus of the visitor center is George Rogers Clark, but its association with all the Clarks is strong and makes this a very worthwhile site to visit on your trip.

It is located at 561 Blankenbaker Road in northeastern Louisville.

Clark's Cabin and Lewis and Clark Plaza, Clark's Point

This site served as the home of George Rogers Clark. William Clark and York also lived there prior to meeting Lewis and their subsequent departure in October 26, 1803. An old log cabin, similar in construction and size, has been erected and furnished on the site. This is where Lewis and Clark recruited additional members for the Corps of Discovery—"the nine young men from Kentucky." Down the hill from the cabin, the Plaza commemorates the site where Lewis and Clark, now joined, departed with their new recruits. A video presentation on the nine men from Kentucky is shown at the Falls of the Ohio Center.

Falls of the Ohio State Park and Interpretive Center

This fine center overlooks the river, the falls, and the fossil beds. One of the main permanent exhibits focuses on the Lewis and Clark Expedition and the roles played by the different members of the Corps of Discovery that were recruited in the area. For those interested in geology and natural history the site offers a 400 million year old 200-acre fossil reef. It has been a focus of study since colonial times. There are a variety of exhibits relating to the area's natural and cultural history that are very interesting. It has video presentations on both the geological history and on Lewis and Clark.

The center is located at 201 West Riverside Drive off I-65, Exit 0 in Clarksville, Ohio.

FILSON HISTORICAL SOCIETY

This privately supported historical society houses and displays a number of Lewis and Clark documents and artifacts. One, a horn of a bighorn sheep is thought to be one of the few items from the expedition still in existence.

The Filson is located at 1310 South Third Street, Louisville.

There are numerous other sites in the surrounding countryside of Kentucky and Indiana associated with brothers Joseph and Ruebin Field, John Shields, William Bratton, and Charles Floyd, all members of the Corps of Discovery that should also be visited. Information is available in the Clark & Floyd Counties Convention & Tourism Bureau, at 315 Southern Indiana Ave. in Jeffersonville, Indiana, near the Falls of the Ohio.

FORT MASSAC STATE PARK, METROPOLIS, ILLINOIS

Originally built by the French in 1757, won by the British during the French and Indian War, it became a possession of the Americans after the Revolutionary War. Lewis and Clark visited the fort November 11-13, 1803. They came to pick up more men for their expedition. George Drouillard, one of the most important members was recruited at the fort. The reconstructed fort is open to the public. While its focus is on its earlier military history, the exhibits do include information about Lewis and Clark.

Fort Massac State Park is east of Metropolis on U.S. 45. Camping is also available.

RED HOUSE, CAPE GIRARDEAU, MISSOURI

Lewis visited with Louis Lorimier on November 23, 1803. Lorimier was an old, knowledgeable trader, and a relative of George Drouillard. Lewis was interested in finding out as much as he could about the

Missouri River and Indians. Lorimier's home has been reconstructed and can be visited.

The Cape Girardeau Cape River Heritage Museum has exhibits on the Mississippi River transportation and the Cape's history. It is located at 538 Independence Street.

For those interested in the Indian removal policy of the U.S., the Trail of Tears State Park, about ten miles north on Missouri 177, marks the trail of the Cherokee on their forced trip to Oklahoma in 1838-9.

FORT KASKASKIA STATE HISTORIC SITE, ELLIS GROVE, ILLINOIS

This site was where additional members of the Corps of Discovery were recruited. Today nothing is left of the fort visited by Lewis and Clark.

ST. GENEVIEVE, MISSOURI &
FORT CHARTRES STATE HISTORIC SITE, ILLINOIS

The Corps camped on the shore opposite the village of St. Genevieve, and the next morning passed the old fort a few miles north. The Corps did not stop and visit either, but travelers today can. A visit to St. Genevieve is most enjoyable. It still has old buildings that pre-date Lewis and Clark and its French heritage is still very evident. The site of Fort Charters, with its partial reconstruction can also be visited and relates information about its history.

St. Genevieve is located on U.S. 61 and Fort Chartres, north of Fort Kaskaskia State Historical Site, on Highway 155.

GREATER ST. LOUIS AREA

This area includes a wide variety of sites and centers associated with Lewis and Clark. Just as Lewis and Clark spent a long time here preparing for their journey, the modern traveler should do the same. Some of the sites are in Illinois and some in Missouri. This is not a place where you can see it all in one day!

GATEWAY ARCH/JEFFERSON NATIONAL EXPANSION MEMORIAL

This is the location of the gigantic silver Gateway Arch commemorating St. Louis as the "Gateway to the West." It is located on the site of old St. Louis that was visited by Lewis and Clark. The Museum of Westward Expansion is beneath the Arch. There a statue of Jefferson serves as the point from which western expansion flows. Rightly so, for the Lewis and Clark Expedition is part of the first of many concentric circles from which emanates the expansion of the United States westward. As one walks out and around, the whole story of the West unfolds through the use of artifacts and life-like exhibits—the native people, the explorers, fur trappers and traders, emigrants, settlers and gold seekers, cattlemen and homesteaders, military and Indians. There is also a special exhibit on the history and use of peace medals. In addition there is an I-Max theater and a ride to the top of the Arch for a breathtaking view of the area.

The northern part of the park grounds and parking lot was once the site of William Clark's residence and gallery/museum. There he kept many of the artifacts and presents he received while he lived in St. Louis after his return from the journey. Unfortunately, nothing of this remains as years ago the structures were destroyed and his collections dispersed, stolen or lost.

The memorial park is located on the Missouri side of the Mississippi River just off I-55 and I-70 at 11 North Fourth Street.

The Bellefontaine Cemetery is the final resting place of William Clark. It is located at 4947 West Florissant Avenue.

The Old Courthouse Museum shows how early St. Louis appeared about the time of Lewis and Clark. It is located west of the Arch at 11 North 4th Street.

MISSOURI HISTORICAL SOCIETY MUSEUM

This museum contains both permanent and special exhibits. The focus is on the history of St. Louis and Missouri through state-of-the-art displays and interactive exhibits using thousands of artifacts. The past, present, and future and their inter-relationship are examined. Some of the special exhibits focus on the Indians, Lewis and Clark, Western Expansion, and Charles Lindberg.

The museum is located in Forest Park at Lindell Boulevard. and DeBaliviere, the site of the Louisiana Purchase Centennial Exposition.

CAHOKIA, ILLINOIS AREA
CAHOKIA VILLAGE & CAHOKIA MOUNDS STATE HISTORIC SITE

Cahokia Village was established in 1698 by the French. Lewis and Clark arrived in December 1803. They used this area as their post office and supply area during their five months in Camp Dubois. Today you can visit two buildings visited by Lewis and Clark. The Cahokia Courthouse exhibits the services it provided for U.S. territorial citizens, artifacts and early maps. The Holy Family Church whose history includes the Spanish, French, British and American periods still has the Latin mass. The buildings are located a couple of blocks from each other in Cahokia at 107 Elm Street off ST3 and 157.

The present Jarrot Mansion was built in 1807. In 1802 Lewis had often visited Nicolas Jarrot, a noted fur trader in the area. The original home was replaced by this house. It is now open to the public and can be visited. It is next to the church.

During the Corps' stay in Camp Dubois Clark visited some of the old "Indian Fortifications" which were the ruins of a Mississippian Culture village. Today a large and impressive visitor center tells the story of the Mississippian culture and the Cahokia Mounds. Tens of thousands of Indians inhabited this urban area known as the "City of the Sun." The site is a world heritage site. Life-sized displays depict the daily life of the Indians. The multi-media center provides for even greater understanding of the mound people and culture. Visitors can climb Monk's Mound, the largest and most impressive of the earthen mounds. Many of the surrounding mounds in nearby areas have been destroyed as the area has developed.

The Cahokia Indian Mounds are located at 130 Remey Street, off the I-55/70 exit 6 in Collinsville.

LEWIS AND CLARK VISITORS CENTER & CAMP RIVER DUBOIS, HARTFORD, ILLINOIS

This is the site that commemorates where the different recruits began their process of being molded into a single unit known as the Corps of Discovery. This new multi-media center tells the whole story of the Lewis and Clark Expedition, but its main focus is on their training and preparations made during their five months in the camp. There are a variety of displays explaining how the men lived and trained, but it is the unique cut away full-sized keelboat and the life-sized reconstruction of Camp Dubois that allow for a special experience.

Nearby is the Corps of Discovery Monument commemorating the beginning of the journey and the states that made up the Louisiana Territory. It is located along the Mississippi, in the vicinity of the mouth of the Wood River and across from the mouth of the Missouri. Clark noted in his journal, *The mouth of the River Dubois is to be considered as the point of departure.*

The center and monument are located off State Road 3 near Hartford.

LEWIS AND CLARK BOATHOUSE AND NATURE CENTER, ST. CHARLES, ILLINOIS

St. Charles was founded in 1769. It is the oldest town on the Missouri River. South Main Street is on the National Register of Historic Places. This is where Lewis rejoined the Corps after completing last minute business in St. Louis. They were given their last celebration and party before continuing on up the Missouri River. The Lewis and Clark Center explains the story of the Corps of Discovery through the use of displays, artifacts and miniature dioramas. Full size replicas of the keelboat and pirogues are housed here when not on the river.

The center is located at 1050 Riverside. The whole of South Street and the riverside allows the visitor to experience the charm of this unique historic town.

Frontier Park, with its large statue of Lewis, Clark, and Seaman, is found along the river. The western portion of the park represents the approximate location where the Corps of Discovery camped while they stayed in St. Charles.

KATY TRAIL STATE PARK, MISSOURI

For those travelers who want to hike or bike along part of the Lewis and Clark Trail, the Katy Trail offers them a chance to do so. This old railroad bed parallels the Missouri River on the north side from St. Charles to New Franklin where it crosses over to Boonville a few miles east of Arrow Rock.

One of the stops west of St. Charles on the trail is the town of Defiance. This was the home of one of America's other great explorers, Daniel Boone. Boone and his family moved to the area in 1799 when it was still Spanish territory. The home he built in 1803 is open to the public and is deserving of a visit. Defiance is about sixteen miles west of St. Charles on State Road 94.

ARROW ROCK STATE HISTORIC SITE
INTERPRETIVE CENTER, ARROW ROCK, MISSOURI

This historic village is most associated with the early years of the Santa Fe Trail. The town was founded in 1828. The Corps had camped on an island nearby when they passed.

The Arrow Rock State Historic Site Interpretive Center and its displays relates to the history of the area including the Missouri and Little Osage Indians, the early explorers, and Lewis and Clark. Camping is also available.

FORT OSAGE , SIBLEY, MISSOURI

This fort was originally constructed in 1808 under the direction of William Clark. It was the first post established in the newly acquired Louisiana Territory and part of the U.S. government's system of trade factories to control the trade with the Indians. The fort was first called Fort Clark, but then changed to Fort Osage after the local Indians. It was shut down in 1822, and its military role ended in 1827. A large portion of the fort has been reconstructed, some right on the original foundations. The focus of the exhibits is on its role with the Indian trade and then the Santa Fe Trail. It has living history programs that make a visit very interesting.

The fort is located in Sibley, almost three miles north off Highway 24.

KANSAS CITY/INDEPENDENCE AREA
NATIONAL FRONTIER TRAILS CENTER

While the focus of this center is on the Santa Fe-Oregon-California trails, it has a fine exhibit on Lewis and Clark. Included are reproductions of some trade goods and equipment that the Corps brought with it. The exhibits on the Oregon-California-Santa Fe trails are excellent.

This center is located a few blocks south of Independence Square at 318 West Pacific.

Also on the grounds is the headquarters of the Oregon-California Trails Association. It is dedicated to the identification, preservation and improved interpretation of the western emigrant trails and their role in American history.

Nearby are numerous other historic sites related to Independence's varied history, including President Harry Truman's home and library.

CLARK'S POINT & STATUE

High on a bluff overlooking the junction of the Kansas and the Missouri rivers is the large statue of Lewis, Clark, Sacagawea, York and Seaman. Looking down at what once was the stockyards and over at the junction of the rivers is the area where the expedition camped from June 26-29, 1804 and also stopped briefly on September 15, 1806. Clark climbed a high hill and noted that it provided a *commanding situation for a fort*.

The statue is located in Case Park at 8th and Jefferson Street.

FORT LEAVENWORTH, LEAVENWORTH, KANSAS

This is the oldest military post in continuous use west of the Mississippi River. It was established in 1827 and replaced Fort Atkinson. The fort is the center for the Command and General Staff College for advanced military training.

The Frontier Army Museum has a variety of displays and artifacts dealing with Lewis and Clark and continuing through the settlement and development of the West. Special emphasis is on the role of the military in U.S. history.

The museum is located on Reynolds Avenue on the fort's grounds.

Other sites and displays on the grounds relate to the Santa Fe, Oregon, California, and Mormon trails and Buffalo Soldiers.

LEWIS & CLARK STATE PARK, RUSHVILLE, MISSOURI

Travelers can camp on a lake near where the Corps traveled and camped on July 3, 1804. The river has meandered much in the valley. This was the area where Clark noted the many geese and named a lake, Gosling Lake. Lewis and Clark Lake and village in the state park is located very near where the Corps camped.

The park is located off U.S. 59, south of Rushville, Missouri and east of Atchison, Kansas off State Road 45 on State Road 138.

INDEPENDENCE PARK, ATCHISON, KANSAS

Near here the Corps camped and celebrated July 4, 1804. They named the creek near the present day U.S. 59 bridge "4th of July Creek" where they stopped in the morning. Lewis climbed a high hill and had a good view of the surrounding area. Also in the area is the present day mouth of Independence Creek, which they also named. When the Corps passed the area in 1804, Independence Creek entered the Missouri River almost five miles to the north. Their 4th of July camp was located on the Missouri side of the river where the Atchison/Doniphan county lines intersect the river. The park is located along the Missouri River in Atchison.

For those interested in the history of aviation, Amelia Earhart was born here and her home is now a museum.

ST. JOSEPH, MISSOURI

While today St. Joseph is probably better known for the roles it played with the Pony Express and the Oregon-California trails, the area also played a role in the story of Lewis and Clark. They stopped in the area on the way up in July 1804. On their return trip, on September 12, 1806, they also stopped and met Robert McClellan. He was traveling up the river to trade with the Indians. He brought the Corps of Discovery some of their first news about the events of the past two years.

The St. Joseph Museum is a certified site. It has exhibits that describe the story of Lewis and Clark as they passed through and stopped at St. Michael's Prairie as the area was then known. The museum is located on 11th and Charles Streets.

The area boasts various other museums associated with Jesse James, the Pony Express, fur trade, railroads and emigrant trails. All are worthy of a visit.

**SQUAW CREEK NATIONAL WILDLIFE REFUGE/
BIG LAKE STATE PARK, MOUND CITY, MISSOURI**
The Corps first passed through this area July11-13, 1804. From the
Squaw Creek Visitor Center's Loess Hill Trail, visitors can see the
changes in the geography and plant life typical of this area at the edge
of the plains.

On July 12 the Corps camped on an island just across from the
mouth of the Big Nemaha River. It was here that Alexander Willard
was court-martialed and punished for sleeping while on sentry duty.
Today it would correspond to the area about one mile south of the
southern tip of Big Lake. Travelers can camp on the oxbow lake that
was the old channel of the Missouri River.
Squaw Creek National Wildlife Refuge is located about two miles
west on U.S. 159 off exit 79 on I-29. Big Lake State Park is farther
west, north off U.S. 159 on State Road 111.

**MISSOURI RIVER BASIN & LEWIS & CLARK INTERPRETIVE
TRAIL AND VISITOR CENTER, NEBRASKA CITY, NEBRASKA**
The unique focus of this center is the hundreds of flora (plants) and
fauna (animals) newly identified by Lewis and Clark. Paths through
the woods along the river allow visitors to "retrace" the steps of Lewis
as he searched for specimens along the river. Exhibits show the plants
and animals. A full size replica of the keelboat *Discovery* takes visitors
along the journey through a multi-media presentation.
The center is located at 911 Central Avenue.

OMAHA, NEBRASKA/COUNCIL BLUFFS, IOWA AREA
Both before and after Lewis and Clark, this area is rich in
American history. Indian culture, the fur trade, California-Oregon-
Mormon emigrants, the railroads, homesteading and ranching all left
their imprint on this area and all are represented in the various muse-
ums and centers found here.

WESTERN HISTORIC TRAILS CENTER, COUNCIL BLUFFS, IOWA
This fine center focuses on all of the area's history. All the periods
are show cased with exhibits and hands on displays that help visitors
understand these periods. Special programs are held throughout the
year along with multi-media presentations. The White Catfish Days
are celebrated here. It was only a few miles south where Private Silas
Goodrich caught the large fish and the Corps camped.
The center is located south off I-80, exit 1B at 3434 Richard
Downing Avenue.

JOSLYN ART MUSEUM, OMAHA, NEBRASKA

This art museum houses the work of many famous artists associated with the American West. Perhaps the most important for this book is the collection of Karl Bodmer's works. Many of these works are found in this book. He was one of the few and early painters of the American West. Also housed in the museum are many of the fine works of Alfred J. Miller and George Catlin. Both also painted the West in the 1830s. Some of the works of Frederick Remington are also there.

The museum is located in the downtown area at 2200 Dodge Street.

FORT ATKINSON STATE HISTORIC PARK AND COUNCIL SITE, FORT CALHOUN, KANSAS

This bluff, on the edge of the river, was the site where Lewis and Clark held their first council with the local Indians, the Missouri and Oto. The site was later selected by the military for the construction of Fort Atkinson in 1822. It was abandoned in 1827 when the army moved to Fort Leavenworth. Today much of the fort has been reconstructed. There is a beautiful visitor center and a variety of seasonal living history weekends. The river has since moved east away from the bluff and trees now grow on it. A walking trail takes modern visitors through the area. In the prairie near the visitor center are life-sized statues depicting and commemorating the first council.

The fort is located east of U.S. Highway 75 at 7th and Madison in Fort Calhoun.

Also located in Fort Calhoun is the **WASHINGTON COUNTY HISTORICAL MUSEUM**. In addition to the exhibits relating to local history, with artifacts from prehistoric time, Native Americans, early pioneers and the nearby fort, there are interactive exhibits about the Lewis and Clark Expedition and especially their stay in "Council Bluffs." This smaller museum is located on U.S. Highway 75.

DESOTO NATIONAL WILDLIFE REFUGE & RIVERBOAT MUSEUM, MISSOURI VALLEY, IOWA

The focus of this center is the natural history of the area and also on the *Bertrand*, a riverboat that sunk in 1865 and was recently excavated. The Corps first passed through this area after leaving the council site. It was at a site near here on September 30, 1804 that Joseph Field killed a badger. It was the first of the animal specimens skinned and stuffed by Lewis that was later sent to President Jefferson.

This center is located east of the Missouri River off U.S. 30.

LEWIS AND CLARK STATE PARK AND
INTERPRETIVE CENTER, ONAWA, IOWA

Docked here on Blue Lake are replicas of the keelboat and pirogue that were used by Lewis and Clark. The oxbow was the old river when the Corps camped here on August 9, 1804. Their campsite was near where the road first crosses Blue Lake. Interpretive signs and trails are also found in the park. Camping is available.

It is located about three miles west of Onawa off State Road 125.

BLACKBIRD HILL AND GRAVE SITE,
NEBRASKA, OMAHA INDIAN RESERVATION

While this site is not open to the public, it was noted and visited by Lewis and Clark on August 11, 1804. There is a pavilion on Highway 75, mile 152 north of Decatur, with information about the Omaha Indian culture.

SIOUX CITY, IOWA AREA
FLOYD'S BLUFF AND MEMORIAL

This monument marks the present site of Sergeant Charles Floyd's grave. The original site was closer to the river, but due to erosion over the years the grave had to be moved east to its present spot. Floyd was the only member of the Corps of Discovery to have died on the journey. Today it is believed he died from appendicitis. A beautiful view of the Missouri River can be experienced from the bluff.

The monument is located off exit 143 on I-29 about six miles south of Sioux City just off U.S. 75.

SERGEANT FLOYD WELCOME CENTER

This Iowa Welcome Center is located in a former workboat of the Corps of Engineers. It now houses displays on Lewis and Clark and Sergeant Charles Floyd and on the history of transportation on the river. A life size figure of Floyd is based on a forensic study of his remains before he was re-buried in 1901. It is located off exit 149 on I-29 at 1000 Larsen Park Road.

SIOUX CITY LEWIS & CLARK INTERPRETIVE CENTER

This new center focuses its exhibits and interactive displays on the expedition's journey up the Missouri and the events that occurred in the Sioux City area. It examines the human side of the story. A unique program allows visitors to become a member of the Corps and take one of seven different roles. They can then proceed on through the center from the perspective of the individual's role and learn about their experiences of setting up camp; Sergeant Floyd's sickness, death, and burial; an election of a new sergeant; the court martial of a member; the capture of a prairie dog; and the climb to Spirit Mound.

It is located off exit 149 on I-29 at 900 Larsen Park Road near the Sergeant Floyd Welcome Center.

SIOUX CITY PUBLIC MUSEUM

This museum has an extensive collection of Indian artifacts and exhibits depicting the history of Sioux City as a gateway to the northwest and displays and dioramas on Native Americans.

The museum is located at 2901 Jackson Street.

MISSOURI NATIONAL RECREATIONAL RIVER AND EDUCATION CENTER, PONCA STATE PARK, PONCA, NEBRASKA

Between Ponca and Gavin's Point Dam the river is protected as the Missouri National Recreational River. Here travelers can see the river in its natural state as it was when the Corps passed with its islands, sandbars, chutes, and snags.

The focus of the center and its exhibits is on the river system, its natural habitat, and its many uses by the different peoples and cultures that have occupied the region over time. Camping is also available in the park that is two miles north of Ponca off Nebraska 12.

LEWIS AND CLARK CAMPSITE-HERITAGE PARK, ELK POINT, SOUTH DAKOTA

Two days after Charles Floyd died Patrick Gass was chosen by the men and appointed by Lewis to be the new sergeant. It was near this site that the election of Gass by the men was held. On the return journey, the Corps met a trapper and trader who gave them some news of what had happened since they left.

The site is located in the Elk Point City Park at the west end of town. Every year a re-enactment of the event is held on August 22 during the Lewis and Clark Celebration Days.

W. H. OVER MUSEUM & SPIRIT MOUND
HISTORIC PRAIRIE, VERMILLION, SOUTH DAKOTA

The W. H. Over Museum's mission is to preserve and interpret the land and peoples of southeastern South Dakota. The museum is organized along three themes: the land, the first people, and the new frontier. The natural history and geography of the area has changed extensively. Exhibits describe the native plants, animals, rocks and minerals both past and present. Native Americans have lived in the area for the past 10,000 years. An extensive collection of pre-reservation and early reservation artifacts, including clothing, pottery, tools, hunting equipment of Dakota and Lakota are on display. New frontier exhibits include information and artifacts about the explorers, traders, and pioneers. Firearms, clothing, and a fine collection of early photographs chronicling the period of contact with the Indians, the U.S. Army, river trade and mining are also displayed. There is a special Lewis and Clark/Spirit Mound Learning Center.

The year-round museum is located on the University of South Dakota campus at 414 Clark Street off Ratingen Street between Highway 50 by-pass and Highway 50 business. It is well worth a stop. It also sponsors an annual Lewis and Clark celebration.

Spirit Mound was a forbidden place for the local Indians. They believed the mound was inhabited by small large headed eighteen-inch tall "devils," and that they would attack and kill all who climbed the hill. On August 25, 1804 Lewis and Clark and other members of the Corps climbed the hill. They found no small devils, but as Clark recorded in his journal, they did get a view of a *most butifull landscape; Numerous herds of buffalow were seen feeding in various direction. . . .* Today one can also hike up the mound and stand at the top. The view is still beautiful, but the buffalo roam no more. The 320 acres that encompass the site are being restored to native prairie.

The mound is located about six miles north of Vermillion off Highway19. Interpretive panels relay information about the site. The experience is worth the short trip and walk to the top through the prairie.

LEWIS AND CLARK VISITOR CENTER/ CALUMET BLUFF – GAVINS POINT DAM, YANKTON, SOUTH DAKOTA

It was about two miles east of this center on August 25, 1804 that the Corps met the Yankton Sioux and held their council at Calumet Bluff. Much of the visitor center deals with Lewis and Clark and their meeting with the Indians. Other exhibits focus on the construction of the dam.

The year-round center is located west of Yankton, just across the dam on the south or Nebraska side of the Missouri River. If you want to camp the nearby Lewis and Clark State Recreation area is perfect. The Lewis and Clark Festival is held annually near the end of August. Re-enactors portray historic figures and events and, thus, make it much easier to understand. The center can also be reached from Nebraska Highway 121, north from Crofton.

Also located in Yankton is the Dakota Territorial Museum.

NIOBRARA STATE PARK, NEBRASKA

It was along the Niobrara River that Clark explored and found an abandoned Ponca Indian village. This is still a wild area much like it was when the Corps passed. Exhibits here focus on the local Indian history. Camping is available as are hiking trails.

The park is located off U.S. 12 west of Niobrara.

FORT RANDALL DAM VISITOR CENTER, PICKSTOWN, SOUTH DAKOTA

There is a small visitor center located on the north side of the dam. It has information on old Fort Randall and some on Lewis and Clark. The section of the river south of the dam to Niobrara State Park is still similar to what it was when the Corps passed through.

To the southeast on the Nebraska side of the river is Old Baldy, the site of the Corps' frustrating, but finally successful, attempt to capture a prairie dog. The site is about eight miles north of Lynch on signed local roads.

ATKA LAKOTA MUSEUM, CHAMBERLAIN, SOUTH DAKOTA

This year-round museum is one of the finest on the trail. The focus of it is on the culture, heritage and history of the Yankton and Teton Sioux. Displays on clothing, buffalo, tipis and tools are only some of the outstanding exhibits in the museum.

The museum is located two miles north off I-90 exit 263 on the grounds of the St. Joseph Indian School.

LEWIS AND CLARK KEELBOAT CENTER, I-90
INFORMATION VISITOR CENTER, CHAMBERLAIN, SOUTH DAKOTA

This unique rest area's structure includes Lewis and Clark displays with a focus on the keelboat and other aspects of their local Missouri River travel—Plum Creek Camp, Indian Encounters, Boatmen's Life and the Land of Plenty. Inside the building is a reconstructed keelboat that continues outside as a balcony. While the keelboat is wider than the one used by the Corps of Discovery, it is similar and one can stand on the stern and view the Missouri below.

This unusual information center is in a rest area on I-90 on the east side of the Missouri River at Chamberlain.

WEST BEND STATE RECREATION AREA, SOUTH DAKOTA

Here is the Grand Detour. The Missouri River makes a twenty-five mile loop and almost returns to the same spot. Clark and a few men crossed the neck of this loop on September 20, 1804. It was a little more than a mile by land, but it took the boats the whole day. The land was dry and the prairie full of prickly pear cactus. The overlook allows for a distant view of the area. This section of the river today, known as Lake Sharpe, is much wider and higher than when the Corps passed.

The site is thirty-five miles southeast of Pierre off State Road 34.

Pierre, South Dakota – Various sites.

It was in this area that Lewis and Clark met the Teton Sioux and had their somewhat hostile encounter. There are also other historic sites in the area.

South Dakota Cultural Heritage Center

This center traces the history of South Dakota from the Lakota culture to the coming of the railroad. One section focuses on the "Oyate Tawicoh'an" meaning "The Ways of the People." Life-size exhibits relate to the religious and social beliefs and life of the Indians. Another section, "Proving Up," chronicles the interactions of the native cultures with the non-native peoples from the mid-eighteenth century to the twentieth century. Other sections are devoted to displaying the museum's vast collection of artifacts and changing exhibits reflecting more recent themes. In addition to the life-sized dioramas, an extensive use of audio-visual presentations brings to life the history of South Dakota.

The center itself is an earth-mounded structure. It is reminiscent of both the earthen lodges of the Indians and sod structures and dugouts of the early settlers. It is located on Governors Drive overlooking the capitol building.

Fort Pierre Chouteau

The fort site is on the west side of the Missouri. It was built by the American Fur Company and was active from 1817-1855. It is an ongoing archaeological project of the state. Although it is not identified as a Lewis and Clark site, is was built near one of their camp site. The fort was one of the first fur trade forts that were established along the Missouri after the return of Lewis and Clark. This was the site visited by George Catlin, and Prince Maximilian and Bodmer.

It is located north of Pierre off Highway 1806.

Wakpa Sica Reconciliation Visitor Center is located near the fort site. It explains the meeting of the Tetons with Lewis and Clark and the history of the Sioux in the area.

Oahe Lake and Dam Visitor Center is a few miles farther north of Pierre on State Road 1806. Also in the general area is the Triple U Ranch with its large buffalo herd. It is northwest off highway 1806 between Lacy and Mission Ridge. The location and the buffalo were used in the film *Dances With Wolves*.

WEST WHITLOCK RECREATION AREA

The Arikara lived along the Missouri and were visited by Lewis and Clark in October, 1804. They lived in earth lodges and farmed. Today one can visit a replica lodge at the recreation area on the Missouri near Gettysburg, north of U.S. 212 on State Road 1804 on the east side of the Missouri. The site of the Lewis and Clark council with the Arikara was actually held north of Mobridge on the present-day Standing Rock Indian Reservation. The site has been flooded by the waters of Lake Oahe.

KLEIN MUSEUM, MOBRIDGE, SOUTH DAKOTA

History comes alive in this fine small museum. A major focus is on the culture of the Sioux and Arikara Indians who lived in the area when Lewis and Clark explored the region. Clothing, beadwork, pottery, tools and other artifacts are on display. A special gallery is devoted to Sitting Bull. Other room exhibits depict life in the area during the nineteenth and early twentieth century. The museum is located on West Highway 12 in Mobridge.

Across the Missouri River south of U.S. 121, four miles on Highway 1806 are the Sitting Bull and Sakakawea monuments.

FORT LISA REPLICA, KENAL, SOUTH DAKOTA

It was near here at original Fort Manuel Lisa that Sacagawea reportedly died in 1812.

BISMARCK/MANDAN, NORTH DAKOTA AREA

Here are found sites associated with the Mandan Indians, Lewis and Clark and the U.S. military.

FORT ABRAHAM LINCOLN STATE PARK AND ON A SLANT VILLAGE

On A Slant Indian Village was inhabited from about 1575 to 1781 by the Mandan Indians. The visitor center has exhibits and programs that depict life in a Mandan village, and today visitors can enter reconstructed earthen lodges. There are also exhibits on Lewis and Clark who camped in the area, and hands on activities for the young. Chief Big White/Sheheke was born in this village around 1760. The expedition noted the ruins of the village from their camp across the river.

For those interested in later military history, parts of Fort Abraham Lincoln have been reconstructed. It was from here that

General George Armstrong Custer and the 7th Calvary rode out to meet their fate at the Little Bighorn.

There is also a modern campground and picnic area along the river. The park is located about seven miles south of Mandan on route 1806.

THE NORTH DAKOTA HERITAGE CENTER

This center is the State Historical Society of North Dakota's showplace. Here one can explore the story of North Dakota's past through a variety of permanent eye-catching, artifact-filled exhibits that make you feel as if you were back in the periods being viewed. Exhibits start with the First People, An Era of Change, which includes Lewis and Clark, the Settlement period and the era of Bright Dreams and Hard Times. In addition, there other special and rotating exhibits.

The center is located on the Capital Complex off State Street in Bismarck.

DOUBLE DITCH INDIAN VILLAGE STATE HISTORIC SITE, NORTH DAKOTA

This is another Mandan village site. It had been inhabited from about 1675-1780 and was abandoned by the time Lewis and Clark passed. They marked its location on their map.

This site is located on Highway 1804 about seven miles north of Bismarck.

CROSS RANCH STATE PARK, NORTH DAKOTA

This former ranch is maintained by the Nature Conservancy. It is located along one of the last free flowing areas along the Missouri River in North Dakota. It includes the physical area where the prairie meets the river bottom. There is archaeological evidence of habitation for over 6,000 years. Hiking trails, and primitive camping facilities allow visitors to get a first-hand view of the river bottom area seen by the Corps of Discovery as they travel along the Missouri River.

The site is on River Road five miles southeast of Hensler, off North Dakota 1806.

NORTH DAKOTA LEWIS & CLARK VISITOR CENTER & FORT MANDAN HISTORIC SITE, WASHBURN, NORTH DAKOTA

This is one of the outstanding centers on the trail and is dedicated to the interpretation of the Lewis and Clark Expedition. While it tells the whole story, its focus is on the Indians they met and interacted with during the long winter of 1804-1805. It has displays and hands-on exhibits that would interest young and old alike. There are rotating exhibits with displays and artifacts from other museums. There is an impressive collection of Karl Bodmer printed artworks. He visited the area with Prince Maximilian in the 1830s and painted scenes along the Missouri River Valley.

Just down the road on the river bottom is the authentically recon-structed Fort Mandan and its own visitor center. A visit to the fort allows one to see what conditions and life was like for the Corps that long cold winter. Re-enactors and special events and programs help visitors better understand and get a more historically accurate expe-rience.

The Lewis and Clark Interpretive Center is located on U.S. Highway 83 and North Dakota 200A in Washburn.

FORT CLARK STATE HISTORIC SITE, NORTH DAKOTA

In 1822 some of the Mandans left their old villages and built a new village of earth lodges on a bluff on the west bank of the Missouri at the confluence of Chardon and Clark's Creek. They called this village "Mitu'tahakto's," meaning first or east village. In 1830-1831 the American Fur Company, hoping to expand its trade with the Mandans, built Fort Clark on the bluff a little south of the Mandan vil-lage. This village and fort were the subjects of many paintings by George Catlin and then Karl Bodmer during his 1833/4 stay in the region. In 1837 smallpox broke out and decimated the Mandans. In 1838 the Arikara moved into the abandoned village. In the 1850s cholera and the smallpox devastated the Arikara. The site was finally abandoned in 1862.

Today the archaeological remains of the village, fort and cemetery are protected and interpretive signs on the grounds help visitors visu-alize the site. The area is open seasonally. It is located north off 200A on an access road about fourteen miles west of Washburn.

KNIFE RIVER INDIAN VILLAGES NATIONAL
HISTORIC SITE, STANTON, SOUTH DAKOTA

This site was the home of the Hidatsa for about 500 years. The site has the remains of three villages. It was at the Awatixa Village that Lewis and Clark met Sacagawea and Toussaint Charbonneau in 1804. It was also the scene painted by George Catlin in 1832. The Big Hidatsa Village, Menetarra, can also be visited. The year-round muse-um is dedicated to interpreting and preserving the culture of the local Plains Indians. It has a fine collection of artifacts and an audio-visual program. There is a reconstructed earthen lodge and tipis. All that exists of the villages today are the extensive earthen depressions from each of the lodge sites. Walking along the interpretive paths one can listen to the singing birds and the blowing wind and easily imagine the sounds of the activity that once filled this historically important area. Take the path by the river and pass the area Catlin painted showing the children playing and swimming.

The Mandan village of Chief Sheheke (Big White) was located about five miles to the southeast where the power plant now is. The actual site of Fort Mandan where the Corps wintered has not been definitively identified, but it was on the east side of the Missouri about three miles downstream from Big White's village.

The Knife River site is located 2.5 miles off 200A on State Road 31 just past Stanton.

THREE AFFILIATED TRIBES MUSEUM, FORT BERTHOLD RESERVATION, NEW TOWN, NORTH DAKOTA

Take a step back in time. This museum focuses on the changes in the life and culture of the Mandan, Hidatsa, and Arikara. Exhibits show life in an earth lodge that was typical of the area before western contact. The impact of contact with the European Americans and, more recently, the harnessing and damming of the Missouri River that led to significant changes to the local tribes is examined through displays and artifacts.

The museum is located in New Town off Highway 23 on the Fort Berthold Indian Reservation.

LEWIS AND CLARK TRAIL MUSEUM, ALEXANDER, NORTH DAKOTA

This interesting museum in the small town of Alexander is housed in the old school. It has eight display rooms inside and more outside with some interesting exhibits on homestead articles, cars, machines, and Lewis and Clark.

It is not located along the river route, but is on the driving route on U.S. Highway 85 and Highway 200. It is a good example of what small towns can do for history.

CONFLUENCE OF THE MISSOURI RIVER AND THE YELLOWSTONE RIVER, FORT UNION AND FORT BUFORD

MISSOURI-YELLOWSTONE CONFLUENCE INTERPRETIVE CENTER

This is one of the newest visitor centers associated with Lewis and Clark. While wintering at Fort Mandan, Lewis and Clark learned of the Yellowstone River. They were told of its source west in the mountains and its large drainage system. However, their mission was to explore the Missouri and follow it to its headwaters. Lewis did note the significance of the junction and believed it would be a natural area for a trading post. During the return trip while at Travelers Rest it was decided that the Corps would be split. Lewis would return by way of the Missouri and Clark would find the route to the Yellowstone and take it back to the Missouri. The two parties rejoined at this point. As it turned out, Clark arrived first and had to move down river. Lewis arrived and finally caught up with Clark five days later August 12, 1806. Both Catlin and Bodmer painted scenes of the area in the 1830s.

The site is located on the north bank of the Missouri off Highway 1804 west of Buford.

FORT UNION TRADING POST NATIONAL HISTORIC SITE

John J. Astor's American Fur Company built Fort Union in 1827. It was the largest trading post on the Missouri River. A reproduction of the fort was built on the actual site after an extensive archaeological study was completed. Today Fort Union focuses on its role in the area fur trade that it controlled from 1827 to 1867. The fort was an oasis of civilization for visitors then, and it still is today. The massive white walls, large Bourgeois House, and tall corner blockhouses of the fort were immortalized in Bodmer's paintings. Today visitors can walk around the fort and museum and even view the fort from the area where Bodmer made his sketches.

The fort is located on Hwy 1806 about twenty-four miles southwest of Williston.

FORT BUFORD STATE HISTORIC SITE

A second fort, Fort Buford, was built in the area in 1866 for military purposes. It was de-activated in 1895. Its functions were to provide protection in the area, serve as a depot for supplies and soldiers during the later Indian campaigns, and also as a detainment area for Indians. Both Sitting Bull and Chief Joseph were imprisoned here for a short time. It has a small museum in one of the original fort buildings. The kitchen, mess, and barracks have been reconstructed. It is located upriver from the new confluence visitor center and downriver from Fort Union.

FORT PECK INDIAN RESERVATION

The Fort Peck Indian Reservation Cultural Center is located in Poplar on U.S. 2. It has information and displays about the Assiniboine and Sioux.

Farther west at the Fort Peck is the dam and the new Fort Peck Museum. It has information about the dam's construction and history of the area. Also nearby there is a wildlife preserve that has a small herd of buffalo and elk that were once numerous in the area.

GREY CLIFF PRAIRIE DOG TOWN STATE PARK, BIG TIMBER, MONTANA
The prairie dog was new to the Corps of Discovery. It was called the barking squirrel. Here you can observe and learn about these little animals in their natural habitat.
   On the return trip Clark's party stopped in the area for lunch. The park is located off the I-90 exit 377.

POMPEYS PILLAR NATIONAL HISTORIC LANDMARK, MONTANA
This large sandstone rock along the Yellowstone was a landmark to the Indians before it became associated with the expedition. Now it became significant to a new people and culture. This site has the only on site physical evidence left by the Corps. William Clark wrote his name and date, July 25, 1805, on the rock. He also named the massive sandstone rock "Pompys Tower," in honor of Sacagawea's son Jean Baptiste, whom Clark had nicknamed Pompy, Shoshoni for "little chief." When the journals were finally published in 1814 the name of the rock formation was changed. Today there is a visitor center that focuses on the site's history. Visitors can take the path up the rock, see Clark's name and date, and then continue up to the top for an impressive view of the area.
   The site is located off exit 23 on I-94.

WESTERN HERITAGE CENTER, BILLINGS, MONTANA
The focus of this center is on the history and cultures found in the Yellowstone River area. It has changing exhibits and audio-visual programs.
   This center is located at 2822 Montana Avenue near the University of Montana.

BOZEMAN, MONTANA

THE MUSEUM OF THE ROCKIES
This is one of the outstanding museums on the trail. It focuses on the history of Montana and the northern Rockies, including the prehistoric period and animals and fossils, local American Indians, early explorers, trappers and traders, emigrants, early modes of transportation and continues until recent times. Changing exhibits are also found. A living history farm is open in the summer.
   The museum is located on the Montana State University campus at South 7th and Kagy Boulevard.

GALLATIN COUNTY PIONEER MUSEUM

This is a fine local museum that has exhibits on local American Indians, early pioneers and the settlement of the area. It is located at 315 West Main Street in the old county jail.

MARIAS RIVER – DECISION POINT, LOMA, MONTANA

At this site at the mouth of the Marias River, the Corps was forced to spend nine days here trying to determine which river was the Missouri. The captains had not been told about this river that entered from the northwest. Nine days of exploration along both rivers were made before the Captains determined which river was the Missouri. The captains chose the correct river. Bodmer traveled to this area and made many paintings of the surrounding area.

Today visitors can visit a small Bureau of Land Management display explaining the significance of the site. It is located about eleven miles east of Fort Benton just off U.S. Highway 87.

FORT BENTON AREA, MONTANA

In October 1976 the section of the Missouri River from the Fred Robinson Bridge to Fort Benton was designated a "National Wild and Scenic River." This 149-mile section is now protected to remain in its natural, free-flowing state. Here the river valley remains much as it was, altered only by nature, as when Lewis and Clark and the Corps of Discovery ventured through it. The area was called the "White Cliffs or Rocks." The unique rock formations, known as LaBarge Rock, Citadel Rock, and Hole in the Wall, were all seen by Lewis and Clark. Today the section of the river, known as the Badlands and the White Cliffs are open during the summer months for float trips, canoeing and camping. Information packets are available through the BLM Lewistown Field Office. Local outfitters and guides are available by contacting the BLM in Fort Benton.

MUSEUM OF THE UPPER MISSOURI

In 1846 the American Fur Company established Fort Benton. It was located at the head of navigation on the Missouri River and was the last stop for steamboats. It became the main hub for trade in the area and west across the Rockies. The site of Fort Benton is an archaeological project and the fort is in the process of being reconstructed.

The exhibits focus on the early history of Montana and the northwest in the nineteenth century including the Lewis and Clark Expedition. The museum is located on the site of Fort Benton along the riverfront.

MUSEUM OF THE NORTHERN GREAT PLAINS

This museum focuses on the development of farming and the economy of the area. Exhibits center on farming practices, machinery, and the overall economy of the whole area. Of special interest is the "Hornaday Buffalo" exhibit. These six Montana buffalo were taken from one of the last wild herds, mounted, and then exhibited at the Smithsonian from 1887 to 1955. They were restored in 1996 and are now in the original poses and positions as when they were first displayed. The museum is located only a few blocks from old Fort Benton.

RIVER FRONT PARK

The park is located in what was the old rough section of town. It commemorates Fort Benton's history. Here can be found a large Lewis and Clark statute, a replica keelboat used in a movie about the fur trade era, and another statue of a dog well known to dog lovers. It is not of Seaman, but of Shep, who was faithful to his master even after his death. The riverfront area has undergone renovation in recent years. The Grand Union Hotel, built in 1880 has been restored in all her splendor.

GREAT FALLS, MONTANA AREA

This area played a significant part in the travels of Lewis and Clark. Lewis and Clark had been told of the Great Falls of the Missouri while they wintered with the Mandan and Hidatsa in 1804-5. Because of the number of falls the expedition had to portage over eighteen miles around them. The process took nearly a month. There are a variety of museums and sites along the river that are all worthy of a visit by Lewis and Clark enthusiasts.

LEWIS AND CLARK NATIONAL HISTORIC TRAIL INTERPRETIVE CENTER

This is one of the best centers on the whole trail. There is a fine audio-visual program, on site re-enactors, life-sized dioramas, and lots of hands-on displays for the young and old. The story of the journey from their departure, travel up the Missouri, portage at Great Falls, continuation and trip over the mountains, and finally their journey down to the Pacific is told with life-sized displays and exhibits of artifacts. Information about specific sites related to the portage is available in the center.

The center is located on the south shore of the river on Giant Springs Road off River Drive.

The center is also the home of the National Lewis and Clark Trail Heritage Foundation. This organization is dedicated to preservation and interpretation of the Lewis and Clark National Historic Trail. It is the perfect organization for anyone interested in Lewis and Clark.

GIANT SPRINGS HERITAGE STATE PARK AND THE FALLS

The Giant Springs was noted by Clark on June 18, 1805. He thought it was one of the largest fresh water springs in the world. The discharge from the spring is estimated at 6.4 million gallons per hour. Today, the spring is surrounded by lush green grass, tall trees, a picnic area and a fish hatchery. However, when Clark visited the springs there was nothing else, no trees or lush green grass.

The spring is located on Giant Springs Road a short distance from the Interpretive Center. Both the spring and the center are open all year round. Also along the river are various overlooks for some of the falls.

RYAN DAM PARK AT THE GREAT FALLS

Here is the Great Falls Lewis saw on June 13, 1805. The splendor of the falls has been greatly diminished by the construction of the Ryan Dam, but it is still interesting to see. Picnic grounds are now located on an island in the river below the falls. The dam and park can be accessed north of Great Falls from U.S. 87 on Morony Dam Road to Ryan Dam Road.

Other interpretive displays along the river are located at Rainbow Dam and Overlook, West Park, and the Broadwater Portage Overlook. Maps and literature are available at the Lewis and Clark National Historic Trail Interpretive Center.

C. M. RUSSELL MUSEUM

Charlie Russell was one of the great American western artists. He painted many of the subjects and events associated with the Lewis and Clark Trail. The museum holds many of his paintings and has other changing displays. Russell's home and studio are included in this facility.

This newly expanded museum is located at 400 13th Street North and is well worth the stop.

HOLTER LAKE RECREATION AREA,
GATES OF THE MOUNTAINS, MONTANA

Upper Holter Lake contains the area called "gates of the rocky mountains" by Lewis on July 19, 1805. Arrangements can be made for regular or chartered tours of the river to view the area. Camping and picnic areas are also available.

The area is about ten miles southwest of Craig on Missouri River Recreation Road.

BROADWATER COUNTY MUSEUM, TOWNSEND, MONTANA
This small county museum has exhibits and displays that focus on local Indians and early frontier life.
It is located at 133 North Walnut.

MONTANA HISTORICAL SOCIETY MUSEUM, HELENA, MONTANA
This fine museum houses a major exhibit focusing on the Lewis and Clark Expedition. Other galleries of general interest focus on the art of Charles M. Russell and on the early photographs of Yellowstone by F. Jay Haynes.
The museum is located in the Capitol Complex at Sixth and Roberts. Other large murals painted by Charles Russell and Edgar Paxson can be viewed in the House chamber and lobby of the State Capitol Building.

THREE FORKS, MONTANA
After traveling up the Missouri the Corps came to a range of hills that the river broke through and opened onto a small plains. There was no single channel, but a maze of rivers and channels. This site is where three rivers join to form into one. It is also the site where the Shoshoni were camping when the Hidatsa raided and captured Sacagawea.

MISSOURI HEADWATERS STATE PARK
Lewis named these rivers the Jefferson, Gallatin, and Madison. Today the area includes interpretive signs about Fort Rock, Lewis's Rock or Hill, and other aspects of the area. Picnicking, camping, hiking paths, and floating facilities are also found in the area. The immediate area probably looks much as it was when the Corps of Discovery passed.
The site is north of the Three Forks' I-90 exit.

HEADWATERS HERITAGE MUSEUM
This town museum has exhibits pertaining to local history and early pioneer life. Included in its artifacts is the anvil from the 1810 trading post at Three Forks.
It is located at 415 East Elm.

For those interested in staying in historic hotels, and looking for a nice place to relax, eat, and sleep, the old Sacajawea Hotel is located in Three Forks. The hotel dates back to the 1880s and the early railroad days.

VIRGINIA CITY AND NEVADA CITY STATE HISTORIC SITE, MONTANA

For those who might want to take a break from Lewis and Clark a side trip to Virginia City can be fun for the whole family. Montana has been active in restoring and preserving this site that is a symbol of Montana's western history. This was the location of the 1864 gold rush and is west of Ennis off U.S. 287 on State Road 287.

BEAVERHEAD ROCK STATE PARK, MONTANA

As the Corps worked its way farther up the Missouri and entered the Three Forks region Sacagawea began to recognize the area. The Corps knew they were close to the Shoshoni lands. However, it was the landmark known as Beaverhead Rock that told her she was only days away from her homeland. From the proper perspective the huge rocky formation looks like a swimming beaver. If the display in the Great Falls center is viewed, it is even easier to recognize the form. Look closely at it as you approach it from the north.

The landmark is located on Highway 41 about thirteen miles north of Dillon. An interpretive sign and overlook is south of the rock, but from this side the formation loses its "shape."

BEAVERHEAD COUNTY MUSEUM
CLARK'S LOOKOUT STATE PARK, DILLON, MONTANA

This is another of the fine local museums. Its focus is on the history of the area and it does include information about the expedition. Nearby is also a visitor center with information about the expedition and Lewis and Clark sites in the area.

The museum is located in the town at 15 South Montana.

Clark climbed this hill on August 17, 1804, to view the area and take some compass bearings. It is about a mile north of Dillon, west off State Road 91 just across the river.

CAMP FORTUNATE OVERLOOK

This is the area where Lewis and Clark had their meeting with Shoshoni Chief Cameahwait, Sacagawea's brother, and obtained some of the horses that were needed. The specific area is now flooded, but one can still get an overview. Picnicking, camping, and boating are available.

The overlook is off I-15 at the Clark Canyon Dam exit on Highway 324.

LEMHI PASS SITE, MONTANA/IDAHO

For those who want to experience both the exhilaration of reaching the Continental Divide and the western boundary of the Louisiana

Territory, but also the disappointment after seeing what lay ahead, just as Lewis did on August 12, 1805, the trip up to and over Lemhi Pass is a must. The dirt road west off Highway 324 has been improved and takes travelers on what for the most part, is a gentle climb towards the pass. However, as it gets nearer the pass itself the road gets narrower and steeper and is subject to the impacts of weather. It can be a little rough. For those who continue, the view from the top is breathtaking with mountain after mountain still facing you. There are interpretive signs at the pass. A short distance from the summit is Sacagawea Camp and the spring that is the source for Trail Creek that Lewis thought was the source of the Missouri River. The road west down the pass is steep for cars, but for the Corps of Discovery it was even more challenging. A few miles down the west slope is the campsite where Lewis reached the first waters running to the Pacific.

SALMON, IDAHO AND LEMHI COUNTY

This area was the homeland of the Lemhi Shoshoni and birthplace of Sacagawea. It was one of the major goals for Lewis and Clark. The captains knew they would need horses to cross the mountains and that the Shoshoni had horses. Cameahwait agreed to provide horses and also a guide, Old Toby, to guide them north and then across the Bitterroot Mountains.

LEMHI COUNTY HISTORICAL SOCIETY AND MUSEUM

This houses the nation's largest collection of Lemhi Shoshoni artic-facts. It is located on Highway 93, 210 Main Street.

SACAJAWEA INTERPRETIVE, CULTURAL AND EDUCATIONAL CENTER, SALMON, IDAHO

This is another of the newest centers associated with the expedition. The focus of this center is to tell the story of the Shoshoni people, their culture, and also the significant role they played in the success of the Lewis and Clark Expedition. A path leads to various outdoor exhibits depicting their way of life.

The center is located on Highway 28 at the eastern edge of the town.

RAVALLI COUNTY MUSEUM, HAMILTON, IDAHO

The Corps of Discovery traveled up the Bitterroot Valley following the general route of U.S. Highway 93 from the Idaho-Montana border to Lolo. It was here that they met the Salish Indians who provided more horses for the Corps. There are a variety of sites on or near the highway.

Another of the small worthwhile museums, it has exhibits on Lewis and Clark in the Bitterroot Valley, and the local Indians—Salish, Shoshoni, and Nez Perce.

The museum is located at 205 Bedford Street in the large old courthouse.

FORT OWENS STATE PARK & HISTORIC
ST. MARY'S MISSION, STEVENSVILLE, MONTANA

St. Mary's Mission was founded by Father DeSmet in 1841. Exhibits focus on the culture and history of the local Indians—Salish, Kootenai, Flathead, and Blackfeet.

The mission museum is located at 315 Charles Street.

TRAVELERS REST STATE PARK, LOLO, IDAHO

This is where the expedition turned west to follow the old Nez Perce trade and hunting route across the Bitterroot Mountains to the Clearwater River. The site was a camping ground for the expedition on the journey both out and back. Here they recruited September 9-11, 1805, to prepare for the hard journey ahead of them. Here too they rested after crossing the mountains from west to east June 30-July 3, 1806. It was also here that the captains decided to split their party. Lewis would take the Indian trail east and then explore the Marias River, while Clark would return and find a route to the Yellowstone and explore it. They were to rejoin at the junction of the Yellowstone and Missouri rivers on August 1, 1806.

An interpretive sign at the intersection of U.S. 93 and U.S. 12 commemorates the site and events. Travelers Rest State Park is located just off Highway 93 on Mormon Creek Road. Recent archaeological work has identified the latrine and main cooking sites. The interpretive center is focused on the Corps stay in the area and there is an ongoing development program for the site.

LOLO HOT SPRINGS / LOLO PASS
VISITORS CENTER & LOLO TRAIL, IDAHO

The hot springs that the members of the Corps of Discovery bathed in are now commercially developed. Some establishments, such as The Fort-Lewis and Clark Center, have displays devoted to the Lewis and Clark Expedition. The site is located on U.S. Highway 12 about twenty-five miles west of Lolo.

LOLO PASS VISITOR CENTER & LOLO TRAIL

Another of the centers redeveloped for the bicentennial, The Lolo Pass Visitor Center focuses on the Lewis and Clark experience across the Lolo Trail, the flight of the Nez Perce during the 1877 war, and the

Wayne Cornell

Lolo Pass Visitors Center

area in general. For Lewis and Clark this crossing itself was truly a life and death struggle. The weather was cold, it snowed, and providing food for all the members and horses was extremely difficult. For the brave and hearty, the trail follows U.S. Forest Road 500, also known as the Lolo Motorway. It is a seasonal unimproved single lane dirt road that closely approximates or parallels the original Nez Perce Trail. Originally it was only a foot and animal trail along the mountain ridge tops. Because of the nature of the road you should check with the Forest Service in the center for information about traveling the road and sites associated with Lewis and Clark. There has even been some talk of restricting travel on the road during the bicentennial. For the real Lewis and Clark fans you may want to hike or ride the trail on horseback.

The center is located on U.S. Highway 12, west of Lolo, at the Montana/Idaho state line.

POWELL RANGER STATION, IDAHO

The expedition had a terrible time crossing the Bitterroot Mountains in 1805. Lack of sufficient food was only one of the problems the Corps faced. The name given to a creek near their camp reflected their hardship and solution. It was called "Colt Kill Creek." Exhibits in the station explain their stop and experiences in crossing the mountains.

The station is located about twelve miles west of Lolo Pass just off U.S. 12.

WEIPPE DISCOVERY CENTER, WEIPPE, IDAHO

Weippe Prairie is at the western end of the Lolo Trail. This is where Clark's advance party met the Nez Perce after the Corps' terrible crossing of the Bitterroots. Interpretive signs relate to the Nez Perce culture and their contact with Clark.

The discovery center has information about the Nez Perce and also Lewis and Clark. It is located on State Road 11 and Wood Street.

LONG CAMP SITE
NEZ PERCE NATIONAL HISTORIC PARK, KAMIAH, IDAHO

A small interpretive sign explains the Corps stay near here on their return journey. They waited weeks in the area for the snow to melt in the mountains. The sign is on U.S. 12 about a mile east of Kamiah.

CLEARWATER HISTORICAL MUSEUM
AND CANOE CAMP, OROFINO, IDAHO

It is near this area that, after following the Nez Perce or Lolo Trail, Lewis and Clark again came to a river, the Clearwater, which enabled them to continue west by water to the Pacific.

This is another of the fine small local museums. Its focus is on the history of the Clearwater River basin, including Nez Perce culture, Lewis and Clark, and mining and logging.

Situated along the Clearwater River is the Canoe Camp site where the members of the Corps of Discovery learned a new method of building canoes. They camped here from September 26, 1805 to October 7, 1805. It is located four miles west of Orofino on U.S. 12.

NEZ PERCE NATIONAL HISTORICAL PARK, SPALDING, IDAHO

The mission of the park is to protect and interpret the thirty-eight sites under its jurisdiction that have "exceptional value to the Nez Perce people and nation as a whole." The main museum houses collections of tribal artifacts and photographs relating to the Nez Perce culture, the Lewis and Clark Expedition, the fur trade era, the Spalding Mission, mining and logging, and the Nez Perce War of 1877.

The year-round museum is located about eleven miles east of Lewiston on the south side of the Clearwater River on U.S. 95, 8 1/2 miles southeast towards Spalding. (Some of the Nez Perce sites, such as Long Camp, Weippe Prairie, and Canoe Camp that are under the jurisdiction of the Nez Perce tribe are also related to Lewis and Clark.)

NEZ PERCE COUNTY HISTORICAL
SOCIETY AND MUSEUM, LEWISTON, IDAHO

This fine small museum has exhibits depicting the development of Nez Perce County, including Lewis and Clark's influence. It also has some hands-on exhibits for children.

The museum is located on 3rd Street a few blocks north of Highway 12.

Pioneer Park at 2nd and 5th streets has some interpretive signs on the expedition.

APPALOOSA MUSEUM AND HERITAGE CENTER, MOSCOW, IDAHO

When Lewis and Clark met the Nez Perce in 1805 they noted the fine spotted horse the Nez Perce bred. While off the Lewis and Clark Trail, this museum is included because of its focus on these spotted horses noted by the expedition and later called the Appaloosa.

The center is located west on Pullman Road as it nears the Idaho/Washington state line.

LEWIS AND CLARK DISCOVERY CENTER, CLARKSTON, WASHINGTON

This interpretive center has information and displays about the local Nez Perce, Chief Timothy, and the meeting of the Nez Perce and Lewis and Clark.

It is located in Clarkston off U.S. 12 at 721 6th Street.

LEWIS AND CLARK TRAIL STATE PARK, WAITSBURG, WASHINGTON

About five miles east on U.S. 12 is the Lewis and Clark Trail State Park. This forested area on the Touchet River was what the Corps wrote of and camped by. Interpretive signs tell about the area and the 1806 return journey through the area. Picnic and camping sites are available in the area.

The park is located on U.S. 12 about five miles east of Waitsburg.

FORT WALLA WALLA, WALLA WALLA, WASHINGTON

Lewis and Clark did not pass this area, but the museum has displays and exhibits on them. The museum is comprised of a number of original, reconstructed and modern buildings. They focus on the early settlement and economic development of southeastern Washington and they house some very interesting displays about the area.

The museum is located at 755 Myra Road.

SACAJAWEA INTERPRETIVE CENTER
AND STATE PARK, PASCO WASHINGTON

This park is at the confluence of the Snake and Columbia rivers. This is where the expedition spent two days hunting, repairing equipment and meeting with local Indians. Here you too can enjoy a picnic as you journey west along the rivers towards the Pacific. The small interpretive center has an outstanding collection of stone and bone artifacts of the Columbia Basin Indians, and also exhibits that highlight the role of Sacajawea to the Lewis and Clark Expedition. The park is located off U.S. 12 on Sacajawea Park Road

Also north of the area on Lake Sacajawea on the Snake River is the Ice Harbor Lock & Dam which also has displays on Lewis and Clark.

HAT ROCK STATE PARK. OREGON

While going down the Columbia River on October 19, 1805, Clark noted a geological structure near the river and called it "Hat Rock." When visiting the park one can easily see why the rock was properly named. There is a picnic area in the park. Unfortunately, the site is being "housed in" on a couple of sides.

The park is located nine miles east of Umatilla, off U.S. 730.

MARYHILL MUSEUM OF ART
CELILO FALLS OVERLOOK, WISHAM, WASHINGTON

Lewis and Clark encountered many different Indians on their trip down the Columbia River. In their journals they described many Indian artifacts. This museum houses a fine art collection and outstanding examples of baskets, stone tools, and other Indian artifacts of the Columbia Plateau and Pacific Northwest.

The museum is located off Washington State Road 14 east of Wisham at 35 Maryhill Museum Drive.

From this overlook on highway 14 one can see the former site of the Celilio Falls, the Great Falls of the Columbia. Since 1957 these falls have been inundated by the waters of The Dalles Dam. The Corps was forced to portage around part of them. The site was important to the local Indians for its fishing and also as a trading area for the Indian above and below the falls.

THE DALLES, OREGON

When Lewis and Clark came down the Columbia River there were a number of falls and rapids. Near The Dalles were also the Short Narrows and the Long Narrows. They were a few miles down river from Celilo Falls. As with Celilo Falls, both The Short Narrows and the Long Narrows are now under the water behind The Dalles Dam.

The Lewis and Clark Rock Fort site with its interpretive sign is located north off exit 83 on I-84 near the river. The Corps camped there after making it through the Narrows, and again in 1806 on their return journey.

Nearly a half century later The Dalles would also play a significant role in the story of the Oregon Trail and the settlement of Oregon and Washington.

The Columbia River Gorge Discovery Center & Wasco County Historical Museum

This museum complex provides visitors with exhibits on a variety of themes. The focus of the center is the Columbia River Gorge and local history. The history of the gorge is examined starting with its formation, how the Indians and their cultures related to it, the period of exploration including Lewis and Clark, then how those came to settle the area interacted with it, and finally the impact of how they tried to harness it and the river's future uses. There are excellent exhibits about the different Indians who inhabited the area who were met by the Corps of Discovery. The museum is also working with state-of-the-art equipment to locate Lewis and Clark campsites along their route. Many of the outdoor exhibits relate to the Oregon Trail period when The Dalles was the end of the wagon route.

The center and museum is off I-84 at exit 82 near the mouth of Chenoweth Creek.

Columbia River Gorge Interpretive Center, Stevensville Washington

The focus of this center is to preserve, conserve, exhibit and interpret the cultural and natural history of the Columbia River Gorge. Many of the river gorge displays center on the Native American cultures that lived there, the river as a route for Lewis and Clark and later Oregon bound emigrants.

The center is located off I-84 exit 44 across the Bridge of the Gods, east a few miles on Washington State Road 14.

Bonneville Lock & Dam Visitor Centers Oregon & Washington

There are visitor centers on both the Washington and Oregon sides of the river at the Bonneville Dam. Each has exhibits about the river, fish, the workings of the dam and locks, and also about Lewis and Clark. On the Washington side just west of the visitor complex is the Fort Cascades Historic Site. On the grounds is the site of an old Chinook Indian village that may have been visited by Lewis and Clark.

They are located in Bonneville off I-90 and in North Bonneville off Washington Highway 14.

BEACON ROCK STATE PARK, WASHINGTON

As the Corps traveled farther down the Columbia it came to a large rocky formation on the north side of the river. It was here that they began to notice the tidal nature of the river. They knew they were now close to completing their journey to the Pacific. Clark named the formation Beacon Rock.

Today a state park has been developed around the rock. It has a picnic area and hiking trails. It is even possible to go to the top of it. The park is located off Washington Highway 14, eight miles west of Stevenson, or about thirty-five miles east of Vancouver.

COLUMBIA RIVER GORGE, OREGON SIDE
MULTNOMAH FALLS AND ROOSTER ROCK, OREGON

These are two other stops travelers can make today. Multnomah Falls is located at an I-84 rest stop. There is no record of the Corps stopping there, but they must have seen the falls. Rooster Rock State Park is also on 1-84 a few miles farther west at exit 25. The Corps stopped and camped at the rock. Today there is a large picnic area, swimming beach and boat launch ramp.

OREGON HISTORICAL SOCIETY MUSEUM, PORTLAND, OREGON

Portland has developed into a major seaport for the United States at the junction of the Willamette River and the Columbia. It was not until their return journey that the Corp discovered the mouth of the Willamette. Yet, in a sense, Portland signifies one of the main goals of the expedition—the expansion of U.S. trade in the west and its extension to Asia. Portland does that today.

The Oregon Historical Society Museum has a wide variety of displays and exhibits that tell the story of all of Oregon's history and development.

The museum is located near the downtown area at 1200 Southwest Park Street.

FORT VANCOUVER NATIONAL
HISTORIC SITE, VANCOUVER, WASHINGTON

Fort Vancouver itself did not exist when Lewis and Clark passed through the area. In 1825 the British Hudson's Bay Company built the fort. The fort's establishment reflects one of the primary motives that originally caused Jefferson to send the Lewis and Clark Expedition, namely the desire to control the fur trade in the west before the British could gain complete control over the area. Today you can visit the partially reconstructed fort. It was started in 1964 and is an ongoing project. While its focus is on the post-Lewis and Clark period of fur trade, it provides a wealth of information about the conflict between the British and the Americans on their overlapping claims in the Northwest/Oregon territory.

The fort is located east off the I-5 at exit 1c on East Mill Plain Boulevard.

The Pacific Ocean and Coast

This was one of the goals of the Lewis and Clark Expedition. Here there are numerous museums and interpretive centers that relate to the Corps of Discovery.

Fort Canby State Park, Ilwaco, Washington

Within the park boundaries is the Lewis and Clark Interpretive Center. The fort was established during the Civil War and received its name in 1875. The fort was deactivated at the end of WWII. The area itself was named Cape Disappointment in 1788 by the English sea captain John Meares. Today the interpretive center has a multi-media program about the journey and displays about the different individuals, their foods, medical treatments, daily life and contributions of the whole journey. Other exhibits relate to the fort's more recent historic periods. Camping and picnic sites are available.

The fort is located two miles southwest of Ilwaco, Washington off highway 101. Also in the vicinity are two other parks. **Lewis and Clark Campsite State Park** is where the Corps camped from November 15-24, 1805. Here a poll was taken to determine where to build their winter camp. This is the first recorded "vote" by a woman, an Indian, and a black person in American history. Also at the **Fort Columbia State Park Interpretive Center**, in addition to its primary exhibits on coast artillery, is a large exhibit about the Chinook Indians. Both parks are located on U.S. 101 southeast of Chinook.

Fort Clatsop National Memorial - Lewis and Clark National and State Historical Park, Astoria, Oregon

Here is the reconstructed replica of Fort Clatsop, the winter quarters for the Corps of Discovery in 1805-06. By visiting both the center and the replica you can get a better feel for the life and hardship the Corps faced during that winter. There are excellent exhibits and an audio-visual presentation in the center that tells the story of the stay here the winter of 1805-06 and their interaction with the local Indians. The rooms in the fort are appropriately furnished as they might have been and the living history programs help interpret the site and provide a variety of demonstrations of frontier skills. The spring site and area where the canoes were kept can also be seen.

The fort is located about four miles southwest of Astoria off business U.S. Highway 101.

Fort Astoria was built by John Astor's Pacific Fur Company in 1811. It was located near where the expedition camped before building Fort Clatsop. A small portion of Fort Astoria has been rebuilt. This was the first American establishment in the Oregon Country and helped to establish our claim to the area. It is located at 14th and Exchange.

Also nearby is the Clatsop County Historical Society located at 1618 Exchange Streets.

There are additional site areas along the Oregon Pacific Coast off U.S. 101.

Seaside was the site of a small Clatsop village visited by members of the expedition. Near here they established the Salt Camp where they undertook the task of making salt during the winter of 1805-06. The Salt Works Memorial with its interpretive display is on the south end of the Promenade on Lewis and Clark Way.

Tillamook Hook and Clark's Point is in Ecola State Park. Here Clark climbed the hill and had a spectacular view of the Pacific and surrounding area.

Near Ecola Creek in Cannon Beach members of the expedition, including Sacagawea, came to see the great fish (whale) that had washed ashore. Clark traded for about 300 pounds of blubber and a few gallons of whale oil.

GRINDERS STAND, HOHENWALD, TENNESSEE

The listing of historic sites would not be complete without this one. Whether by his own hand or someone else's, this is where Lewis died on October 11, 1809. A monument marks his gravesite. Today you can visit a reconstruction of Grinders Inn, read about Lewis's life and death, and see his grave.

The site is located on the Natchez Trace Parkway about 70 miles southwest of Nashville, Tennessee.

In addition to these museums, centers and sites, there are numerous other highway signs, small museums, and new ones being developed. Be sure to keep your eyes open and take advantage of them. They all deepen your understanding, broaden your mind, and give you a chance to get in a little exercise. Take advantage of all of them.

Additional reading

Since the approach of the Lewis and Clark Bicentennial, it has been almost impossible to keep up with the huge number and variety of publications dealing with Lewis and Clark that have been produced. Some are re-prints of older editions that were out of print a few years ago, but many are new. Some focus on recently discovered materials, specific individuals, or specific aspects of their journey, while others have colorful photographs taken along the route as it exists today; and, thankfully, some are appropriate for students and schools. There are, however, a number of books that pre-date the bicentennial celebration that deserve your attention because of their scholarship and interest that they spurred.

Stephen Ambrose's *Undaunted Courage* has probably sparked more interest in Lewis and Clark in recent years than any of the other books available. His book covers the story of the expedition along with the historic background. It is his style, and the enthusiasm he shows, that makes this volume exciting and a must for anyone starting to study Lewis and Clark. Another book, which in a sense complements it, is his *Lewis & Clark, Voyage of Discovery*, published by National Geographic. It includes some of the same materials, but also has extensive photos along the route by Sam Abell.

Even though it is over fifty years old, Bernard DeVoto's edited edition of *The Journals of Lewis and Clark* is one of the best single volume versions of Lewis and Clark's journals. DeVoto provides the reader with both historic background information and then a journey to the Pacific and back is depicted by using the journal entries of members of the expedition. He relied primarily on the entries of Lewis and Clark, but does include some of those from other members. His work was based on the 1904-05 Rueben Gold Thwaites edition of Lewis and Clark's journals, using more than a third of the materials. Thus, even though a daily approach to the journey was used, DeVoto noted that he did not include entries for every single day.

As noted before, the earliest published account of the journey was by Patrick Gass. *The Journals of Patrick Gass: A Member of the Lewis and Clark Expedition*, edited by Carol Lynn MacGregor is an expanded version of his journal that includes additional documents and information relating to Gass's life a number of years after the expedition. While not as detailed as the journals of Lewis and Clark, it should still be considered as a basic reading.

Roy E. Appleton's *Lewis and Clark's Transcontinental Exploration, 1804-1806* was originally published in 1975 as Volume XIII of *The National Survey of Historic Sites and Buildings*. This reprinted volume will provide the readers and travelers with important site information. It includes forty-two historic sites identified with Lewis and Clark. The sites are associated with the National Park Service, National Historic Landmarks or other historic sites. Most of them are of specific locations, such as the Sergeant Floyd Monument and Lemhi Pass, but some relate to general areas such as the Lolo Trail, about 160 miles in the Bitterroot Mountains, or to the Missouri River Breaks, the approximately 140-mile corridor along the Missouri River known as the Badlands and White Cliffs sections. Appleton provides information about the site's location, its relation to the expedition, and its state today. Additional site locations can be found in the Historical Background section. However, one must remember that the information is now over a quarter of a century old and some things have changed. In addition to his examination of the historic sites, he provides historic background information about the whole topic including Jefferson, the Louisiana Purchase and the expedition. In fact, there are more pages devoted to the historic background than to the historic sites.

One of the goals set by Jefferson was to find out information about the Indians who inhabited the newly acquired territories. For those who are interested in the ethnic aspects of the Lewis and Clark Expedition, James Rhonda's *Lewis and Clark among the Indians* is the book. Here the focus is not on the journey itself, nor a description of the cultures of the Indians, but rather on the contacts that the Corps made with the Indians at various times during the journey. Included are an examination of those contacts and an explanation of the different cultural basis for the relationships and interactions that occurred between the captains, other Corps members, and the various tribal groups. It examines the contacts from both sides, the description of which was not common at that time. It is this approach that makes this book so worthy of your time.

It has often been noted that for a journey so long in time and distance, and one faced with such a wide variety of hazards from the weather, geography, wild animals, hours of hard labor, malnutrition, disease, and accidents, it is a wonder that the expedition succeeded and almost everyone returned in reasonably good health. Eldon G. Chuinard's *Only One Man Died: The Medical Aspects of the Lewis and Clark Expedition* will provide the reader with an examination and explanation of that aspect of the journey. Out of print until just recently, this volume provides valuable information and insight into the medical knowledge and practices of the time and reviews the great variety of health problems endured daily and the treatments given to the members of the expedition and also to the Indians. One can acquire a true appreciation for their daily progress, endurance and achievements. Considering all this information, the question arises "Could we so endure today?"

For those who really want to delve into the whole Lewis and Clark experience the present series, *The Journals of the Lewis and Clark Expedition*, edited by Gary Moulton is a must. The work was started in the mid-1980s and is now complete. It is a thirteen-volume work that includes the various journals, and field notes, charts and graphs and associated maps. Volume I is a compilation of the various maps, Volumes 2-8 comprise the journey starting when Lewis left Pittsburgh on August 31, 1803 until the return to St. Louis on September 26, 1806. Volumes 9-11 include all the known diaries of the enlisted men by Ordway, Floyd, Gass, and Whitehouse. Volume 12 is devoted to scientific listing and study of the various plants recorded, and Volume 13 is an index. Throughout the series Moulton's annotations provide extensive additional information. While the original series was published in cloth, a more economical series in now available in paper. For the average reader the sheer number of volumes may seem to be almost too much, but it will provide the readers with much more insight into the expedition than a single volume or other series.

However, if one is looking for an even less expensive series, there is a new facsimile reproduction of the 1904-05 Reuben Gold Thwaites eight-volume *Original Journals of the Lewis and Clark Expedition.* This series includes a map volume and others which are devoted to the journals of the captains and many of the journals of the enlisted men. Missing because of discoveries in the past century are those of Lewis's Ohio River journal, Ordway's, parts of Clark's field notes, and portions of Whitehouse's journal. Gass was not included by choice since it was already widely available. This series does provide a good framework and a basis for seeing how history can "change" over time.

For those who can read topographical maps and want to examine the route of the expedition today, but can't leave their home, or for those who want to really follow the route, the new three-volume set, *Lewis and Clark Trail: A Cartographic Reconstruction*, by Martin Plamondon II, will provide hours of enjoyment and much useful information. I found it fascinating both in relation to Clark's original work and also to that of the author's. The maps represent the whole journey starting from Camp Dubois. Volume I goes up the Missouri to Fort Mandan. Volume II continues from Fort Mandan up the Missouri, then along the land route to the Clearwater and down the water route to the confluence of the Snake and the Columbia, Volume III will complete the rest of the journey down the Columbia to the Pacific and also the return overland routes once the captains split the Corps at Travelers Rest with Lewis heading north to explore the Marias and Clark returning southeast to follow the Yellowstone. The maps show both the present course of the rivers and the course of the rivers as mapped by Lewis and Clark. The maps are fairly narrow and usually include only about one to five miles on either side of the rivers or route. Sometimes this makes it somewhat difficult to use with ordinary maps. However, also included are the campsites as can best be determined and short journal entries about the general area or daily happenings as the Corps passed along that particular area.

For those interested in other documents that shed light onto the expeditions, there is the 1962 edition of Donald Jackson's ed. *Letters of the Lewis and Clark Expedition with Related Documents*. It includes information about 428 additional letters and documents that complement the published journal. Many of these had been unpublished at the time. More recently is James Holmberg's *Dear Brother: Letters of William Clark to Jonathan Clark* that includes forty-seven more letters and other documents. They provide some additional information and insights and also confirm many of the previous ideas about Clark and the expedition. Many of Holmberg's explanations are longer than the originals. Both these books provide excellent additional information that will help in understanding not only the expedition, but also its history and a clearer understanding of the peoples involved.

Two recent publications that make extensive use of colorful photographs similar to the National Geographic publication is the Ken Burns and Dayton Duncan's book, *Lewis & Clark, The Journey of the Corps of Discovery, An Illustrated History*. It was published to complement the Ken Burn's PBS documentary program on Lewis and Clark. The other is *The Saga of Lewis and Clark into the Uncharted West* by Thomas and Jeremy Schmidt.

Two books appropriate for middle/high school students and teachers are Janis Herbert's *Lewis and Clark for Kids* and my *Following Lewis and Clark's Track*. Each provides basic information about the expedition and has activities for young people. *Lewis and Clark for Kids* have related activities and projects, while *Following Lewis and Clark's Track* has activities based on the topics and information provided. Addition projects or topics for study are also provided that reinforce and expand on the materials discussed. New from Carol MacGregor, are two books for youngsters that deal with the expedition: *Shoshoni Pony* and *Lewis and Clark's Bittersweet Crossing*.

For those interested in basic information about the journey of Prince Maximilian and would also like to see more of the works of Bodmer, *Karl Bodmer's America* will provide more than enough information with lots of paintings and sketches.

For those interested in driving along the trail I have listed a number of pamphlets in the bibliography some of which have recently been published that will be very helpful. Barbara Fifer's *Along the Trail with Lewis and Clark* provides narrow maps that show the trail, historic sites, and modern paved highways with notations from the journals. Also included are other places to visit, places to stay or eat and other helpful information—a most useful edition for those traveling today.

For those brave enough to canoe down the Missouri through the White Cliffs there is Glenn Monahan and Chanler Biggs' *Montana's Wild and Scenic Upper Missouri River*. Couple that with the Missouri River maps available through the Bureau of Land Management and the traveler will have an almost mile-by-mile approach to the river and its history. Add a good outfitter and the canoe trip will be truly enjoyable.

All these books will enable both the armchair traveler and the trail traveler to experience the Lewis and Clark Trail in a manner that is both exciting and informative. For those considering delving further into different aspects of the trail, another great source for additional readings are the bibliographies of the books mentioned above. These provide a goldmine of other primary and secondary source materials to examine, especially if a specific topic has caught your interest.

And, for those who would like to become life long readers of Lewis and Clark, membership in the Lewis and Clark Trail Heritage Foundation will provide the quarterly publication *We Proceeded On*.

This is full of new articles and information related to all aspects of the Lewis and Clark Expedition, and also about the organization and local chapters. That will keep the reader looking forward to always being able to "Proceed On."

Happy Reading! Happy Traveling! Happy Trails!

Bibliography

Books & booklets

Albers, Everett C. *The Saga of Seaman*. Bismarck, ND: Northern Lights, North Dakota Press, 2002.

Alinder, James, ed. Carleton E. Watkins, *Photographs of the Columbia River and Oregon*. The Friends of Photography, Inc., 1979.

Ambrose, Stephen E. *Undaunted Courage*. New York: Simon & Schuster, 1997.

Ambrose, Stephen E. *Lewis & Clark, Voyage of Discovery*. Washington, DC: National Geographic Society, 1998.

Anderson, Irving W. *A Charbonneau Family Portrait*. Fort Clatsop Historical Association, 1988.

Appleman, Roy E. *Lewis & Clark Transcontinental Exploration 1804-1806*. Washington: DC, United States Department of the Interior, National Park Service, 1975.

Betts, Robert B. *In Search of York: The Slave Who Went to the Pacific with Lewis and Clark*. Colorado Associated University Press, 1985.

Bodmer, Karl. *Karl Bodmer's America*. Lincoln: University of Nebraska Press & Joslyn Art Museum, 1984.

Brodie, Fawn McKay. *Thomas Jefferson, An Intimate History*. New York: W. W. Norton & Co., Inc., 1974.

Catlin, George. *Letters and Notes on the Manners, Customs and Conditions of the North American Indians, Vols I & II*. Dover Publications, Inc., 1973.

Chuinard, Eldon G. *Only One Man Died: The Medical Aspects of the Lewis and Clark Expedition*. Glendale, California: Arthur Clark Company, 1980.

Coues, Elliott, ed. *The Expedition of Zebulon Montgomery Pike*. Minneapolis: Ross and Haine, 1965.

DeVoto, Bernard, ed. *The Journals of Lewis and Clark*. New York: Houghton Mifflin Co., 1997.

Dillon, Richard H. *Meriwether Lewis, A Biography*. Coward-McCann, 1965.

Duncan, Dayton and Ken Burns. *Lewis & Clark. The Journey of the Corps of Discovery, An Illustrated History*. New York: Alfred A. Knopf, 1997.

Fifer, Barbara & Vicky Soderberg. *Along the Trail with Lewis and Clark*, Great Falls: Montana Magazine, 1998.

Fisher, Ron, and John Hess. *Into The Wilderness*. Washington, DC: National Geographic Society, 1978.

Gass, Patrick, *A Journal of the voyages and travels of a corps of discovery, under the command of Capt. Lewis and Capt. Clarke*. Pittsburgh: David M'Keehan, 1807.

Gilbert, Bil. *The Trailblazers*. New York: Time-Life Books, 1973.

Hassrick, Royal B. *The George Catlin Book of American Indians*. New York: Promontory Press, 1977.

Herbert, Janis. *Lewis and Clark for Kids*. Chicago: Chicago Review Press, 2000.

Hill, William E. *Following Lewis and Clark's Track*. Independence, Missouri: Oregon-California Trails Association, 2000.

Holmberg, James, ed. *Dear Brother: Letters of William Clark to Jonathan Clark*. New Haven:Yale University Press / Filson Historical Society, 2002.

Jackson, Donald, ed. *Letters of the Lewis and Clark Expedition with related Documents*. Urbana: University of Illinois Press, 1962.

Keats, John. *Eminent Domain, the Louisiana Purchase and the Making of America*. New York: Charterhouse, 1973.

Lewis, Meriwether, *History of the expedition under the command of Captains Lewis and Clark*...Volumes I & II. New York: Bradford and Inskeep and Abm. H. Inskeep, 1814.

Lewis, Meriwether and William Clark. *The Journals of the Lewis and Clark Expedition*, Vol. 1-13. Edited by Gary E. Moulton. Lincoln, Nebraska: The University of Nebraska Press, 1983-2001.

Lewis, Meriwether. *The Expedition of Lewis and Clark, Vols. I & II*. March of America Facsimile Series No.56. Ann Arbor: University Microfilm, Inc., 1966.

MacGregor, Carol Lynn, ed. *The Journals of Patrick Gass, Member of the Lewis and Clark Expedition*. Missoula: Mountain Press Publishing Co., 1997.

McCracken, Harold. *George Catlin and the Old Frontier*. New York: Bonanza Books, 1959.

Monahan, Glenn and Chanler Biggs. *Montana's Wild and Scenic Upper Missouri River*. Anaconda, Montana: Northern Rocky Mountains Books, 1997.

Norona, Delf. *Moundsville's Mammoth Mound*. West Virginia Archeology Society, 1997.

Peterson, Donald A. *Early Pictures of the Falls. Great Falls: The Portage Route Chapter*, Lewis and Clark Trail Heritage Foundation, 1998.

Peterson, Merrill D. *Thomas Jefferson & the New Nation*. New York: Oxford University Press, 1970.

Plamondon II, Martin. *Lewis and Clark Trail Maps, A cartographic Reconstruction, Vol. I*. Pullman, WA: Washington State University Press, 2000.

_____. *Lewis and Clark Trail Maps, A Cartographic Reconstruction, Vol. II*. Pullman, Washington: Washington State University Press, 2001.

Ryan, Mary C. *The Louisiana Purchase*. Washington, DC: National Archives and Records Administration,. 1987.

Rhonda, James P. *Lewis and Clark Among the Indians*. Lincoln: University of Nebraska Press, 1984.

Schmidt, Jerry & Thomas. *The Saga of Lewis and Clark into the Uncharted West*. New York: DK Publishing,1999.

Talbot, Agnes Vincen. *The Truth about Sacajawea*. Jackson, Wyoming: Grandview Publishing Co., 1997.

Thwaites, Reuben Gold, ed. *Original Journals of the Lewis and Clark Expedition, 1804-1806*, Vol.1-8. New York: Antiquarian Press LTD, 1959.

Thwaites, Reuben Gold, ed. *Maximilian Travels in North America 1832-34, Early Western Travels, 1746-1846*, Vols. 22, 23, 24 & 25. The Arthur H. Clark Co., 1904.

Truettner, William H. *The Natural Man Observed: A Study of Catlin Indian Gallery*. Washington, DC: Smithsonian, 1979

Yater, George H. and Caroln S. Denton. *Nine Young Men From Kentucky*. WPO Publication No. 11, Lewis and Clark Trail Heritage Foundation, Inc. May, 1992.

The Lewis and Clark Expedition's Newfoundland Dog, WPO Publication No. 10, Lewis and Clark Trail Heritage Foundation, Inc., September 1990.

Members of the Corps of Discovery, North Dakota Lewis & Clark Bicentennial Foundation, 1999.

Articles

Anderson. Irving W. and Schroer, Blanch, "Sacagawea, Her Name and Her Destiny," *We Proceeded On*, Vol.25, No.4, November 1999, pp.6-9.

Benson, Keith R., "Herpetology on the Lewis and Clark Expedition, 1804-1806," *We Proceeded On*, Vol.25, No. 4, November 1999, pp.24-29.

Brown, Jo Ann, "George Drouillard and Fort Massac," *We Proceeded On*, Vol. 25, No.4, November 1999, pp 16-19.

David, Marshall B., "Carl Bodmer's Unspoiled West," *American Heritage*, Vol. XIV, No. 3, April, 1963, pp. 43-65.

Cleary, Rita, "Charbonneau Reconsidered," *We Proceeded On*, Vol. 26, No. 1, February 2000, pp. 18-23.

Duncan, Dayton, "Toilsome days and wristless nights," *We Proceeded On*, Vol26, No.4 November 2000, pp.18-26.

Gatten, Jr., Robert E., "Clark Land in Virginia and the Birthplace of William Clark," *We Proceeded On*, Vol. 25, No.2, May 1999, pp.-6-10.

Guice, John D.W., "A Fatal Rendezvous: The Mysterious Death of Meriwether Lewis," *We Proceeded On*, Vol. 24, No.2, May 1998, pp 4-12.

Grinnell, Calvin, "Another View of Sakakawea," *We Proceeded On*, Vol. 25, No.2, May 1999, pp. 16-19.

Hinds, V. Strode, "Reconstructing Charles Floyd," *We Proceeded On*, Vol. 27, No.1, February 2001, pp.16-19.

Holmberg, James J., "Seaman's Fate?" *We Proceeded On*, Vol. 26, No. 1, February 2000, pp.7-9.

_____, A Man of Much Merit," *We Proceeded On*, Vol. 26, No. 3, August 2000, pp.8-12.

Hunt, Robert R., "Luck or Providence? Narrow Escapes on the Lewis and Clark Expedition," *We Proceeded On*, Vol.25, No. 3, August 1999, pp. 6-11.

_____, "For Whom the Guns Sounded," *We Proceeded On*, Vol. 27, No. 1, February 2001, pp. 10-15.

Merritt, J.I., "A New Portrait of Patrick Gass," *We Proceeded On*, Vol. 27, February 2001, pp. 26-30.

Moore, Bob, "A Closer Look at the Uniform Coats of the Lewis and Clark Expedition," *We Proceeded On*, Vol. 24, No 4, November 1998, pp.4-8.

_____, "Pompey's Baptism," *We Proceeded On*, Vol. 26, No1, February 2000, pp.10-17.

_____, "Corps of Discovery Gravesites," *We Proceeded On*, Vol. 26, No. 2, May 2000, pp. 5-9.

Morris, Larry E., "Dependable John Ordway," *We Proceeded On*, Vol. 27, No. 2, pp. 28-33.

Moulton, Gary E., "Lewis and Clark on the Middle Missouri," *Nebraska History*, Vol. 81 No. 3, Fall 2000, pp.90-105.

Poter, Joseph C., "Marvelous Figures, Astonished Travelers," *Montana*, Vol. 41, No.4, Autumn 1991, pp. 36-53.

Ronda, James P., "'A Knowledge of Distant Parts' The Shaping of the Lewis and Clark Expedition," *Montana*, Vol. 41, No. 4, Fall 1991, pp.4-19.

Walcheck, Ken, "Pronghorns," *We Proceeded On*, Vol. 24, No. 3, August 1998, pp.4-9.

_____, "Wapiti," *We Proceeded On*, Vol. 26, No.3, August 200, pp. 26-32.

Pamphlets

The Lewis and Clark Trail, National Park Service.

The Eastern Legacy of Lewis and Clark, Lewis and Clark Trail Heritage Foundation/ Philadelphia and Ohio River Chapters.

The Beginning of the Great Expedition, U.S. Army Corps of Engineers.

Discovering the Legacy of Lewis and Clark, Bicentennial Commemoration 2003-2006, Lewis and Clark Interagency Partnership.

Lewis and Clark at the Falls of the Ohio, NPS, Falls of the Ohio Lewis and Clark Bicentennial Committee & other partners.

The Illinois Lewis and Clark Trail Guide, Illinois Lewis and Clark Bicentennial Commission.

Trail of Lewis and Clark - Nebraska & Iowa, Nebraska Division of Travel and Tourism / Iowa Division of Tourism.

Guide to Following the Lewis and Clark Trail between Sioux City and Ft. Randall, Yankton Lewis and Clark Bicentennial, Inc.

Lewis and Clark Trail, The South Dakota Adventure, South Dakota Department of Tourism.

North Dakota Lewis and Clark Trail Guide, North Dakota Department of Commerce Tourism Division.

Montana's Lewis and Cark trail Through Missouri River Country, Missouri River Country, Travel Montana, Department of Commerce.
Floating the Upper Missouri, Bureau of Land Management.

Lewis and Clark's Montana Journey, Travel Montana, Department of Commerce.

Lewis and Clark in the Rocky Mountains, U.S. Department of Agriculture Forest Service.

Lewis and Clark Expedition, Lemhi County, USDA Forest Service, Bureau of Land Management, River of No Return Interpretive Association.

Lewis and Clark Across the Lolo Trail, Clearwater National Forest, Lolo National Forest.

Idaho Museums Along the Lewis and Clark Trail, Idaho State Historical Society, Governor's Lewis and Clark Trail Committee.

Lewis and Clark in Washington State, Washington State Parks and Recreation Commission.

Lewis and Clark on the Columbia River, Lewis and Clark Bicentennial Commission in Oregon/ Washington State Governor's Lewis and Clark Committee.

Lewis and Clark, Oregon-Washington, Oregon Tourism Commission/ Washington State Business and Tourism Development.

(In addition to the pamphlets listed, there were many others from the different national, state and local sites and visitor centers.)

THE AUTHOR

William Hill is the author of several books on western trails, including *The Oregon Trail, Yesterday and Today* and *The Santa Fe Trail, Yesterday and Today*, published by Caxton Press. He has devoted many years and traveled thousands of miles collecting material for his guides.

Born in Pennsylvania, Hill earned his B.A. in history from the University of Minnesota. He also attended Hofstra University, where he obtained his M.S. in secondary education and C.A.S. in educational administration.

Hill's interest in the West dates back to his childhood trips taken there with his family. He is a member of the Lewis and Clark Trail Heritage Foundation, the Oregon-California Trails Association, the Santa Fe Trail Association, Western Writers of America and various historical associations.

Hill is now retired from teaching and he and his wife live in Centereach, New York.

INDEX

Other books about the Pacific Northwest
From CAXTON PRESS

Shoshoni Pony
ISBN 0-87004-431-1

11x8 1/2, 32 pages, full color, hardcover $15.95

Forlorn Hope:
The Nez Perce Victory at White Bird Canyon
ISBN 0-87004-435-4

6x9, photographs, maps,
246 pages, paper, $15.95

Do Them No Harm
Lewis and Clark among the Nez Perce
ISBN 0-87004-427-3

6x9, 350 pages, paper $16.95

On Sidesaddles to Heaven
The Women of the Rocky Mountain Mission
ISBN 0-87004-384-6

6x9, 268 pages, illustrations, maps, paper $19.95

Dreamers: On the trail of the Nez Perce
ISBN 0-87004-393-5

6x9, 450 pages, illustrations, maps, hardcover, $24.95

Our Native American Legacy
Northwest Towns with Indian names
ISBN 0-87004-401-x

6x9, 312 pages, illustrations, map, paper $17.95

For a free Caxton catalog write to:

CAXTON PRESS
312 Main Street
Caldwell, ID 83605-3299

or

Visit our internet web site:

www.caxtonpress.com

Caxton Press is a division of The CAXTON PRINTERS, Ltd.